3 200401 603

C000215271

| 15 | | |
|---|---|---|
| HOOK NORTON LIBRARY HIGH STREET HOOK NORTON OX15 5NH TEL: HOOK NORTON 737 | KENNINGTON LIBRARY THE VILLAGE HALL KENNINGTON ROAD KENNINGTON OXFORD OX1 5PG TEL: OXFORD 730769 | |
| 17. FEB 2003 | | |
| 28. JUN 2003 | 20. NOV 09. | |
| 08. SEP 2003 | 18. JUN 11 | |
| 01. APR 05. | 17. MAR 12 | |
| 23. APR 05. | | |
| 10. JUN 05. | | |
| 21. FEB 09 | | |
| | | |
| | | |

390.9094257BLO
BLOXHAM, C.G.
May Day to mummers: folklore and
traditional customs of Oxfordshire

**Please return / renew this item by the last day shown**

 OXFORDSHIRE
COUNTY COUNCIL
CULTURAL SERVICES

# May Day
# to
# Mummers

## Folklore and traditional customs
## in Oxfordshire

*Christine Bloxham*

| OXFORDSHIRE COUNTY COUNCIL | |
| --- | --- |
| 3200401603 | |
| Cypher | 16.12.02 |
| | £12.99 |
| | |

THE WYCHWOOD PRESS

Our books may be ordered from bookshops or (post free) from
Jon Carpenter Publishing, Alder House, Market Street, Charlbury,  OX7 3PH
01608 811969

e-mail: wychwood@joncarpenter.co.uk

Credit card orders should be phoned or faxed to 01689 870437 or 01608 811969

We would like to acknowledge the assistance of the Greening Lamborn Trust in
enabling the publication of this work

First published in 2002 by
**The Wychwood Press**
an imprint of Jon Carpenter Publishing
Alder House, Market Street, Charlbury, Oxfordshire OX7 3PH

The right of Christine Bloxham to be identified as author of this work has been
asserted in accordance with the Copyright, Design and Patents Act 1988

All rights reserved. No part of this publication may be reproduced, stored in a
retrieval system or transmitted in any form or by any means electronic,
mechanical, photocopying or otherwise without the prior permission in writing
of the publisher

ISBN  1 902279 11 5

Printed in England by Antony Rowe Ltd, Chippenham SN14 6LH

# Contents

# Acknowledgements

**My interest in folklore was inspired by Mrs Ethel Rudkin, author of** *Lincolnshire Folklore*, who took me under her wing when I worked at Scunthorpe Museum. When I moved to Oxfordshire I was fortunate to meet Christina Hole, the noted folklorist and author – who when she died left me her Oxfordshire notes – and Miss Stanley Smith, a former County Librarian. I have collected local material since the early 1970s, but I am sure there are still gaps in my knowledge.

I am not the first to have collected local information, and I have drawn extensively on the collection made by Percy Manning at the end of the 19th century, intended for a county folklore book which was never written and now housed in the Bodleian Library, and the collections made by Christina Hole, Miss Stanley Smith, the Oxfordshire and District Folklore Society, the work of Keith Chandler on Morris dancing, Roy Judge on Oxford May Day and Jack-in-the-Green, the Pitt Rivers Museum, the Centre for Oxfordshire Studies (including the Oxfordshire Photographic Archive) and many local history books written over the years. John Blair very kindly let me use material from his unpublished manuscript on Bampton. Dr Martin West of All Souls kindly vetted my section on the Mallard custom and gave me information about the 2001 celebration. Dr Malcolm Graham and Hugo Brunner kindly helped with a grant application, and we are pleased to acknowledge the assistance of the Greening Lamborn Trust without whose help much of this material could never have been published.

Arthur MacGregor of the Ashmolean Museum generously supplied the photograph of Guy Fawkes' lantern, and All Souls lent me photographs of the Mallard medals. The Pitt Rivers Museum kindly supplied a copy of the photograph of Whit horns in their collection. David Watts lent me photographs of the Kirtlington lamb ale and the garlands in Charlton-on-Otmoor church. Rosemary Arnold and Sheila Stephens gave me much information about May Day in Somerton, and provided photographs. Lesley Argyle of the Abingdon morris men and John Graham of the Headington morris men generously lent morris photographs. The Oxford Stamp Centre was a source of many useful photographs. Other people who kindly lent photographs include Russell Auger, the Bodleian Library, Freda Kitcher, the Salisbury and South Wiltshire Museum, H. A. Shatford and Baroness von Maltzahn. In respect of quotations from *A Kind of Magic* by Mollie Harris, acknowledgement is made to Pollinger Ltd and the Estate of Mollie Harris. Elizabeth Swaffield kindly gave permission to use quotations from Flora Thompson's *Lark Rise to Candleford*.

On a personal level, I would like to thank all who have helped me in the course of my research, my publisher Jon Carpenter, who was very patient with me, and my family, who have at times been neglected in favour of my writing.

C.B.

# Introduction

**Customs and folklore are not the easiest subjects to study, as the** information is scattered in diverse sources, and because they are local and personal matters they are seldom mentioned in official documents, so the survival of information can be patchy. Very little information can be found before the fourteenth century, when household accounts, corporation and parish records and literature begin to give clues. During the middle ages the parish replaced the manor as a basic unit of society, and ritual began to be used to enhance status and diffuse tensions. From the mid-fifteenth century seasonal customs were used to raise money for the church. Over the last 150 years the parish has become a less important element, and customs have become more family-centred. Interpretation is not always easy either, and the emphasis has changed over recent years from a desire to establish pagan roots for many customs to a more social-historical approach, which looks critically at the evidence and places it in a more historical context, refusing to suggest that it goes back beyond the information available. This has led to the somewhat surprising conclusions that some customs which appear to have strong pagan elements, such as the Morris and the mummers, only go back to the 16th and 18th centuries respectively.

However there are certain themes which can be found in the material. The early church did take elements and dates of many pagan customs, to ease the change to Christianity – the spring festival of May Day and the celebration of Christmas at midwinter are examples of this, expressing a natural human desire to celebrate the coming of spring and derive comfort during the depths of winter. However, as will be seen, the ethos behind these and the way in which they were celebrated changed greatly over the centuries.

Customs were a way of defining the calendar in the days before most people had access to newspapers, radio and television. Rural customs fitted neatly into the farming year, taking place at times when there was a lull in farm work, such as Christmas, or becoming part of it, as with harvest customs. Our very word 'holiday' is derived from the 'holy days' of the church, which exercised a strong influence over the development of customs, encouraging some and condemning others – the Puritans officially condemned the celebration of Christmas during the Commonwealth. At other times the church profited from customs, as with church ales, where home brew was sold, amidst suitable jollifications, to raise money for the church. Other customs such as beating the bounds had a practical purpose, enabling people to see which parish they lived in and to whom they should pay their tithes in the days before readily-available maps.

Customs have not remained static – that would have led to their stagna-tion and disintegration – so they have either adapted to changing social beliefs or died out. The sixteenth and seventeenth centuries saw a lot of changes with the Reformation and the influence of the Puritans, particularly during the Commonwealth. The newly reformed church was trying to eliminate the paganism left in religion, and loudly condemned activities such as May Day which were thought to encourage lewd behaviour, although the custom staggered on despite this. With the rapid changes in religion during the Tudor period people must have been in a constant state of confusion over ecclesiastical ritual and custom, and what was permitted, as beliefs see-sawed between Catholicism and Protestantism.

Changes in social beliefs were influential too, in a less formal way. As Britain became more industrialised and people moved away from the land, rural customs declined, hours of work became more rigid as manufacturers wanted to keep their machines working, and open drunkenness, which was a feature of many customs such as Whitsun Ales and Morris dancing, was actively disapproved of and discouraged, particularly by the Temperance movement, and these went into decline. In the Victorian era moral standards rose, and many country customs were looked on with great disapproval, and as these feelings filtered down through society, the customs died.

Customs have also served as a way of sharing money between rich and poor in a period before the formal umbrella of social security. The poor were able to go to their richer neighbours to ask for alms on occasions like St Thomas' Day. Labourers' children received little if any pocket money, particularly after their parents lost independent sources of income after enclosure, so it can be no accident that many of the begging rhymes such as the May Day and Valentine ones date from the 19th century, the greatest period for enclosure.

Paternalism was obvious in some customs, as in Kirtlington where the Dashwood family of Kirtlington Park subsidised the local Morris men, giving the men joints of beef to enhance their strength for dancing. Many poor people visited the great houses and the wealthier inhabitants in the villages in the course of the year, begging for money or food.

Another important element was that before there was much organised entertainment, people had to provide their own, and the organisation of this must have helped to hold local communities together. Fairs used to be a major source of entertainment, as well as having the practical hiring element, but now that we have so much on offer, they are an anachronism, albeit a pleasant one, in the early years of the 21st century, and there are regular dark mutterings about how they disrupt the traffic flows in towns. Perhaps they will not last out the century.

Different elements of the population have been involved in customs at different times – it was the young adults who took part in many such as May Day in the late middle ages and up to the mid-17th century, and after the decline in the 18th century it was the children who took over in the 19th, much encouraged by increased rural poverty, and later in the century the custom was largely taken over by the schools, some of which still hold May celebrations today.

The twentieth century saw the end of most traditional mumming and much Morris dancing, but from the 1950s there were revivals, though often with different personnel. Morris dancing, instead of being a pastime for agricultural labourers, was taken up by 'yuppies' and townsfolk. Events such as the Festival of Britain in 1951 and the Millennium encouraged people to look for elements of the past to bring into the future.

The sources of information for the study of customs are diverse, as exemplified in the text and the bibliography. However those who would like to pursue the subject further can look out for reports in local newspapers, local histories, local diaries, local government papers, ecclesiastical papers, and periodicals in addition to the usual sources.

# The Return of the Light

## Plough Sunday and Plough Monday

*Plough Monday next after that Twelfthtide is past,*
*bids out with the plough, the worst husband is last.*
*If ploughman gets hatchet or whip to the shrene*
*maids loseth their cock if no water is seen.*

Thomas Tusser, c. 1580

**After Twelfth Night (January 6th) life went back to normal following** the traditional break taken in rural communities over the twelve days of Christmas. The following Sunday was known as Plough Sunday, which was followed by Plough Monday. The success of the harvest was of vital importance to the agricultural community, so every effort was made to ensure the fertility of the fields. Before the Reformation plough lights were kept burning in many churches, sometimes cared for by the plough guilds, which were suppressed in 1538. In some cases real ploughs were kept in the church to symbolically bless the ones used in the fields. This was condemned by the Protestant John Bale during the reign of Edward VI who described it as 'conjuring of ploughs'.

Such practices ended with the Reformation, but the need to bless the plough was still felt, and they were often brought into church to be blessed on Plough Sunday. Plough Sunday services were revived in 1951 at Aston Rowant, where an old plough was kept in the nave, by Rev. Frank Martin, and at Coombe in 1954. In 1956 the service at Coombe was attended by the Bishop of Oxford, Dr. H. J. Carpenter.

The ploughmen themselves enjoyed Plough Monday celebrations. In many areas, as Thomas Tusser described in the rhyme quoted above, the men were challenged to get to the farmhouse hearth before the servant girl had risen, lit the fire and boiled a kettle on it, and to prove they had been there put something on the screen or settle. If they succeeded, they expected the gift of a cock for their next feast. As they paraded the plough round the village soliciting money for that feast, they often threatened to plough up front lawns if they were refused!

Oxfordshire records only describe their gallivanting in the late 19th century. In the Asthal area near Burford, according to Ambrose Preston (who was aged 83 when his information was recorded for the Percy Manning Collection in 1903) ploughing apparently restarted on the first day after New Year, and that morning they paraded round armed with a plough hatchet, shouting:

Rain, hail or shine,
The best cock in the yard's mine.

They expected the mistress of the house to come out bearing a quart of beer containing toast, and if this was not forthcoming the boys went into the farmyard and pretended to hunt cocks until the beer arrived. This practice was called 'wind the cock'.

At nearby Minster Lovell, according to Mr Williams' *Minster Lovell Memories* (undated typescript), carters went round carrying a piece of plough, reciting a similar rhyme:

Hail, rain, snow or shine
The finest cock on the farm is mine.

Rev. C. E. Prior recorded that until about the 1860s farm boys in Checkendon in South Oxfordshire dressed up for their Plough Monday celebrations, but he does not record what they did. (Oxfordshire Archaeological Society Report for 1906, Banbury 1907.)

## Hunting the Mallard

This curious custom at All Souls College is said to have been an annual festivity at one time, but is now celebrated once a century and was last performed on 14th January 2001. It involves a hunt through the college, from cellars to the roof, peering into all the nooks and crannies, over several hours, for a large mallard duck, which was said to have been found in the drains during the laying of the college foundations in 1438. In another version, a pastiche of a medieval chronicle, written by Benjamin Buckler in the 18th century, it was suggested that Archbishop Chichele, founder of the College, dreamt that when the foundations were dug 'a swapping mallard' would be found 'imprisoned in the sink or sewer, wele fattened and almost ybosten' – which is said to be what happened. Whatever its origins, the Mallard ceremony became part of All Souls life, and after feasting at the Gaudy held on 14th January, the beginning of the Hilary term, it became the custom to hunt for the mallard.

The earliest references so far found to the Mallard Night are in 1616 and 1632 in the Warden's Punishment Book. The latter was quoted by Martin West in *The All Souls Mallard* (2000), was on 20th January 1632:

Wch day and yeare it was agreed by Mr Warden and ye Deanes that Mr ffleetwood Mr Barker and Mr Prestwitch should bee put out of Commons for a weeke for disturbing ye fellowes tempore dormitionis, et hospitando peregrinos et portando arma invasiva in damnum et scandalum Collegii, and likewise yt they should pay four shillings apeece towards dilapidations done about the seaventeenth of January.

Rich: Astley custos
ffran: Gerald Decan: Jurist
Samuel Kinaston Decan: Artist

'Mallard-dyzers' was written in the margin. The men in question were elected fellows in November 1630, and were therefore celebrating the end of their probationary period. During their antics they were accused of disturbing the sleep of members of the College, permitting strangers into the College overnight and carrying arms. This was probably the episode referred to by the Visitor, Archbishop Abbot, who reproved the college in 1632 for riotous behaviour 'under pretence of a foolish mallard'. He wrote:

Salutem in Christo. The feast of Christmas growing now to an end, doth putt mee in minde of the great outrage, w[ch] as I am informed was the last yeere committed in your College. Where allthough matters formerly had bene carryed w[th] distemper, yet men never did breake forth into that intolerable liberty, as to teare of[f] the doores and gates w[ch] are the fences of the College, and so to disquiett their neighbours as if it had bene in a Campe or Towne of warre, to the greate disgrace of the government of that University. Civill men should never so farre forgett themselves under pretence of a foolish mallard, as to do thinges barbarously unbeseeming, from w[ch] I advise men warily to abstaine, lest otherwise they make themselves unworthy of any habitation in the house of the Muses, w[ch] I forewarne will bee the yssue of those w[ch] heerafter shall transgresse that way.

Quoted in Martin West, The All Souls Mallard (2000)

The 17th century chronicler Anthony Wood wrote:

14th January at night used to be called Allsoules College mallard night, that is, I suppose, no other than the 'Fresh night'. For that day those candidates, which had been chosen on Allsoules day going before, were admitted; and that daye or soone after the probationers for the yeare before going were to be admitted fellowes. those that were thus admitted fellowes were brought from their chambers in the middle of the nighte, (having neither gowne or band on), sometimes on a coule-staffe, and so led in the hall and about the college. Before whome some of the junior fellows, sometimes disguised, would sing a song in praise of the mallard ... I take to be made much about the restauration of Charles II.

Andrew Clark, The Life and Times of Anthony Wood, antiquary of Oxford, 1632-1695, described by Himself, Oxford 1894, pp 513

This makes Mallard Night sound more like an initiation rite, and behaviour on that night had perhaps been moderated by the disapproval of the 17th century Puritans.

Anthony Wood has perhaps the earliest version of the song in his manuscript, though it lacks the chorus:

The griffine, bustard, turky, and capon,
Lett other hungry mortalls gape on
And on theire bones with stomacks fall hard
But lett All Souls men have the mallard.

The Romans once admir'd a gander
More than they did their best commander
Because hee saved, if some dont fooll us

6

The place named from the scull of Tolus.

The poets fain'd Jove turn'd a swan
But lett them prove it if they can
So mak't appeare its not att all hard
Hee was a swapping, swapping mallard.

Some storys strange are told I trow
By Baker, Holinshead and Stow
Of Cocks and Bulls and other queire things
That happen'd in the reigne of theire kings.

Hee was swapping all from bill to eye
He was swapping all from wing to thigh
His swapping toole of Generation
Oute swappe`d all the wingge`d nation.

Then let us drink and dance a galliard
In the remembrance of the Mallard,
And as the Mallard doth in poole
Let's dabble dive and duck in Boule.

The coule-staffe he referred to was a pole on which a large bucket was carried on a pole by two men. Being carried on such a pole was a feature of punishing scolds and the 'rough music' played to cuckolds and adulterous couples. 'Swapping' probably comes from Middle English, meaning 'swooping'. The verses are found in different orders in the various texts. The verse about English chroniclers was abandoned in 1752 and the 'swapping' verse in 1821. It has in recent times become customary for the Lord Mallard to write a topical new verse on each occasion to replace the indecent one.

The custom was performed annually during part of the 17th century but only the song is known from the eighteenth. Writing in 1722, Thomas Hearne commented:

The Mallard was found in the sink when the workmen were repairing it. It had continued there for several years, I think almost from the first Foundation of the College for about twenty years current or more.

Montagu Burrows suggested an alternative origin for the Mallard Hunt, which he postulated only began in the 17th century, following the discovery in a college drain of a 13th century seal with a design depicting a griffin, with four legs, outstretched wings, a curly tail and a vulture-like beak, with the legend 'S. Guil. Malardi clici', probably an abbreviation of 'Sigillum Guilliemis Malardi Clerici' – i.e. the seal of clerk William Malard. There is an impression of this seal illustrated in Alderman Fletcher's copy of Anthony Wood's *History and Antiquities of the University of Oxford*, edited by J. Gutch (1786). Burrows suggested that 'some wit of the College' invented the Mallard and wrote the song. There is no further information to confirm or deny this proposition, apart from the fact that the first known information about the custom dates from the 17th century.

The first detailed description of the Mallard Hunt is that of Thomas Baskerville of Sunningwell (who, as he had not attended the University himself, obtained his information from two All Souls fellows), written about 1682:

As touching the first institution of this Ceremony (which is very ancient saith Mr Stedman) I cannot give any account of it, but when they have a mind to keep it, the time is always within a night or two of All Souls. Then there are six Electors wch nominate ye Lord of the Mallard, wch Lord is to beare the expences of the Ceremony. When he is chosen, he appoints six officers, who march before him with white staves in their hands, and meddalls hanging upon their breasts tied with a large blew ribbond. Upon ye meddalls is cut on the one side the Lrd of the Mallard with his officers, on the other ye mallard as he is carried upon a long Poll.

When ye Ld is seated in his chair with his officers of state (as above sd) before him, they carry him thrice about the Quadrangle and sing this song:

Griffin Turkey Bustard Capon
Let other hungry mortalls gape on
And on their bones with stomacks fall hard
But let All Souls men have the mallard
Hough the bloud of King Edward, by ye bloud of King Edward
It was a swapping swapping Mallard.

Stories strange were told I trow
By Baker, Holinshead and Stow
Of Cocks and Bulls and other quere things
That were done in the Reignes of their Kings,
Hough the blood etc.

Swapping he was from bill to eye
Swapping he was from wing to thigh
His swapping toole of generation
Out swap'd all the winged Nation
Ho the bloud etc.

The Romans once admir'd a Gander
More than they did their Chiefe Comander
Because it sav'd if some don't foole us
The p[lace] called from ye head of Tolus.
Ho the bloud etc.

The poets fained Jove turned a swan
But let them prove it if they can
As for our profe tis not at all hard
That twas a swapping swapping mallard,

Then let us sing & dance a Galliard
To the remembrance of the mallard

And as the mallard does in Poole
Let's dabble dive and duck in Bowle
Ho the bloud etc.

The mallard song being sung by one man, all the rest yt are present bearing the Chorus, when that is done, they knock at the middle Chambers, where most of ye Seniors lodge, of whome they demand Crowns a piece (I suppose a forfeiture for not assisting at the Ceremony) wch is readily given, then they go with 20 or 30 Torches (which are allways carried before them) upon the Leads of ye Colledge where they sing their song as before. This ended, they go into their common rooms, where they make themselves merry with what wine every one has mind to, there being at that time great plenty of all sorts. When they have sufficiently refresh'd themselves, to conclude all they go into the Buttery where every one has his Tumbler of Canary or other wine. Then he that bore the Mallard chops of his head, dropping some of the bloud into every tumbler, which being drunk off, every one disposeth of himselfe as he thinks fit, it being generally day-brake.

MS Rawlinson D810, Bodleian Library, quoted in Lilian M. Quiller Couch, ed., Reminiscences of Oxford by Oxford Men,<br>Oxford Historical Society, 1892, pp 243-246

This contains some significant points. It gives a different date – around All Souls day, 1st November, rather than 14th January. It also gives details of the people participating in the ceremony – largely the younger fellows, who demanded money from their seniors – and the procedure and a slightly different version of the Mallard song. This version is thought to date from around the time of the Restoration in 1660, but may have replaced an earlier one. It is not known which King Edward is meant in the chorus – there was not a King Edward on the throne when the college was founded. Perhaps as they mention his blood, the reference could be to the Saxon King Edward the Confessor, who was patron saint of England before St. George. Montagu Burrows suggests that it could refer to Edward I, who features in several medieval songs. Edward VI has also been suggested.

Martin West has suggested in *The All Souls Mallard* (2000) that the differences in the descriptions and the dates indicate that there may have been two different ceremonies – the initiation of novices, who are humiliated by being dragged round in a state of undress by men in disguise, as described by Anthony Wood and the Mallard ritual of Baskerville, which has similarities with begging rituals such as hunting the wren, when a dead wren was carried in procession on a pole or in a cage and the protagonists begged for money.

Thomas Hearne wrote of the Mallard Hunt in his *Diary* on 18th January 1723:

Last Monday, the 14th inst. (the 14th being always the day), was All Souls College Mallard, at which time 'tis usual with the Fellows and their friends to have a Supper, and to sit up all night drinking and singing. Their song is the Mallard, and formerly they used to ramble about the College with Sticks & Poles, etc. in quest of the Mallard, and they had a Lord of the Mallard, but this hath been left off many Years.

This illustrates how customs change and adapt – the night on which the custom is held has now been established as 14th January, but it had been modified to exclude the hunt round the college. However this aspect reappeared in 1801, when more medals were struck – those of 1801 show the Lord Mallard and his officers wearing gowns and wigs and carrying staves on one side, and the Mallard bearer on the other side, carrying a flat-topped staff with a mallard on top. All Souls College collections include medals struck to celebrate the ceremony possibly for 1701 (but more likely to be from the 17th century), and definitely 1801, 1901 and 2001.

The 1801 ceremony was witnessed by the future Bishop Heber, who wrote to John Thornton:

THIS ELECTROTYPE OF THE UNIQUE SPECIMEN OF THE PEWTER MALLARD MEDAL OF 1701, NOW IN THE HUNTERIAN CABINET, GLASGOW.

An electrotype of the lead medal said to have been struck for the Mallard ceremony in 1701, but possibly earlier.

... I write under the bondage of a very severe cold, which I caught by getting out of bed at four in the morning, to see the celebration of the famous All Souls' Mallard Feast. All Souls is on the opposite side of Ratcliffe (sic) Square to Brazen Nose, so that their battlements are in some degree commanded by my garret. I had thus a full view of the Lord Mallard and about forty fellows in a kind of procession on the library roof, with immense lighted torches, which had a singular effect. I know not if their orgies were overlooked by any uninitiated eyes except my own; but I am sure that all who had the gift of hearing, within half a mile, must have been awakened by the manner in which they thundered their chorus 'O by the blood of King Edward'. I know not whether you have any similar strange customs in Cambridge ...

'Mrs Heber's Life of Heber', quoted in Lilian M. Quiller Couch, *Reminiscences of Oxford by Oxford Men*, Oxford Historical society, 1892, p.241.

Cosmo Gordon Lang, Fellow of All Souls and later Archbishop of Canterbury, superintended the Hunt in 1901, and wrote:

The most outstanding and historic duty of the Lord Mallard is to take charge of the Mallard Feast, once frequent and disorderly, and now restricted to the opening year of each century. I prize the memory that it fell to me in January 1900 [1901] to do this great thing... Suffice it to say here that I was carried in a chair by four stalwart Fellows - Wilbraham, Gwyer, Steel-Maitland and Fossie Cunliffe, I think they were - for nearly two hours after midnight round the quadrangles and roofs of the College with a dead mallard borne in front on a long pole (which I still possess), singing the Mallard Song all the time, preceded by the seniors - such grave and reverend persons as Warden Anson, Dicey, Holland and the like - and followed by the juniors, all of them carrying staves and torches, a scene unimaginable in any place in the world except Oxford, or there in any society except All Souls. The whole strange ceremony had been kept secret; only late workers in the night can have heard the unusual sound, though it is said that Provost McGrath of Queen's muttered in his sleep: 'I must send the Torpid down for this noise.'

Quoted in J. G. Lockhart, *Cosmo Gordon Lang*, 1949, pp57-8

Obverse and reverse of the medals struck to commemorate the 1801 and 1901 Mallard ceremonies.

Photos courtesy of All Souls.

Lang imprinted some of his own ideas on the ceremony:

I thought it unseemly that surplices should be worn and we contented ourselves with black gowns. There seemed something approaching irreverence in the notion of making the junior Fellows eat of the mallard's flesh and drink its blood so as to be incorporated into the spirit of All Souls. Instead of this I had a small silver mallard made and filled with wine, which the juniors drank. But when the bird was burned in the small hours in a bonfire, some of them could not be restrained from eating portions of his charred flesh. Quoted in J. G. Lockhart, op. cit., p58

11

Warden Anson also described the ceremony in his diary:

We dined at 7 o'clock, being a party of 36. Before dinner Oman distributed medals with blue ribbons and each of us wore one round his neck.

After dinner and common room I went home for a little while and then came out to find the procession forming in the large Quadrangle. Lang was seated in a chair borne by Steel, Wilbraham, Cunliffe and Alington. Liddell carried in front the Mallard on a long staff: the others carried torches.

The procession passed round the old Quadrangle, and once and a half round the large Quadrangle, ending at the Chapel door. They then ascended to the roof. Bramston and I remained below. The scene of the perambulation on the roof was very picturesque. The line of figures, the strange effects of light produced by the torches among the pinnacles, the splendid voice of Lang chanting the Mallard song, and the solemn chorus made up a singular and impressive ceremony.

When they had descended the stairs leading past the Muniment room, the procession was again formed, with the Lord Mallard in his chair, and moved, singing all the way to the corner of the Quadrangle by the Hall and Common-room passage. There the torches were piled to make a bonfire, the wings and head of the Mallard were cut off and the wings burned; and the party joined arms and danced slowly round the fire singing 'Auld Lang Syne', and then we adjourned to the Buttery for the 'Mallard Potation'.

A small silver salt cellar, in the figure of a Mallard, given by Buchanan for the Mallard's table, was filled with madeira, and a few drops poured into each man's glass of port by Lang, while Lane on this occasion chanted the song. This was a symbolic drinking of the Mallard's blood, as it was agreed that the old practice of carrying alive Mallard, cutting off his head and drinking of cups into which his blood was dropped had become barbarous.

After this there was a supper in the Hall, and the signatures of those who had taken part in the ceremony were recorded and attested by the seal of the Lord Mallard.

The menu for the dinner that night consisted of:

Potage des Tourterelles du Siècle Nouveau
Tourbot, Sauce du Warden
Éperlans à la Custodes Jocalium
Vol-au-Vent du Ris de Veau à la Sub-Warden
Filets de Boeuf de L'Estates Bursar
Châpons Rôtis à la Roi Edouard
Jambon d'Yorck
Selle du Mouton
Mallards Swapping Sauce
Pouding d'All Souls
Gâteau de Chichele
Sardines de Gaudy
Merluches. Salade des Junior Fellows
Dessert du Common Room

Although the occasion was not officially witnessed by members of the public, M. J. Lancashire, her mother and sister went down Catte Street and hovered outside the College. At eleven o'clock in the evening their patience was rewarded, and through the iron gate they saw groups of men with torches, talking and laughing, preparing to start the procession:

> ... Soon someone gave the order and off they started.
>
> A beautiful voice [that of Cosmo Gordon Lang] rang out on the night air singing the old Mallard Song which is peculiar to All Souls. We could hear every word distinctly as he sang in a rich clear voice, which seemed exactly suited for the occasion ... But the effect when the words were taken up by the whole College was magnificent,
>
> O by the blood of King Edward,
> O by the blood of King Edward,
> It was a swapping, swapping Mallard.
>
> The words echoed out again and again, sometimes faint while the procession moved into the farther quad, and becoming louder again as the procession slowly approached us ...

> Quoted in J. G. Lockhart, *Cosmo Gordon Lang*, 1949, pp463-4

Mrs Lancashire watched a procession led by torchbearers, one of whom carried a stuffed mallard on a long pole, followed by the Lord Mallard, carried shoulder high in his chair by four men, while two others carrying wands walked beside them and two in front to steady the chair if required. Behind Lord Mallard came the members of the College in gowns with caps or top hats. When the procession had been all round the quads and over the roofs, the torches were thrown down in a heap to make a bonfire and Auld Lang Syne was sung, and then a final rendition of the Mallard song. The proceedings ended at 12.15 am.

It must have been a bitter-sweet occasion for those connected with All Souls who were unable to attend the ceremony. One, George Curzon, Viceroy of India, was apprised of the event by a cable sent after dinner which contained the single word 'Swapping' from the chorus of the Mallards Song, and immediately returned his reply: 'It was.'

The sculptor John Tweed was commissioned to design a medal to commemorate the Hunt, depicting Lord Mallard Cosmo Gordon Lang in bishop's robes (although he had not at that time reached that rank) and Lang being borne aloft in his chair on the reverse.

Although the Mallard hunt now only takes place once a century, the Mallard song can occasionally be heard at other times. The unofficial office of Lord Mallard is part of College custom, the Lord Mallard acting as a master of revels. Cosmo Gordon Lang was proud to hold it:

> It was my glory to hold that office in the College for some thirty years. It is indeed a strange office. The holder of it is not appointed; he <u>becomes</u>: he takes his place by the informal assent of the College... Thus, when Sir Thomas Raleigh went to India, I acted in his place, and when he returned and was unwilling to continue, I <u>became</u> Lord Mallard.

> J. G. Lockhart, op. cit., pp56-57

Lang served as Lord Mallard from 1898 to 1928. The Lord Mallard would sing the Mallard Song at the All Souls Day Gaudy and again at the annual Bursar's Dinner.

The custom of singing the Mallard Song at gaudies was still thriving in 1955 when it was reported in *The Sunday Times* of 13th November 1955 which contained a note:

NEW LORD MALLARD

If you had passed down Oxford's Catte Street on Saturday evening a week ago you might have wondered what on earth were the boisterous and far from academic sounds leaking from the ancient grey stones of All Souls. You were hearing the Fellows and quondam Fellows of the College, at their annual gaudy on the Saturday next after All Souls day, singing the chorus of the ancient Mallard song:

Oh, by the blood of King Edward!
Oh, by the blood of King Edward,
It was a swapping, swapping mallard.

And the singer of this strange ballad was the new Lord Mallard, the College's master of the revelries, filling the place of the late Sir Douglas Malcolm, who twenty-seven years ago followed in the office Archbishop Lang. When Lang was translated to Canterbury he had to vacate this dearly beloved role on thus becoming ex officio the College's Visitor. The latest in this eminent succession is no less a person than Lord Somervell.

Other twentieth-century Lord Mallards included Lord Hailsham, Dr. Alan Tyson and Professor John Vickers.

The Mallard was hunted according to custom on 14th January 2001, when the Lord Mallard was Dr. Martin West, who was appointed Lord Mallard in 2000. Proceedings began with Evensong in the college chapel, at which the former Warden Lord Neill read the lesson and the choir from St Barnabas' Church sang. This was followed by drinks in Hall, to which former fellows were invited. The total number participating in the formal dinner was 120, so the only room large enough to take them was the Library, which was lit largely by candles. This year, for the first time, female fellows also took part. The dress code was black tie, and academic dress. The tables were laid out in two long parallel rows. The menu (see Appendix 1) was carefully selected and laid out to make the word 'Mallard'. A large two-handled loving cup containing punch was passed round the table. The person on each side of the drinker and the one opposite stood up and all bowed. After the meal the guests received chocolates with a white chocolate mallard decoration, which are commonly served at gaudies.

After the meal the company assembled outside the library wearing caps and gowns and Martin West as Lord Mallard encouraged his companions to hunt with him. A three-dimensional painted wooden mallard was attached to a red pole, and this was carried at the front of the procession, followed by the Lord Mallard carried in a chair from the common room which was used in the 1901 ceremony, by six strong fellows. Two fellows carried poles with balls and crosses on top. Other members of the procession were armed with theatrical flaming torches to light their way. The

procession set off from the library, where Dr West sang a new verse of the song:

> Our famed Procession now appears:
> we do it every hundred years.
> We re-create the old effects,
> but this time plus a whole new sex.

They processed round the Great Quad and the Front Quad, keeping to the left, singing as they went. Some, including the Lord Mallard, climbed up the tower, where the college flag was flying. Those who climbed the tower sang verses of the song from there while those below in the quad sang the chorus, giving a fine antiphonal effect.

The procession continued, still keeping to the left, back to the Great Quad, where there was a fireworks display

Top. Obverse of the 2001 Mallard medal, with a duck and a drake as there are now two sexes represented among the Fellows of the College, with the inscription reading 'All Souls' College Oxford in Latin.

Bottom. Reverse of the 2001 medal, depicting the sundial designed for the College by Christopher Wren, with a quotation from Martial about the hours of life: They perish but they are charged to your account.
Photographs courtesy of All Souls' College.

based around a wooden model of a mallard. It was considered too dangerous for the procession to go over the lead roofs as was done in the past.

A new medal (see photographs on page 21) was designed for the occasion, and about 200 were struck. The design shows two ducks on the obverse – to indicate that two sexes are now involved in the custom, and the college sundial designed by Christopher Wren on the reverse. They are hung on yellow ribbons with a central red stripe, the college colours (this marks a departure from the blue ribbons used in the past).

The custom remained a private college one, the only onlookers being members of the college staff.

## Candlemas Day: February 2nd

This Christian festival has been celebrated in England since the 7th century AD, when the Venerable Bede described a ritual candlelit procession. It derived from the story in St. Luke's Gospel describing how Mary took Jesus to the Temple at Jerusalem for purification forty days after his birth. There an old man proclaimed him as Messiah, describing him as a 'light to lighten the Gentiles'.

In the medieval Sarum Use the candles were venerated and each parishioner brought a candle to church and paid a penny for the priest to place them by the altar, where he sprinkled them with holy water and incense and blessed them which explicitly gave the candles the power of frightening away devils. After Mass the candles were carried round the church again, then some were burned in front of a statue of the Virgin Mary while others were taken home and carefully preserved, being brought out and lit if someone in the house was sick or dying or there was danger from storms. At the Reformation the blessing of candles was banned as pagan superstition but Candlemas remained a holy day, gradually decreasing in importance from the 17th century.

According to tradition it was light enough by Candlemas Day to eat the evening meal without lighting candles, as a rhyme remembered in Stratton Audley and Wendlebury states:

Candlemas Day
Throw beans in the clay,
Put candles and candlesticks all away.

This indicates that it was also considered a good day for planting beans. In the days before newspapers were common, people worked much more from the country calendar, and saints' days and church festivals were easy to remember as dates for performing particular tasks.

Candlemas Day has weather lore attached to it, like this rhyme from Forest Hill, quoted by Ella Miller in the *Forest Hill Village Book* (1933):

If Candlemas Day be dry and fair
The half o'winter's to come and maire;
If Candlemas Day be wet and foul
The half o' winter's gane at Yule.

It was also believed that if the Christmas decorations had not been taken down by Twelfth Night, they should be taken down at Candlemas:

Tuesday being Candlemas Day, according to ancient custom, the ostlers of this place were on their patrole to the several inns to get drunk, and see if the servants had taken down their Christmas evergreens.

*Jackson's Oxford Journal, 16.2.1761*

## St Blaise's Day: February 3rd

February 3rd is no longer significant in the country calendar, but from the 17th century it was celebrated by those connected with the woollen industry, being dedicated to St Blaise, a bishop from Cappadochia who was the patron of wool-combers, wax-chandlers and wild animals.

Dr Plot in his *Natural History of Oxfordshire* (1677) commented on how the day was celebrated in Oxfordshire:

When countrywomen went about and made good cheer, and if they found any of their Neighbour-women a Spinning, set their Distaff on fire; that feast being celebrated on the third of February.

The day was vigorously celebrated in many areas which specialised in the woollen industry in the 18th and 19th centuries, but seems not to have taken root in Oxfordshire.

## St Scholastica's Day: 10th February

St Scholastica, who lived from about 480-543, was the sister of St Benedict; she became the first Benedictine nun and is patron saint of convulsive children. Her feast day, 10th February, became notorious in Oxford because of a major riot between the University and the Town which took place in 1355.

There was much discord between the fledgling university and the town of Oxford in the middle ages, as the university acquired a stranglehold, eroding the town's jealously guarded privileges. The bad feeling flared up when students and clerks, including Walter de Springheuse and Roger de Chesterfield, drinking in the Swyndelstock Tavern at Carfax, began to argue with the innkeeper, John de Croydon, unwisely and intemperately questioning the quality of his wine. He responded with 'stubborn and saucy language' and someone threw a quart pot of wine at his head. Several townsmen, including the owner of the inn, John de Beresford, sprang to his assistance and the town bell of St. Martin's was rung to summon further town help: men rushed up armed with bows and arrows and attacked the unarmed scholars. The chancellor of the university made a vain attempt to calm matters, but was forced to flee and more students, summoned by the bell of St. Mary the Virgin, and this time armed, entered the fray, so the fighting continued until night.

The St Scholastica's Day riot began in an argument in the Swyndlestock Tavern on the corner of Carfax, commemorated by this plaque.

Photograph: Christine Bloxham

THIS WAS THE SITE OF THE SWINDLESTOCK TAVERN 1250-1709

Edward III was staying at Woodstock so the mayor rode to see him the next day to explain the town's grievances. Meanwhile in Oxford fighting resumed, more townsmen having been summoned to the fray by the bailiffs, supported by others hired from the surrounding neighbourhood. Anthony Wood described the scene in his *History and Antiquities of the University of Oxford* (1674):

In dinner time the Townsmen subtilly and secretly sent about fourscore men armed with bows and arrows, and other manner of weapons into the parish of St. Giles in the north suburb; who, after a little expectation, having discovered certain Scholars walking after dinner in Beaumont (being the same place we now call St Gile's field) issued out of St Gile's church, shooting at the said Scholars for the space of three furlongs: some of them they drove into the Augustine Priory, and others into the Town. One Scholar they killed without the walls, some they wounded mortally, others grievously and used the rest basely. All of which being done without any mercy, caused an horrible outcry in the Town ...

Scholars armed with bows and arrows tried to block the town gates, where they and the townsmen fought until vespers, when two thousand country people broke in through the west gate, so the scholars fled back to their lodgings, but found no safety there, as Anthony Wood wrote:

Finding no Scholars in the streets to make any opposition, [they] pursued them, and that day they broke open five Inns, of Hostles of Scholars with fire and sword ... Such Scholars as they found in the said Halls or Inns they killed or maimed, or grievously wounded. Their books and all their goods which they could find, they spoiled, plundered and carried away. All their victuals, wine, and other drink they poured out; their bread, fish etc., they trod under foot. After this the night came on and the conflict ceased for that day ...

More Scholars' houses were broken into when rioting continued the next day, and Scholars were thrown into lavatories and buried in dunghills and some unfortunate chaplains had their tonsures flayed. By the time peace was restored three scholars and several townsmen were dead and many others injured.

An enquiry was held, lasting a year, during which time the town was under inderdict, which closed all the churches. Several leading citizens were imprisoned and heavy fines were imposed on the town – an immediate payment of 500 marks and an annual payment of 100 marks in compensation for property damaged. The University gained even more power as the Chancellor took over some town functions. The humiliation of the town continued for the next five centuries until 1825, as on the anniversary of St Scholastica's Day the Mayor, bailiffs and burgesses had to walk in procession from the Guildhall to St Mary's Church, where they publicly knelt and prayed for the souls of the victims, each gave a silver penny, and the Mayor swore to uphold the privileges of the University.

On 10th February 1682 Anthony Wood commented on the proceedings of the day:

Friday, the burgess(es) or citizens of Oxford appeared in their full number on S. Scholasticaes day at S. Marie's. Alderman William Wright their oracle told them that if they did not appear, there might some hole be picked in their charter, as there was now endeavouring to be done in that of the city of London. He told them moreover that though it was a popish matter, yet policy ought to take place in this juncture of time.

Andrew Clark, *The Life and Times of Anthony Wood, Antiquary of Oxford 1632-1695*, volume III, 1894, p 4

This shows the spirit of rebellion in the ranks about performing this humiliating ritual, but it was carried on as there was a genuine fear that not to do so might jeopardise the legality of Oxford's charter.

*The Gentleman's Magazine* of 1738 commented on the practice:

Friday Febr. 10. This being St Scholastica's Day, a certain Number of the principal Burgesses [of Oxford] did publickly pay each one penny in Token of their Submission to the Orders and Rights of the University. The occasion of this Custom and Offering was a barbarous and bloody Outrage committed by the Citizens in the reign of Edward III against the persons and goods of several Scholars, which drew a great and just Amercement upon the Criminals. The City pretended they were not able to pay the Fine, without their utter Ruin, and did humbly pray and at last obtained a Mitigation from the University. An annual payment of 100 marks was then accepted: And this, by the farther Favour of the University, was changed into a small yearly Acknowledgement, viz. That the Mayor and sixty two such Townsmen as had been sworn in that year to preserve the Privileges of the University, should Yearly upon that day repair to St Mary's Church, and should then and there offer sixty three Pence, in Memory of the barbarous Murder of sixty three innocent Scholars.

Quoted in Montagu Burrows, *Collectanea II*, Oxford 1890

# March 1st: St David's Day

St David's Day is a Welsh celebration, commemorated in Oxford at Jesus College, which has a strong Welsh leaning, having been founded in 1571 by Welshman Hugh Price, a self-made man who rose to wealth from being the son of a butcher. He decreed that Welsh scholars should be educated there.

It was customary for a green leek to be attached to the tassel of each college member's cap by the college servants first thing in the morning, and this was worn to chapel and lectures. The custom died out around 1875, but leeks have sometimes been worn since.

Another more convivial custom was recorded in W. Hone's *Year Book* of 1838:

An immense silver gild bowl, containing ten gallons, which was presented to the College by Sir Watkin Williams Wynne in 1732, is filled with 'Swig', and handed round to those who are invited to sit at the festive and hospitable board.

# Love's Messenger

## St Valentine's Day

**February 14, the feast of St Valentine, has retained its popularity** over the centuries, although the customs have varied. Although named after St Valentine – two saints of that name were martyred in the 3rd century: a Roman priest martyred in AD 269 and an Umbrian bishop executed in AD273 – neither St Valentine had any particular connection with love. This aspect has become attached to their name because their saint's day coincided with the Roman festival of Lupercalia, a fertility festival which featured the sacrifice of dogs and goats to protect flocks and herds. Two young men of high rank carrying goat-skin thongs chased young women to whip them to ensure their fertility. This did not form part of the festival over here, but another facet, that of young people drawing lots to ascertain their partner for the day, was practised in England at least from the later Middle Ages until the 18th century.

Samuel Pepys made several references to the custom in the mid 17th century in his Diaries, when drawing lots on 13th February for your valentine was common practice, and the man was expected to buy his valentine a gift. Pepys had mixed feelings about it as he had an aversion to spending money on such fripperies. When he visited Sir William Batten on St Valentine's Day he cautiously enquired who was the other side of the door before he entered, in case it was a woman who would expect a gift. An indication of how seriously it was taken is given in his diary entry for 1662, when he wrote that his wife had arranged for her valentine, a wealthy young man from whom she expected a generous gift, to visit her on the morning of 14th. However when she awoke she heard noises downstairs and realised that she had workmen regilding her mirror frames. She felt compelled to go around with her eyes covered until her true valentine arrived, because if she saw one of the workmen first he would become her valentine instead, and she would not receive such a good present! Several pairs of gloves were often given as presents.

Francis Misson, a French traveller, described the practice of lot drawing in 1719 in his *Memoirs and Observations in his Travels Over England*:

On the eve of the 14th of February, St. Valentine's Day, a time when all living nature inclines to couple, the young folks in England, and Scotland too, by a very antient custom, celebrate a little festival that tends to the same end. An equal number of maids and bachelors get together, each writes their true or some feigned name upon separate billets, which they roll up, and draw by way of lots, the maids taking the men's billets and the men the maids', so that each of the young men lights upon a girl he calls his Valentine, and each of the girls upon a young man whom she calls hers. By this means each has two Valentines, but the man sticks faster to the Valentine that is fallen to him, than to the Valentine to whom he is fallen. Fortune having thus divided the company into so many couples, the Valentines give balls and treats to their mistresses, wear their billets several days upon their bosoms or sleeves, and the little sport often ends in love. This ceremony is practised differently in different counties, and according to the freedom or severity of Madam Valentine. There is another kind of Valentine, which is the first young man or woman that chance throws in your way in the street or elsewhere on that day.

Chaucer, who lived in the 14th century, did not refer to lot drawing, but wrote of St Valentine as master of love:

> Ye known well, how on St Valentine's Day,
> By my statute and through my governance,
> Ye doe chase your Makes, and after flee away
> With hem as I prick you with pleasaunce.

Valentine gifts are recorded in the middle ages, such as when Sir Henry Willoughby, a Warwickshire gentleman spent two shillings and threepence on one in 1523 – unfortunately no details remain of how he spent his money.

An Oxfordshire omen maintained that if a dark man crossed the threshold on February 14th, he would marry one of the daughters living there during the coming year.

Hand-written cards and notes were written from the 17th century, but it was not until the 19th century that printed valentines became popular. Some were beautifully decorative, concocted from paper lace, which was sometimes decorated with silver or gold leaf, dried flowers and leaves, fabric leaves and flowers similar to those used on wedding cakes, coloured scraps, usually with designs of flowers, ribbon, net, feathers and even human hair. An examination of the extensive collection in the John Johnson Collection in the Bodleian Library revealed that many were made up from the same materials, but put together in slightly different ways, suggesting that they were probably made by outworkers. From the 1860s parfumiers such as Rimmel of Paris introduced perfumed sachet valentines.

Although most cards were decorative, the so-called 'comic' valentines made before about 1850 insulted the recipient, who, to add insult to injury, had to pay to receive letters rather than to send them at that time.

Few towns can boast valentines designed specially for them, except Oxford. The Oxford valentine was printed about 1870 and has sepia drawings depicting an academic young man and woman playing each other at chess, with the Oxford University coat of arms above them, and four views around them showing favourite spots for courting couples – the ruins of Godstow nunnery, punting on the River Cherwell, Addison's woodland walk and the Chinese bridge next to the Botanical Gardens near Magdalen Bridge. It has a quotation from Swinburne's poem *A Match* handwritten below:

> If love were what the rose is,
> And I were like the leaf,

Our lives would grow together
In sad or singing weather,
Blown fields or flowerful closes,
Green pleasure or grey grief;
If love were what the rose is,
And I were like the leaf.

Many country people could not afford to buy Valentines, so they devised their own. 'Country Kate' described hers:

The only two Valentines I ever had were both from crafty-jokers. One was a bit of leather with the branded inscription: 'You are a good sole', and the other were a shrivelled pig's tail, tied with just the ticket, 'You are THE END.'

Sheila Stewart, *Country Courtship*, 1975, p 76

The role of children in St Valentine's Day probably dates from the 19th century when, particularly after enclosure, the agricultural labourers were impoverished, so there was no pocket money for the children. They then began to recite or sing little rhymes at various times of year, hoping to be given a penny or so. A number of Oxfordshire rhymes survive. John Brand recorded in 1849 in *Observations on the Popular Antiquities of Great Britain* that Oxfordshire children sang as they went round collecting pennies:

Good morrow, Valentine,
First 'tis yours, then 'tis mine
So please give me a Valentine.

A totally different version, more like a Shrove Tuesday rhyme, was recorded from Berkshire and adjacent parts of Oxfordshire by Ian Yarrow, in *Berkshire Scrapbook*:

Knock the kittle agin the pan,
Gie us a penny if 'e can;
We be ragged and you be vine,
Plaze to gie us a Valentine.
Up wie the kettle an'

A Victorian perfumed sachet Valentine made from paper lace embellished with cut out printed flowers, enclosing a satin sachet containing perfume, printed with the poem 'Remembrance':

Forget me not', an echo lives – In friendship's feeling
heart, – Respecting sweetest
symphonies, Where absence
makes it smart. – Oh, simple
words with love imbued, -
How hearts respond to
thee, – In cadence soft
through struggling
fears, My friend
remember me.

Bloxham collection

22

down wie the spout,
    Gie us a penny an we'll gie out.

In 1902 the children in the Baldons recited:

The rose is red, the violet's blue,
The carnation's sweet, and so are you.
And so are they that sent you this,
And when we meet we'll have a kiss.

Percy Manning Collection

Bodicote children had a variant on this, according to O. V. Aplin's *Reminiscences*:

The Oxford Valentine, printed around 1870, shows an academic courting couple playing chess, together with the favourite local spots for romantic assignations: Godstow Nunnery ruins, punting on the River Cherwell, Addison's woodland walk and the Chinese bridge near the Botanic Garden, together with a quotation from Swinburne's poem 'A Match'.

John Johnson Collection, Bodleian Library.

The rose is red, the violet's blue
Carnation's sweet and so be you,
So plaze to give us a Wolentine.

If they were refused, the children changed the second line to:

The Devil's black and so be you!

The Bucknell valentine rhyme, recorded in the *Oxfordshire Archaeological Society Reports* for 1903, reflects the superstition that St Valentine's Day influences the weather:

To-morrow, to-morrow Valentine,
Mr March has had his line,
Please give us a Valentine.

C. M. Pumphrey wrote that the variant sung by the Charlbury children was:

Good morrow, Valentine,
I'll be yours if you'll be mine,
Good morrow, Valentine.

A very similar version was chanted in Islip, according to J. O. Halliwell's *Popular Rhymes and Nursery Tales* (1849):

Good morrow Valentine,
I be thine and thou be'st mine,
So please give me a Valentine.

George James Dew, a resident of Lower Heyford, made few references to Valentine's Day in his Diaries, but the entry for 1867 reads:

Feb 14: Thursday, Valentine's Day. The children as usual went round to receive their Valentines (cakes etc. etc.) Had a most ridiculous Valentine with Bicester post mark on it. On a piece of paper was written 'I sent it, the Postman brought it and the fool took it.'

ed. Pamela Horn, *Oxfordshire Country Life in the 1860s*

Before 1867, when the village school first opened, Lower Heyford children went round in groups singing:

Morrow, morrow Valentine,
I'll be yours if you'll be mine,
So please to give me a Valentine.

However after 1867 the rector exerted his influence through the school and he made it clear that he objected to begging, and requested that the farmers send nuts or cakes to the school for distribution to the children. After a few years the teacher, Mrs Dew, asked the farmers' wives to send cakes, originally dough cakes, which were a great treat for the children. When Lower Heyford school closed and the children transferred to Steeple Aston school, the tradition continued there.

Food was apparently a common gift for the children. At Milton they were given an egg each, which is mentioned in their song:

I choose you if its not too late.
If 'tis too late what shall I do?
I hope its not too late, for I've come to have an egg or two.

Percy Manning Collection

At Shipton under Wychwood Mrs Groves recalled that around 1900 the children used to sing verses such as:

Roses red and violets blue,
Sugar is sweet, and so are you.

By 1900 the Shipton children were usually given little presents such as boxes of chocolates rather than money. Other songs, very similar to the ones mentioned already, were used in other villages.

The town of Chipping Norton boasted a curious valentine custom which may be unique. Sydney Scarsbrook, who was born in Chipping Norton about 1925, said that he was one of the children who used to gather together before school and go up and down the main streets, visiting each shop, where they chanted in unison:

I'll be yours if you'll be mine
Please to give me your Valentine.

Valentining at Chipping Norton: primary school children are shown in the High Street on the morning of 14th February, collecting their hot pennies and penny loaves from the local shops.

Most shopkeepers threw out a shovelful of halfpennies and at Pettifers the bakers they received stale buns. He remembered it continuing until 1940, but said that the custom had disappeared when he came back in the mid 1940s. However an informant from the Chipping Norton Local History Society added that the children were thrown hot pennies (presumably hot to prevent them from being too greedy), and that the custom did not cease until the early 1950s, when a new headmaster at the primary school expressed his disapproval and stopped his own children participating.

# Lenten Fast and Easter Frolics

Snick, snack, the pan's hot,
We're come a shroving
Strike while the iron's hot –
Something's better than nothing.
Flour's cheap and lard's dear
And that's why we come ashroving here.

Rhyme from Drayton near Abingdon, quoted in Berkshire Federation of Womens' Institutes, *The Berkshire Book*, 1939

**The ecclesiastical calendar had a strong impact on the division of** the year, and consequently on calendar customs, particularly in the Middle Ages, but continuing through the centuries. Lent was the most serious and sober time, leading up to the dark day of Good Friday and the celebrations of Easter Sunday. In Europe the pre-Lent period was enthusiastically celebrated with Carnival, but in England Shrove Tuesday was the only day when people let their hair down before the privations of Lent. The date on which it falls is determined by the date of Easter.

Pre-Lent celebrations began on the Saturday before Shrove Tuesday, known as Egg Saturday, or in Oxford *Festum Ovorum*, as it was the last day on which the scholars at the University were given eggs to eat before Easter. Anthony Wood described it in his *Life and Times*, volume II:

1664 Feb 2. Festum Ovorum. This feast I have heard Mr John Wilton say that when he came to the University I Jacobi [1603] all the Bachelors that were presented to determine did after their presentation goe to every College where there were determining, and there make a feast for the senior Bachelors, viz of muscadine and egges, figges, reasons [raisins] and almonds, sack, and such-like; which expense was afterwards put down, and the money given to the library. It was an ancient custom.

Collop Monday, which preceded Shrove Tuesday, was so called because that day the last of the meat – 'collops' of bacon and mutton – were consumed, as eating meat was prohibited by ecclesiastical law during Lent. This was referred to in the 14th century in Langland's *Piers Plowman's Vision*:

And yet I say by my soule, I have no salt baconn,
Ne no kokenayes, bi Cryst, coloppes for to maken.

26

There was a practical element to the prohibition on eating meat, as in the middle ages most animals were killed off in the autumn as there was not enough winter feed, and what remained of the preserved meat could have become quite inedible by spring.

On Shrove Tuesday most people worked until 11 a.m. when the Pancake Bell was rung from each church tower, often for about an hour, as a signal to cease work, and the men then headed home to eat their pancakes. At Charlton on Otmoor it was commented in the *Oxfordshire Archaeological Society Reports* for 1903 that 'It was a good morning's work for the farmers' wives to make them.' Before the Reformation everyone confessed their sins to purify themselves for the holy season of Lent. Then the fun could begin. The custom of making pancakes was eminently practical, as during Lent the eating of eggs and drinking of milk was often prohibited (so that the hens could breed chicks and the cows use their milk for feeding their calves).

A publication entitled the *Oxford Sausage* (undated) wrote of pancakes:

Let glad Shrove Tuesday bring the Pancake thin,
Or Fritter rich, with Apples stored within.

John Taylor, the London poet, wrote satirically about Shrove Tuesday pancakes in *Jack a Lent his Beginning and Entertainment* (1621):

... then there is a thing called wheaten flour, which the sulphury Necromantic cooks do mingle with water, eggs, spice and other tragical, magical enchantments, and then they put it by little and little into a frying-pan of boiling suet, where it makes a confused dismal hissing (like the Lemean snakes in the reeds of Acheron, Styx or Phlegeton) until at last, by the skill of the cooks it is transformed into the form of a Flap-Jack, which in our translation is called a Pancake, which ominous incantation the ignorant people do devour very greedily.

Pancake Day was a great treat for the children. Mollie Harris described in *A Kind of Magic* (1969) how she enjoyed Shrove Tuesday as a child in Ducklington in the early 20th century:

The excitement of pancake day in our house has to be seen to be believed. For no other day in the year could we afford such luxuries. The fun began as soon as our mother brought her big wash-stand jug from the bedroom and set it on the kitchen table. Into it went a quart of skimmed milk that one of us had fetched from Sarah Clarke's, and several eggs from our own hens, all whipped up together with plenty of plain flour into a creamy frothy mixture.

A new frying pan – another annual event for the great day – and a pound of best lard to cook the pancakes in, and we were all set to begin ... The fire burnt fiercely so that she had to hold the pan above the flames. As each pancake was cooked it was doled out to the members of the family in turn, according to one's age, the eldest first.

It was customary to eat the pancakes before 8 o'clock in the evening to bring good luck – this was probably also because the Curfew Bell was rung at that time, after which all fires and lights were extinguished, so it would not be possible to cook them. Although regulations about dowsing fires and lights had long since lapsed, the curfew bell continued to be rung in some places, such as Charlbury, in the 19th century.

Traditional pancake races are largely associated with Buckinghamshire, where the Olney pancake race boasts that it began in 1445, but a number of pancake races were run in the latter part of the 20th century in Oxfordshire, largely to raise money for charity. The Wallingford pancake race was organised for a number of years by the Wallingford District Lions Club, and is still popular. At Eynsham races were organised from 1978 by the playgroup.

Country children chose Shrove Tuesday to go round begging either for money or for ingredients to make their pancakes, and many local rhymes survive. Brand recorded an Oxfordshire version in *Popular Antiquities* (1870):

Knick, knock, the pan's hot,
And we be come a-Shroving;
A bit of bread, a bit of cheese,
A bit of barley dumpling
That's better than nothing,
Open the door and let us in,
for we be come a-pancaking.

Angelina Parker recorded another in *Folklore* (1913):

Pit a pat, the pan's hot,
And I be come a srover,
Eat a bit and bite a bit,
And then 'tis all over.

The children sang the song and asked for pennies.

S. Jackson Coleman in *Tales and Traditions of Berkshire*, which covered the Vale of White Horse area, recorded a song about Poor Jack, a similar version of which has also been found in Worminghall, just over the Oxfordshire border into Buckinghamshire:

Shrove Tuesday, Shrove Tuesday,
Poor Jack came from sea,
His mother made pancakes
And fried them for tea.

The host baked them, she tossed them,
She turned them all black,
She put in some pepper,
And poisoned poor Jack.

Another Berkshire version, probably known in the Vale, was:

Snick-snock, the pan's hot,
We be come a-shrovin',

Plaze to gie us zummat,
Summat's better n' nothin',
A bit o' bread, a bit o' chaze,
A bit o' apple dumplin' plaze.

This was recorded in Ian Yarrow's *Berkshire Scrapbook* (1952). Yarrow commented that after dark on Shrove Tuesday the children went round throwing stones at people's doors.

The children of the Baldons are recorded as singing the following verse in 1895:

Pit-a-pat, the pan's hot,
I be come a Shroving,
Catch a fish afore the net,
That's better than nothing.
Eggs, lard and flour's dear,
This makes me come a-Shroving here.

If this plaintive verse did not persuade people to give them money, the children continued:

Pit-a-pat, the pan's hot,
I be come a Shroving,
A bit of bread and a bit of cheese,
That's better than nothing.
For eggs, lard and flour's dear,
So I be come a Shroving here.

*Folklore*, volume 14, 1903, p168

The Checkendon version was:

Knick, knock, the pan is hot,
Here I come a-shroving.
Lard is scarce and flour is dear,
That brings me a shroving here
Up with the kettle, and down with the pan,
Give me a penny, and I'll begone.

C. E. Prior, *Oxfordshire Archaeological Society Reports*, 1906

The custom of collecting buns from Hendred House in the Vale on Shrove Tuesday is said to go back to the mid-16th century – each child was given a bun and a half-penny in return for reciting a rhyme. Several rhymes were used but each contained a line requesting a penny, a pancake or similar. It became an organised event, with the children setting off together for Hendred House at noon, singing as they walked:

Pit-pat, pan's hot, here we come a' shroving,
With a butcher up my back,

A ha-penny's better than nothing.

S. P. B. Mais, *Our Village Today*, 1956 and Oxon and District Folklore Society *Annual Record*, 1965

The custom is carried on by the current owner, Thomas More Eyston, who has personally been giving buns and pennies to pupils of St Amands Roman Catholic School and Hendred Nursery and Primary Schools for forty years.

The Islip version, has undertones of nursery rhymes:

Pit a pat, the pan is hot,
We are come a shroving,
A little bit of bread and cheese
Is better than nothing.
The pan is hot, the pan is cold,
Is the fat in the pan nine days old?

J. O. Halliwell, *Popular Rhymes*, 1849

The Islip rhyme has some similarities with the version from nearby Weston-on-the-Green:

Pitter patter pancake.
I be come a-shroving.
Is the pan hot, is the pan cold?
I can eat pancakes hot or cold.

*Oxfordshire Archaeological Society Reports*, 1903

Two rhymes were sung in Sunningwell:

Beef and bacon's
Out of season,
I want a pan
To parch my peas in.

The children here also threw stones at doors. The other rhyme, recorded in 1878, printed in A. R. Wright and T. E. Lones, *British Calendar Customs*, ran:

Pitt a patt, a pan's hott,
I am come a scroving.
Lard's scarse and flour's dear,
That's what makes me come to scrowing here.
Eggs in the trencher,
Bacon in the pan,
All in the cellar
And I can carry the can.
As black as a rook,
As speckled as a pie,
I cannot sing no longer,
My throat is so dry.

The householders came out and gave the children cakes and money.

Pancakes were traditionally given to all farm workers, as was the custom at Oddington. Pancake Suppers were given for the shepherds and all who had helped with the lambing on Shrove Tuesday.

Making pancakes was not the only way in which Shrove Tuesday was celebrated. Dr Plot recorded that in the 17th century men and women used to bind one another, which sounds like a variant of the Easter Lifting, another way of raising money. Dunkin, in his *History of Bicester* (1812), describes sports:

> The sports of this day were very considerable before the Reformation, and intended as an indulgence previous to the approaching season of Lent. Their commencement is still announced by the ringing of 'the pancake bell' at eleven o'clock, the ancient hour of dinner. At the first sound of this bell, the young people formerly left their employments, and after a hasty dinner, hied away to their various amusements, which consisted in the barbarous practise of throwing at cocks, or the more active sports of jumping, wrestling, ringing of bells etc. On this day the parish clerk still considers himself entitled to the profits arising from ringing of the bells, and accordingly they are let by the hour to those who prefer that exercise. For a trifling sum others are permitted to walk on the tower or on the leads of the church. But though these and most other amusements exist, so much have they declined of late years, that at present they are chiefly practised by children, and in a short time it is probable that they will be discontinued and forgotten.

Throwing at cocks was a widespread pastime on Shrove Tuesday, as was walking on the leads of the church roof, recorded at several places in Oxfordshire, such as Spelsbury (where women used to dance on the roof), Bloxham and Upper Heyford, where participants carved the shape of their shoes on the leads, with their initials, but in these places it was more connected with repairs to the roof, or national celebrations such as commemorating the victory at the Battle of Waterloo in the case of Spelsbury, rather than being a specifically Shrove Tuesday custom.

Walking on the leads of the church roof was sometimes permitted on Shrove Tuesday, and often commemorated by carving the shape of a shoe with initials and a date. This decorated lead from Upper Heyford Church is now on the Oxfordshire Museum collection, accession number 76.413.1.

31

## Oxford University Shrove Tuesday Customs

Anthony Wood wrote that in the 17th century the freshmen at Merton College and perhaps others paid the cooks to make a brass pot of caudle (a warm, sweet, spiced drink) on Shrove Tuesday and:

Afterwards every freshman, according to seniority, was to pluck off his gowne and band, and, if possibly, to make himself look like a scoundrell. This done, they were conducted each after the other to the high table, and there made to stand on a forme placed thereon; from whence they were to speak their speech with an audible voice to the company, which if well done, the person that spoke was to have a cup of caudle, and no salted drinke; if indifferently, some caudle and some salted drink, but if dull, nothing was given to him but salted drink, or salt put in College beer, with tucks to boot. [Tucks – set of thumbnail marks under chin]. Afterwards when they were to be admitted into the Fraternity, the Senior Cook was to administer to them an oath over an old shoe, part of which runs thus: 'Item tu jurabis, quod Penniless Bench non visitabis etc.' After which spoken with gravity, the freshmen kissed the shoe, put on his gowne and band, and took his place among the Seniors.

*The Life of Anthony a Wood*

In 1722 Hearne recorded that the scholars had their dinners on Shrove Tuesday at 10 a.m., when the pancake bell rang from St Mary's Church, and their next meal at 4p.m. He went on: 'and it was always followed in Edmund Hall, as long as I have been in Oxford, till yesterday, when they went to dinner at twelve, and to supper at six, nor were there any fritters at dinner as there used always to be.' (*Reliquae Hearnianiae*, ii, 156, quoted in Percy Manning, *Seasonal Customs*, MS Top Oxon, d 199.)

Brasenose College participated in Shrove Tuesday by serving cakes and either college-brewed ale or Lamb's Wool at dinner, and special ale verses were written and printed. A correspondent in *Notes and Queries*, 7th Series, February 28 1901, page 166 noted:

This year [1887] at Brasenose College an ancient custom has vanished. The Shrovetide cakes and ale, and the rhyme in their honour, failed to appear on Shrove Tuesday last for the first time. The college brewhouse was pulled down last summer to make room for new buildings, and with it has gone the whole of the Shrovetide ceremony. Another ancient custom died away at St John's College, when the mid-Lent refreshment of frumenty was discontinued by the fellows.

## Quill Winders and Tuckers in the Witney Blanket Industry

The quill winders who worked in the Witney blanket industry used to present the sticks used in quill winding to the millowners on Shrove Tuesday, and in return were granted a feast of pancakes and ale. The Tuckers in the blanket industry also had a feast on Shrove Tuesday:

Shrove Tuesday seems to have been a settling day between the Manufacturers and Tuckers' (or Finishers), when it was the custom for the former to give the latter a dinner. Our firm has never let this old custom drop, but every Shrove Tuesday we hold what is known as the 'Tuckers' Feast'. This year (1898) about 50 of us sat down to a substantial dinner, one old pensioner taking his seat at the table for his 66th 'Tuckers' Feast', never having missed one in all these years.

Charles Early & Co., *A Visit to Witney and Witney Mills*, 1898

After the meal the men used to be given one clay pipe for each year that they had attended the Feast. The Tuckers' feast was still celebrated in the late 1960s, when it was recorded in Alfred Plummer and Richard Early, *The Blanket Makers* (1969):

The tradition of a tuckers' feast is still preserved in Witney every Shrove Tuesday, when the employees in the finishing departments are entertained to dinner by their employers, Charles Early and Marriott (Witney) Ltd. It is the custom on this occasion to sing the song 'Wonderfully Curious', which was composed by Joseph Fowler, a tucker, sportsman and musician, said to have been born about the time of the battle of Waterloo, who used to bring his hymnbook to work with him. The occasion is invariably a jolly one, but nobody now comes on a donkey and we are assured that everyone returns home the same night.

After Fowler's death the song was sung by John Seacole, then Fred Middleton and after his death in 1947 by Jack Tooley. At one time the Tuckers' feasts were held in May and November, and sometimes lasted several days, including games of cricket and skittles in the event as well as eating and drinking.

Plummer and Early recorded the words of the song 'Wonderfully Curious':

The wondrous globe on which we live
Is quite surrounded everywhere
With something quite invisible
It's called the atmospheric air.
The air is fluid light and thin,
Which forms of gas it does combine;
It Carries sound in order well
When put in motion it is wind.
   *Chorus:*
   Oh! how curious, wonderfully curious,
   The laws of nature are indeed
   Most wonderfully curious.

The wondrous globe on which we live
The seaman spreads his canvas sail
And as it moves on quick or slow
He calls it breeze, or storm, or gale.
But when it blows with so much power
Till all resistance is in vain
Blowing at 80 miles an hour

He calls it then a hurricane.
*Chorus*


The winds, the seas, the tempest blown
Are very changeable indeed...
But in the torrids they are known
One way for six months doth proceed,
Oft does the wind make ruins lie,
But their usefulness has been understood,
For in the Bible we are told
God guides the wind and rules the flood.
*Chorus*

# Lent

Until the 17th century Lent referred both to the Christian build-up to Easter and to the coming of spring. Ecclesiastical regulations covering Lent have varied considerably over the centuries. In the 6th century AD Pope Gregory the Great prohibited the eating of meat, eggs and dairy produce: milk, cheese and butter. In the late 10th century Aelfric added the stricture that no food should be eaten except by the old and sick until after evensong. He added wine to the list of prohibitions, and exhorted people that during Lent they should not fight, they should go to confession each Sunday, and abstain from all sexual intercourse. King Canute instituted fines for those found guilty of fighting or intercourse.

Gradually regulations were relaxed, so that by the end of the Middle Ages only meat, cheese and eggs were prohibited during Lent, and marriage and sexual intercourse were still forbidden. Henry VIII permitted people to eat dairy produce because the price of fish was very high. His daughter Mary restored Catholicism and the prohibition on eating fish, but Elizabeth I, in reinstating Protestantism only prohibited the eating of meat. Sometimes the regulations were more political than ecclesiastical, as when Charles I wanted to strengthen his navy and the shipping industry in 1644 and so encouraged the eating of fish during Lent. The Puritans abolished Lent after the Civil War, and although it was restored by Charles II the observance of Lent became a matter of personal inclination.

Some curious little customs are associated with Lent locally.

## *Claymond's Dole, Magdalen College*

An ancient dole, Claymond's Dole is presented in Magdalen College Chapel on the first Sunday in Lent. John Claymond (1448-1537), a humanist and friend of Erasmus, was a fellow at Magdalen and president from 1507-1516, when he left to become the first president of Corpus Christi. He joined with John Higden, his successor at Magdalen, and Robert Morwent, his successor at Corpus Christi, to set up the dole. The preamble from the text is read out by the Dean of Divinity before he moves round distributing the dole:

Since in the changes and chances of this mortal life there is no tie so strong and firm as the tie of true friendship, we ... have determined, so that not even death shall annul our union, to leave behind us a monument, that shall endure for ever, as a testimony of our sincere attachment...

It was decreed that £3 should be distributed annually, with 16 (old) pence for the president, 8 pence for each fellow, 4 pence for each demy, twopence for each chorister and 20 pence for the sacristan. Any money left over was to be sent to Oxford prison to purchase straw for the prisoners.

## Ash Wednesday

In the Middle Ages, when people went to church on Ash Wednesday it was gloomy, as all the images of Christ and the saints were veiled, as were the lectern and the rood screen, and the whole chancel was hidden from the congregation in the nave, making the church a sad and solemn place throughout Lent. To emphasise this the priest blessed ashes and sprinkled holy water over them, then either dabbed some on each person's forehead or gave them some, saying 'Remember O Man that thou art dust and to dust thou shalt return.'

Hallowing the ashes was banned in 1548, and the use of veils ceased in the 1570s, when the feelings of awe for Lent were inspired by sermons instead. However traces of this practice can be seen in the custom recorded as recently as the 1950s in Bloxham, when children brought an ash twig into school. Each child in turn would dip one end of this in black ink, and if any trace of white twig could be seen through the black of the ink that child was pinched.

# Lent Sundays

The Sundays during Lent were nicknamed Tid, Mid, Miserae, Carling, Palm and Paste Egg Day. The first three were named after Latin texts: Te Deum, Me Deus and Miserere Mei, while Carling or Care Sunday was named from the grey carling peas often eaten that day. Care Sunday indicated a time of anxiety before the crucifixion. Palm or Passion Sunday was named for the palms given out in church and Paste Egg referred to the eggs of Easter Sunday.

## Mothering Sunday

The fourth or mid-Lent Sunday was known as Mothering Sunday. It began as an ecclesiastical ceremony, when, until the Reformation, people from outlying churches visited the mother church of their diocese. The harsh Lenten fast was relaxed for the day. In the Middle Ages waffles used to be given as a treat that day, and young female servants often gave them to their mothers, so the day acquired its alternative name of Refreshment Sunday. Servant girls would try to come home to visit their mothers.

The poet Robert Herrick wrote around 1648:

I'le to thee a simnell bring,

'Gainst thou go'st a mothering,
So that, when she blesses thee,
Half that blessing thou'lt give me.

Although the custom of giving simnel cakes was more prevalent in the western parts of England, the Oxford and District Folklore Society *Annual Record* of 1950 records them being given in Oxfordshire. Chambers described them in *Book of Days* (1864) as 'a sort of rich and expensive cakes ... raised cakes, the crust of which is made of fine flour and water, with sufficient saffron to give it a deep yellow colour, and the interior is filled with the materials of a very rich plum cake, with plenty of candied lemon peel and other good things. They are made up very stiff, tied up in a cloth, and boiled for several hours, after which they are brushed over with egg, and then baked. When ready for sale, the crust is as hard as if made of wood...'

There were three different types of simnel cakes: the Shrewsbury version had a crown made from almond paste, the Devizes type was star shaped and had no crown and the Bury simnel was a flat spicy cake filled with currants, almonds and candied peel.

There are various theories as to the origin of the name. One is that it was named after Lambert Simnel, the son of an Oxford baker, who pretended to be one of the sons of Edward IV murdered in the Tower of London. However the cakes predate his exploits by many centuries, being referred to in 1062 in the reign of Edward the Confessor. Another legend says that the cakes were named after two individuals, Sim and Nell, who disagreed about how to cook the cakes – one wanted to boil them and the other bake, so they compromised and did both. It is said that the hard crust sometimes caused consternation in the recipients, one lady being unsure what it was and using hers as a footstool!

Mrs Sansom of Stratton Audley commented in 1949:

The custom was for boys and girls, grown up and away at work, to visit their mothers and take a fruit cake and a bunch of violets and primroses that they had picked up in the fields and hedgerows on their way. This custom ... is still observed by a good many people in this district.

This custom of coming home for the day is echoed in a rhyme:

On mothering Sunday, before any other
Every good child should dine with his mother.
Middle Lent tear away,
Palm Sunday, Easter Day
Are sure to drive all care away.'

ed. J.R. Wodhams, *The Midland Garner*, Vol. II, 1884

Frumenty, a traditional dish at Magdalen College, was eaten on Mothering Sunday. It was made from parboiled whole wheat grains which were strained, boiled in milk, and sugar, cinnamon and other spices added.

Mothering Sunday was a day for enjoyment. At Chalgrove until the end of the 19th century the villagers used to walk to an old clay pit, said to be the burial site of those killed at the Civil War battle of Chalgrove Field, about a mile and a half from the village where the men played cricket and the women bat and ball. They relaxed their fast and ate and drank freely, the latter often leading to fights.

Mothering Sunday has been combined with an American custom – that of Mother's Day. This was initiated by Miss Anna Jarvis from Philadelphia, who had lost her mother. Miss Jarvis petitioned the Senate and House of Representatives to have the second Sunday in May dedicated to the commemoration of mothers. This was agreed in 1913. In America it was customary for flags to be displayed, but when the custom was introduced to England by the American forces stationed here during the Second World War, it was the idea of cards that caught on, and instead of giving them on the second Sunday in May they were given on Mothering Sunday. Perhaps inevitably, the day became more commercialised. As early as 1951 Joan Eltenton commented that in Oxford shops were advertising Mothering Sunday gifts and the cost of flowers rose for the occasion.

## Palm Sunday

Palm Sunday: Palm cross given out in Sibford church to commemorate Palm Sunday. Such palms are distributed to the congregation in most churches.

During the Middle Ages religious processions were held on Palm Sunday (or Passion Sunday) with participants carrying blessed palms and small palm crosses. Henry VIII allowed the blessing of palms and crosses, but denied that this gave them any sanctity, but in 1548 under Edward VI they were banned altogether. With the roller-coaster of religious tenets in the 16th century the use of them was restored under Mary and banned again in 1559 under Elizabeth. Even after the custom had been abolished ordinary people carried on visiting the woods three or four days before Palm Sunday to collect green branches of willow, hazel, box and yew to decorate their houses and the church. The sallow willow, Salix caprea, which has golden catkins, was often known as the English Palm. It was believed that branches gathered specially for Palm Sunday would, if kept in the house throughout the year, help to protect it. Palm crosses used to be hung on the walls of houses, and occasionally they were thrown into wells for divinations. Palm crosses are still distributed in church on Palm Sunday.

The day is sometimes known as Fig Sunday, as mentioned by William Framer in *Notes and Queries* Volume I, 1856:

In parts of Oxfordshire, figs are eaten on Palm Sunday, which is thence called Fig Sunday. This I suppose to be in remembrance of the fig tree without fruit which was cursed for its barrenness.

People ate both cooked and uncooked figs, and cooked them in pies and puddings. Flora Thompson wrote about Palm Sunday in *Lark Rise to Candleford* (1945), describing her childhood in Juniper Hill and Cottisford in the 1880s:

Palm Sunday, known locally as Fig Sunday, was a minor harvest festival. Sprays of soft gold and silver willow catkins, called 'pal' in that part of the country, were brought indoors to decorate the houses and be worn in buttonholes for church-going. The children at the end house loved fetching in the palm and putting it in pots and vases and hanging it over the picture frames. Better still, they loved the old custom of eating figs on Palm Sunday. The week before, the innkeeper's wife would get in a stock to be sold in pennyworths in her small grocery store. Some of the more expert cooks among the women would use these to make fig puddings for dinner and the children bought pennyworths and ate them out of the screws of blue sugar paper on their way to Sunday school.

Palm Sunday service at Chipping Norton, complete with donkey.
Oxfordshire Photographic Archive.

The gathering of the palm branches must have been a survival from the old Catholic days, when, in many English churches, the willow served for palm to be blessed on Palm Sunday. The original significance of the day had long been forgotten; but it was regarded as an important duty, and children ordinarily selfish would give one of their figs, or at least a bite out of one, to the few unfortunates who had been given no penny.

A custom found on Palm Sunday and at several other times of year in Wychwood Forest is that of making Spanish water. This custom was found in the Midlands and parts of Yorkshire, but in Oxfordshire was confined to the forest area. Leafield children used to put sticks of Spanish liquorice into empty bottles and take them to Uzzel Well, where they walked round the well, then filled the bottles with water, shook them up thoroughly and drank the liquid. They sometimes called the day Spanish Sunday. Katharine Briggs, in *Folklore of the Cotswolds*, says this was done on Easter Monday.

# Lent Crocking

When the children broke up from school for the Easter holidays, in some areas it was treated as another excuse to go round rattling little clacks of wood at each door begging for food or money. The rhyme sung in the Bletchingdon, Weston and Charlton area in the 17th century, as recorded in John Aubrey's MS *Lansdowne*, was:

Herrings, herrings, white and red,
Ten a penny, Lent's dead;

Rise, dame, and give an egg,
Or else a piece of bacon.
One for Peter, two for Paul,
Three for Jack-a-Lent's all.
Away, Lent, away.

Aubrey commented:

They expect from every house some eggs, or a piece of bacon, which they carry baskets to receive, and to feast upon at the week's end. At first coming to the door they all strike up very loud 'Herrings, herrings, etc.,' often repeated. As soon as they receive any largess, they begin the chorus:
'Here sits a good wife,
Pray God save her life;
Set her upon a hod
And drive her to God.'
But if they lose their expectation, and must goe away empty, then with a full cry:
'Here sits a bad wife,
The devil take her life;
Set her upon a swivell
And send her to the devil.'
And in further indignation, they commonly cut the latch of the door, or stop the keyhole with dirt, or leave some more nasty token of displeasure.

Red herrings were the smoked herrings often eaten when fresh fish was not available – so many had been eaten by the end of Lent that people were very grateful not to be compelled to eat any more! If herrings were served at Easter, after the prohibition on meat was lifted on Easter Sunday, they were arranged on a bed of corn to represent horsemen riding away.

This custom of going round asking for food carried on over the centuries, and Ian Yarrow commented that in East Hendred in the 19th century children went from house to house on Maundy Thursday with clappers or rattles shouting 'Money, flour, bacon or eggs.'

## Good Friday

This is the most solemn day in the ecclesiastical calendar, and lengthy services are held throughout the day. The solemnity of the day translated itself into other aspects of life – it was universally considered very unlucky to do the washing on Good Friday, as God would consider you so irreligious that your soap suds would turn to blood and stain your washing! In Berkshire and the Vale it was even considered unlucky to wash on the five Fridays after Easter. It was considered unlucky for blacksmiths to shoe a horse, miners to go underground or housewives to sweep the house.

Conversely, it was an excellent day to plant your parsley, as it was thought that if planted on any other day it took so long to germinate because it had to go to the Devil nine times to ask permission to grow, but if planted on Good Friday it came under God's protection and could grow straight away!

Baking was thoroughly recommended on Good Friday, as to eat a hot cross bun or bread baked on that day was lucky, and special properties were ascribed to buns and bread actually baked on Good Friday. It has been suggested that hot cross buns are the descendants of wheaten cakes made in Roman times and marked with a cross for the spring festival for Diana. The Anglo-Saxons also ate cross-marked cakes at the Vernal Equinox.

Good Friday loaf in the Oxfordshire Museum collection (accession number 78. 107), which was baked on Good Friday 1896, and acquired wrapped up in a white cloth. There are no signs of mould, but a few pins have been stuck in the base, perhaps indicative of some magic belief.

There was a strong tradition that buns and bread baked on Good Friday had the special property of never going mouldy, and that they could be put to medicinal use, crumbled and mixed with milk or water, to cure such diverse ailments as diarrhoea, dysentery and whooping cough. They also had protective qualities, such as deterring rats from granaries and protecting inhabitants of the house from accident and misfortune. Often they were hung in the kitchen to dry out thoroughly, or placed in a close-fitting box in a dry cupboard, so that they could be carefully kept until required.

At Berrick Salome, Miss Stanley Smith recorded that that a Mrs Raymond's grandmother, who worked as a cook at Wadham College, baked a hot cross bun in about 1846. This was preserved by the family over the generations as a charm against fire, and was carefully wrapped up in a silk square and placed in a leather bag.

Mrs Bromley, who was brought up in Banbury, expressed her feelings about hot cross buns in *Cake and Cockhorse*, volume 5, number 2, spring 1972:

Going back to my early childhood one of my first recollections is the cry 'Hot cross buns all hot, all hot!' on Good Friday mornings, from about 6 o'clock, as the bakers' boys went round with baskets or trays of hot cross buns. Each year I went with the maid to Betts the baker in Butchers Row to fetch the buns for breakfast. Great trays of brown buns smelling deliciously warm from the oven and then we scuttled home with the bag to eat them whilst hot.

Good Friday loaves tend to be cottage loaf shaped. An article in the Anthony Wood column of the *Oxford Mail* mentioned a cottage loaf, slightly burnt underneath and made about 1898, which had nail marks, perhaps indicating that it had once been hung on a wall. The Oxfordshire Museums' collection includes a cottage loaf which has an accompanying label to say that it was baked on Good Friday 1896. It was wrapped in a white cloth, and had some pins stuck in the base, which perhaps suggests a sinister aspect.

At Woodeaton there was a special Good Friday dole of bread: until 1854 wheat grown in the parish was used to make enough loaves to distribute one to each householder.

At Brasenose College on Good Friday the Scholars used to be given almonds, raisins and figs for dinner – John Pointer mentioned in *Oxoniensis Academia or Antiquities and Curiosities of the University of Oxford* (1749) that in 1662 the butler Edward Shippery paid John Langley thirty shillings for eleven pounds of almonds, thirty five pounds of raisins and thirteen pounds of figs.

Good Friday was a holiday, and as the weather was often reasonable, it was a good time for outings. Primrosing was evidently a favourite occupation in many parts of the county, for children at Ascott-under-Wychwood and Chilson, and for both adults and children at Launton. At Wytham and Stowood (when it was Crown property) the private woods were opened for the day so that the villagers could collect primroses to decorate the church on Easter Sunday. Mollie Harris wrote about her childhood in Ducklington:

> Just before Easter we children made a pilgrimage to Gorsehill Woods to gather primroses to help decorate the church, bunching them up with the pale green leaves, tying them carefully with wool. Then the Miss Holtons would place them lovingly round the font and surround them with tangy moss. This was our small contribution. There was never any money to chink into the plate...
>
> Mollie Harris, *A Kind of Magic*, Chatto and Windus, 1969

Children from Over Norton used to walk to the Rollright Stones and try to count the allegedly countless stones – of course their answers were always different!

Alice M. Harvey remembered from her North Hinksey childhood that people would walk across seven fields to the Chilswell Hills where entertainments such as donkey races, coconut shies and water squirting were held. A fair was held at the Giant's Cave Field near Banbury on Good Friday afternoon, where entertainments included stalls, swings, games and the girls skipped.

## Easter Sunday

> The Rose is red, the violet's blue,
> The gilly flower sweet and so are you;
> These are the words you bade me say
> For a pair of new gloves on Easter-day.
>
> J.O. Halliwell, *Popular Rhymes*, 1869

The date of Easter can fall any time between 21st March and 25th April, as it was decided in AD 325 at the Council of Nicaea that it should be observed on the Sunday after the first full moon on or after the Vernal Equinox (21st March) unless that moon fell on a Sunday, in which case Easter should fall on the next Sunday.

As a very special day in the church calendar, it is hardly surprising that superstitions have grown up round it. Country people got up very early to see the sunrise, believing that the sun would jump three times into the air for joy. They scanned the skies to check the weather, because various prognostications were based on Easter, such as this one from Stratton Audley, Wigginton, Wendlebury and many other places:

Rain Easter Day,
Plenty of grass but little good hay.

This indicated lots of rain in the early summer. A variation came from Ledwell:

A wet Good Friday and a fine Easter Day,
Plenty of grass and very little hay.

However, in Forest Hill the saying went: 'A Rainy Easter betokens a good harvest' – which would mean good sunny summer weather. Also from Forest Hill came:

If the sun shines on Easter Day, it shines likewise on Whit Sunday.

Another old saying goes:

If Our Lord's Day falls in Our Lady's lap,
England will meet with a great mishap.

This means that if either Good Friday or Easter Sunday fall on Lady Day – March 25th – there will be a national disaster within the next twelve months. In 1951 Easter Sunday fell on Lady Day and King George VI died less than twelve months later on 6th February 1952, and many Oxfordshire country people remarked on it.

It was important to wear something new for Easter, as it was widely believed that if you did not celebrate the day in this way you were profaning it, and as punishment the birds would make droppings on you. In 1949 Mrs Samson of Stratton Audley commented that in Wendlebury it was common practice for people to buy a new outfit for Easter.

## Easter Eggs

Easter eggs predate Christianity, but have become the symbol of Easter. They have been a potent symbol since prehistoric times, regarded by the Chinese as a symbol of the universe and incorporated in spring rites by the ancient Egyptians, Persians, Greeks, Romans and Gauls, often dyed and exchanged as tokens of spring. Heads of households sent platters of hard-boiled eggs to churches in the Middle Ages to be blessed by the priests, who made the sign of the cross over them and blessed them with the words: 'Bless, O Lord, this thy creature of eggs that it may become a wholesome sustenance to thy Faithful servants, eating in thankfulness to Thee, on account of the Resurrection of Our Lord.'

Edward I spent eighteen pence in 1290 on having 450 eggs coloured or decorated with gold leaf, which he then presented to the royal household. The most elaborate decorating of pace eggs by pressing flowers on to them before dyeing was done largely in the north of England, but eggs were often decorated in Oxfordshire, even if only by being boiled in coloured water as they were in Leafield. Onion skins were often wrapped round them before boiling to give orangey-brown swirly patterns. Mollie Harris said that her mother painted or marked the eggs she boiled for the children's breakfast in Ducklington, and sometimes wrote each child's name on. In Eynsham in the mid-20th century faces were sometimes painted on the eggs, and cochineal was often used for dyeing.

Chocolate eggs have become an increasingly important part of Easter, and chocolate eggs have replaced real ones for games like Easter egg hunts round people's gardens.

Egg rolling is said to represent the stone being rolled away from Christ's grave. Many hillsides, including Shotover, on the outskirts of Oxford, were used for egg rolling games.

Eggs were often given to children in church on Easter Sunday. This was done at the early Easter service at Minster Lovell around 1910-20. Since about 1912 everyone in the village of Westwell has been asked to contribute an egg to the church on Easter Sunday. They were divided into brown and white eggs and placed in baskets at the back of each bench. They were later given to Burford Hospital.

## Easter Gifts

The children who attended Stoke Lyne church on Easter morning around the 1880s were each given a currant bun doled out by the vicar from a clothes basket. Bread was given to each parishioner at Easter at Swerford.

In Ducklington in the early part of this century it was apples and pork or veal pies which were distributed. This was an old custom, in which the rector was expected to give £10 a year to buy veal or apple pies to distribute among the parishioners. This was changed before 1842 to giving bread, but evidently changed back to pies at a later date. According to H. Edwards in *Old English Customs* (1842) all the parishioners, whether rich or poor, had a right to take the food. Apparently the Hardwick people were served first but anyone who had been in the parish for at least twelve hours was allowed to participate. William J. Monk commented in *By Thames and Windrush* (1926) that this led to 'the wildest disorder, and not very long ago the charity was diverted into a much more sensible thing, viz., the giving of coal.'

## Easter Cake

At Kidlington the churchwardens paid for the baking of an Easter cake each year, using eight bushels of wheat given by the vicar. In 1800 the Churchwardens' Accounts included fifteen shillings and sixpence for baking and delivering the cake. It was last baked in 1811, and the lapse in 1812 caused controversy. In 1813 the Churchwardens' book contained the following comments:

14. June 'The Easter Cake is not given away by the Parsonage Farm as it used to be.'

21. October 'That the Easter Cake to be distributed annually - has not yet been given, but the Rector promises it shall be done'.

However, it seems that this promise was not kept and the custom lapsed.

## Apple Throwing at Northmoor

Thomas Hearne wrote about a curious custom:

At Northmoor, near Witney, after evening service every Easter Sunday, men and women throw large quantities of apples in the churchyard and those that were married that year are to throw three times as many as any of the rest. After this they all go to the vicar's house and have bread, cheese and ale; the vicar is under obligation to provide the best cheese he can get.

Philip Bliss, *Reliqiae Hearnianae*, vol. 2, Oxford 1857, p552

This was still done in 1822, as Bliss commented:

This custom still prevails: and my good friend the present professor of Anglo-Saxon who is vicar of Northmoor tells me that on Easter Sunday last (1822) being ignorant of the usual warfare, and so neglecting to make good his retreat after evening service, he came into contact with a stray shot or two, much to the entertainment of his parishioners, all of whom, old as well as young, religiously take part in the contest.

Percy Manning, *Seasonal Customs*, MS Top Oxon d. 199

## Clipping the Church

Clipping the Church, a spring custom, is found in several places in England, but in Oxfordshire only at Radley where it died out in the 18th century. The idea was revived on Easter Sunday 1965 and reported in the *Oxfordshire and District Folklore Society Annual Record*: 'The choir boys and all the members of the congregation, young and old, joined hands to make a great ring round the Church, and so walked round it.' In an account of the ceremony printed in the *Oxford Mail* for April 19th, 1965, it is recorded that 'the intention was to dance gaily round the church to express the joy of Easter Sunday, but the quickest were confined to the pace of the slowest, and it resolved itself into a happy but orderly procession.'

## Witney Easter Play

Plays were performed at several times of year, especially around May Day and Whitsun, often to raise money for the church. In Witney a puppet play was performed at Easter in the 16th century, but was probably killed off by the Puritans:

In the days of ceremonial religion they used at Witney to set forth yearly, in manner of a shew or interlude, the resurrection of our Lord and Saviour Christ, partly of purpose to draw thither some concourse of people that might spend their money in the town, but chiefly to allure by pleasant spectacle the common sort to the liking of popish maumetry; for the which purpose, and the more lively thereby to exhibit to the eye the whole action of the resurrection, the priests garnished out certain small puppets, representing the persons of Christ, the watchmen, Mary, and others, amongst the which one bare the part of waking watchman, who (espying Christ to arise) made a continual noise like to the sound that is caused by the meeting of two sticks, and was thereof commonly called Jack Snacker of Witney.

Lambarde, 1601, quoted in J. A. Giles, History of Witney, 1852

## Chopping the Block

University College, Oxford had a custom entitled Chopping or Chipping the Block or Chopping the Tree until 1864, when it was decided in a college meeting that it should be discontinued. According to *Notes and Queries*, Ist series, vol. IX, on Easter Sunday:

> ... the representation of a tree dressed with evergreens and flowers is placed on a turf close to the buttery, and every member there resident, as he leaves the Hall after dinner, chops at the tree with a cleaver. The College cook stands by holding a plate, in which the Master deposits half a guinea, each Fellow five shillings and sixpence. This Custom is called Chopping the Tree.

William Carr at University College, London in 1902 had a different description if it, writing that the cook and his assistants brought a chopping block decorated with flowers (not a tree), and that they presented each member of college as he left hall with a blunt cleaver for him to aim one blow at the block, after which he gave the cook a tip, which seems to have been the principal purpose of the custom. Christina Hole in *English Customs and Usage* (1941) adds that the cooks were dressed in white caps and jackets, and that they carried two pewter dishes, one to take the money and the other bearing the blunt cleaver. She added that there was an old college tradition that anyone who could chop the pole in half with one blow could claim all the College estates, although this was never admitted officially.

# Easter Monday

Easter Monday was a holiday and ball games held sway. At Hook Norton a ball race was run across the park from west to east and back again on Easter Monday or Tuesday, the first prize being a very fine ball made for the occasion. Other prizes such as aprons and garments were given by couples who had married within the last year. Enormous round sweets called 'suck-balls', 'as large as little patty-pans', with a soft, toffee-like consistency were specially made and sold that day.

Until about 1775 the rector of Chinnor entertained parishioners at the Rectory. After that the feast was held at a public house, financed by the vicar.

At Ascott-under-Wychwood and Chilson a watercress tea was held on Easter Monday, the only time the children tasted watercress through the year, and in the evening a 'Service of song' was given by friends from another chapel.

# Easter Tuesday

A Radish Feast was held in the 19th century on Easter Tuesday in the Bull Inn, New Street in St. Ebbe's. Oxford after the annual meeting for the election of churchwardens.

45

# Hock Monday and Tuesday

The Sunday after Easter is known as Low Sunday, and the Monday and Tuesday following were known as Hock Days, when people indulged in fun and games to raise money for the church. The favourite activity was for the men and women to take turns in catching or 'lifting' members of the opposite sex and 'ransoming' them which took place from about the 15th century until the 17th. The earliest local reference to hocking comes from Thame churchwardens' accounts in 1457. Hocking is also recorded in the 1475 Corporation Accounts for Henley-on-Thames:

14. Ed. IV. And at this day there remains in the box in 'Hokmony' collected as well by the men as by the women, this year 14s 7½d.

Quoted by J. S. Burns, A History of Henley, London, 1861

There is another reference in Henry VII's reign:

14.HVII (Agreed that the money remaining in the hands of the collectors of the play of Robyn Hode, and in the hands of the women of Henley for money collected at Hocketyde should be applied at the discretion of the Corporation, for the buying of a thuribulum of silver, to be made against the feast of All Souls next coming). op.cit.

It is not clear from the text whether the Robin Hood plays and Hock Tide are connected – Robin Hood plays were more commonly performed around May Day or Whitsun.

Further references are found from Oxford, like this one from St Mary's parish quoted in Brand's *Observation on the Popular Antiquities of Great Britain*, from Peshall's *History of the City of Oxford*:

1510: Receipts recd. atte Hoctyde of the wyfes gaderynge xvs ijd.
1522-3 Rec. for the wyfes gatheryng at Hoctyde de claro xvis xd.

Hocking was adversely affected by the Reformation, but came back with the Restoration of Charles II in 1660, as Peshall quoted references from St Peter in the East, Oxford:

1662 About that time it was customary for a parish that wanted to raise money to do any repairs towards the church to keep a Hocktyde, the benefit of which was often very great: as, for instance, this parish of St Peter in the East gained by Hocktide and Whitsuntide, anno 1664, the sum of £14.

The year before £6 had been raised, but references to the custom ended in 1667 when £4 10s was collected, and it was held erratically before that as Grossfield's diary for 1631 reads:

Apr 20. Hocking left off in St Peters because of their good stock.

Percy Manning, Seasonal Customs, MS Top Oxon d199

Dr Plot mentioned Hock Days in Oxfordshire in the 17th century, referring to the popular but unverifiable belief that it was in commemoration of the massacre of the Danes on St Brice's Day in 1002 by order of the AngloSaxon king Ethelred the Unready:

... whence it came to pass that the women to this day bear the chief Rule in laying hold on Passengers, and exacting some small matter of them, with part thereof they make merry, and part they dispose of to pious Uses, such as Reparation of their Church etc.

R. Plot, Natural History of Oxfordshire, 1677

Plot commented that the women celebrated Hock Monday in a solemn manner, and on the Tuesday it was the men's turn, and lighter-hearted in character.

## April Fool

The first of April, some do say,
Is set apart for All Fool's Day;
But why the people call it so,
Nor I nor they themselves do know.
But on this day are people sent
On purpose for pure merriment...

Poor Robin's Almanack, 1760

The idea of April Fool or All Fools' Day is widespread throughout Europe, associated with the Vernal Equinox, and resembles the licensed buffoonery associated with the Roman Saturnalia. It may have originated when April 1st was the last of the eight days of celebration for the New Year, when it officially began on 25th March.

Tricks must always be played before twelve noon, or else they rebounded on the trickster, who would in Oxfordshire be greeted by:

April Fool is gone and past,
And you're the biggest fool at last.
When April Fool comes again,
You'll be the biggest fool then.

Angelina Parker, Collectanea, Folk-lore, Vol. 24, 1913

Mollie Harris knew a variant on this from Ducklington:

April Fool's Day's past,
And you're the April Fool at last.

The tricks were usually verbal – famous examples include sending someone to find a left-handed screwdriver or smooth sandpaper, or to buy some pigeon's milk.

St George, whose feast day is celbrated on 23rd April, has a local connection, as according to legend he fought and killed the dragon on the flat topped hill now known as Dragon Hill at Uffington.

Photograph: Christine Bloxham

## St George's Day: April 23rd

St George, the patron saint of England, was the son of the Christian Roman Governor of Jerusalem. He became a cavalry officer commanding 5000 men, and there is a legend that during his military career he visited England. He resigned his post because of the persecution of Christians by Emperor Diocletian, and was arrested and tortured when he tore down an edict against the Christians. He could have saved his life by sacrificing openly to the gods, but refused and was beheaded. During his execution his enemies were struck by lightning and the idols were destroyed. His body was buried in his birthplace (Lydda, Syria) and his head taken to Rome. The rose became his symbol because it is said to have grown over his tomb.

Slaying the dragon became part of his legend only in the 12th century, and it this which gives gives him a local link, as it was claimed that the site where St George killed the dragon was Dragon Hill, a small hill just below the Uffington White Horse. It has a strange bald patch in the grass top, said to be where the dragon's blood was shed, which poisoned the earth so that nothing would grow there. The story that St George was buried under the hill was immortalised in verse by local shepherd poet Job Cork:

> If it is true as I heard say
> King George did here the dragon slay,
> And down below on yonder hill
> They buried him, as I heard tell.

Quoted by Jacqueline Simpson in *British Dragons*, Batsford, 1980

St George became patron saint of England in the Middle Ages through the influence of crusading knights who claimed they were helped to win Antioch from the Saracens by a vision in the sky of St George and St Demetrius charging to their aid with a mighty host, and St George was seen again leading the crusader attack on the walls of Jerusalem. In 1222 the Synod of Oxford declared St George's feast day a holiday, and in 1348 his name was made part of the English battle cry by Edward III. These were among the reasons for his being made formally patron saint in November 1415, when his feast day was made a 'double festival' on which only necessary work was permitted to be done.

There are meagre references to the celebration of his day in Oxfordshire, but perhaps Anthony Wood was more than a lone candle in the wind when he wrote about how he celebrated in Oxford in 1685, when St George's Day coincided with the coronation of James II, which perhaps made the day more special:

April 23. Th. S George's day celebrated in Oxon with great solemnity. Against St George's day I made several badges Of St George of sarcanet and red velvet ribbon; (1) for Dr [John] Coheant, (2) for Proctor [John] Massey, (3) for Mr [Francis] Browne, (4) for Mr [William] Bishop. But they were all ashamed to weare them in publick. (Mr. Brown and Mr. Bishop wore them but hid them). Whereupon I gave Dr. Conant's to Mr [Robert] Whitehall upon his desire and he wore it. I wore mine. and another I sent to widdow Taylor.

Andrew Clark, *The Life and Times of Anthony Wood*, Vol. III, 1894

St George's Day was celebrated in the Middle Ages by the various guilds of St George, but the only relic of him left in Oxfordshire is as hero of many of the mummers' plays performed around Christmas, and perhaps it is his dragon which descends the hill at Burford on St John the Baptist's Day.

# Beating the Bounds:
# Rogation and Ascension

That ev'ry man might keep his own possessions,
Our fathers us'd, in reverent Processions,
(With zealous prayers, and with praiseful cheere,)
To walke their parish-limits once a yeare;
And well-knowne markes (which sacrilegious hands
Now cut or breake) so bord'red out their lands,
That ev'ry one distinctly knew his owne;
And many brawles, now rife, were then unknowne.

*Withers' Emblems, 1635*

**The fifth Sunday after Easter is Rogation Sunday, and it and the** following Monday, Tuesday and Wednesday form Rogationtide. The custom of perambulating round the parish boundaries and blessing the fields was an established church ritual by the fifth century. In England the Council of Cloveshoo of 747 decreed that participants should fast until midday and walk 'with fear and trembling, with the sign of Christ's passion and of our eternal redemption carried before them, together with the relics of saints', rather than disporting themselves with games, banquets and horse-racing.

It was one of few rituals to survive the Reformation, and in 1559 it was laid down that the parish boundaries were to be perambulated by the curate and the important men of the parish on the Monday, Tuesday or Wednesday of Ascension week. The curate, not wearing his surplice, was to give a sermon encouraging people to give thanks for the fruits of the earth and warn them of curses on those who removed the landmarks of their neighbours. No banners or crosses would be carried and the party would no longer stop at wayside crosses.

The main purposes of the perambulation were to ensure that the parish boundaries had not been encroached – important in the days when there were few maps, and the clergy were entitled to tithes from each parishioner – and to bless the crops and pray for good weather. George Herbert in the 17th century gave them additional purposes – the chance for people to get together in a friendly fashion and end any quarrels and for the poor to receive refreshments.

Parish records from 15th and 16th century Oxford record money paid for having the bells rung for the occasion, paying those who carried holy objects in procession in money or food, and sometimes providing a meal for the participants. Puritans viewed the custom with disfavour, and William

Brudenell, the new vicar of Deddington, in 1631 refused to wear his surplice as his parishioners desired or to preach his sermon on the site of a cross carved in the earth, demanding: 'To what end he should read one, and said he would not stand bare to a hole, which any shepherd or boy might make for ought he knew, and said it was Popery to observe old customs; and then read in a book a homily.' (*Oxford Diocesan Papers*, c26,ff 182-4, Bodleian Library.) He refused to go on subsequent perambulations saying there was not sufficient reason for them. The wealthier inhabitants of Goring in the 1620s refused to pay the bill for drink, declaring that they would have to be sued in court to extract it out of them.

In some places the service was more for blessing the crops than for checking the boundaries, as at Drayton St Leonard, reported in the *Oxford Times* of 28th May 1954:

> From the parish church of St Catherine, Drayton St Leonard, the Rector, the Rev. H. A. Best, led the choir and congregation through the village to bless the crops.
>
> The procession halted at the allotments, where villagers stopped work to take part in the hymn, reading and prayer and joined with the Rector in asking God's blessing on the crops.
>
> A short service was held at the War Memorial, and again at the nearby market garden, before the procession reached the grounds of Garden Cottage. The choir stood at the edge of the garden on the bank of the river while the Rector blessed the waters. After a hymn and a prayer, the procession made its way back to the church.

The crops are regularly blessed each Rogation Sunday in Oddington, where the Rector ensures that he touches part of every farm, field, barn and well. At Horton-cum-Studley the crops were also blessed at Ascension, after which the three-day club feast was held.

Gradually villages became less coherent wholes, and many boundary landmarks were destroyed by enclosure, so the custom declined, but never completely died, and in many places where boundaries were changed in 1974 the bounds were perambulated for the occasion. Over the years the ceremony has sometimes been transferred to Ascension Day, also known as Holy Thursday, and become colloquially known as Beating the Bounds, and as in Oxford White Wand Day after the peeled willow wands used to beat each boundary mark.

By the 1680s the date of beating the bounds still varied, sometimes taking place at Ascension and sometimes on Whit Monday in Oxford. Anthony Wood described the ceremony in St John's parish in 1682:

> Whit Monday, June 5, anno 1682, having been appointed and set apart for a procession-day, some of the fellows and some of the parishioners went on procession to take the limits of the parish of St. John the Baptist, viz. in this manner. Wee went out of Merton College back gate and so to the south-east corner of the city wall which includes the College mount and garden. Returning thence wee went through Corpus Christi College back-gate to the President's Lodgings

beyond and on to the west side of that College. Which lodgings wee leaving on the right hand, wee went towards the house of easement and made a cross under C.C.C. [Corpus Christi College] summerhouse and on the wall against it. Thence returning wee went by the said lodgings, went out of his dore by Ch.Ch. [Christ Church] gate w[h]ere wee made a cross. Thence to Oriel College common gate; where wee should have made a + on the south side of it, for the south half or more of Oriel College is in St. John Baptist parish. Thence wee left Oriel College corner on the left and their chappell on the left, and went up Grope Lane where on the wall of Oriel College ball court wee made another cross and then going over the gutter wee made another on the farthest extent northward of the tenement called the Magpie (now the Talbot). Thence wee returned, and went up the street antiently called Kibald's street where the Universitie carrier's stables are, and so to the back-side of Mr Robert a Wood where in the house of easement that stands cross Kybald Street we made another + close by that + which the parishioners of St Marie's make. Thence going through the house on the north side of the tennis court and through the alley that leads into S John Baptist street, wee went into Logic Lane, where in the middle (where an elboe or a turning is) wee made another + upon the farthest extent northwards of a garden ground belonging to Mert. Coll. in the tenure of the said Robert a Wood. Thence going to the east end of St John Baptist street, wee made another + upon Merton College garden wall. Bread and drink to the parish.(1) This procession was performed by John Conant, fellow, and John Duncombe, chaplayne, of Mert. Coll., Anthony a Wood M.A., Robert and Edward a Wood (both the sons of Robert a Wood), Arthur Fowler (under-cook of Merton College), John Badcock, porter, etc.

(1) By ancient custom Certain colleges provide an refection of bread, butter, cheese, cress, lettuce and alike to senior parishioners who have beaten the bounds on Ascension Day e.g Lincoln to All Saints and St Michael's parishes, All Souls to St Mary's, Merton and St John's.

ed. Andrew Clark, *The Life and Times of Anthony Wood*, Vol.3, 1892

This gives a fascinating insight into some back streets of 17th century Oxford. The following year Anthony Wood went in procession on Holy Thursday; he found the hall gate of St Alban's Hall shut to prevent the parishioners of St Peter in the East coming through on their perambulation. Parish boundaries remained unchanged, but the buildings did not, so perambulations became more and more convoluted over the years as parishioners had to climb over walls, walk through buildings etc. This applies today – for example the boundary mark for three parishes is found protected behind a glass screen in the middle of Marks and Spencer's in Queen Street, and seeing the processions rush through must amuse the shoppers!

John Brand wrote in the mid 19th century that during the beating of the bounds 'the little crosses cut in the stones of the buildings to denote the divisions of the parishes were whitened with chalk. Great numbers of boys with peeled willow wands in their hands accompany the minister in the processions.' (*Popular Antiquities*, 1849.)

The peeled willow wands were (and still are today) used to beat the boundary mark – today the choirboys carrying them beat the mark together,

Beating the Bounds of the parish of St Michael at the Northgate in 1964: hitting the boundary mark outside Worcester College with willow wands. Photograph: Christine Bloxham

Boys scrambling for hot pennies at Lincoln College while beating the bounds, early 20th century. Oxfordshire Photographic Archive

shouting 'Mark! Mark! Mark!' as they do it to help them remember the positions of the marks. It is said that originally the wands were used to beat the boys, or they were 'bumped' on the marks.

John Kilvert witnessed beating the bounds on Holy Thursday, 25th May 1876, when he was wandering in Merton College gardens after chapel:

We suddenly became aware that the peace of this paradise was being disturbed by the voices and laughter and trampling of a company of people and immediately there came into sight a master and bachelor of arts in caps and gowns carrying a ladder on their shoulders assisted by several men, and attended by a number of parish boys. Every member of the company bore in his hand a long white peeled willow wand with which they were noisily beating and thrashing the old City walls and Terrace Walls. 'They are beating the bounds!' exclaimed Mayhew. The master of arts was Knox, the Vicar of Merton living and parish of St John the Baptist, the bachelor of arts was one of the Fellows of Merton, and the men in attendance were Churchwardens, clerks, sidesmen and parish authorities.

The ladder was let down over the city walls

at two places where the walls were crossed by the parish bounds and at certain important points which it was desired that the boys should keep in mind they were made to scramble for sweetmeats. We determined to follow the procession and see the end. We came down into Deadman's Walk and then passed up a flight of steps and through an iron gate into Corpus Gardens. Here we were stopped by a gate of which the key could not be found for some time. In this quarter the parish boundary ran through an outhouse where used to be an ancient wheel for raising water. In this outhouse a cross was scratched upon a particular stone to mark where the boundary passed through the wall.

By this time the missing key had been found and we found ourselves in the private garden of the President of Corpus, Matthias Wilson. It seemed to be an ancient custom here that those who beat the bounds should be regaled with bread, cheese and ale from the private buttery of the President of Corpus. Accordingly we gathered under an old archway while the customary dole was handed out to us over the buttery hatch. Here Knox took occasion to remark in his merry laughing mischievous way with a sidelong look at Mayhew and myself that all those who beat the bounds were expected to contribute towards the expenses of the Church. The proposed offertory however produced nothing and when we had finished our bread, cheese and ale we passed on through a pretty conservatory where the President came out of his library to speak to Knox and Mayhew. The boys now led us through an outer court where the parish boys were liberally splashed with cold water by undergraduates from the windows of the upper rooms.

Eventually we emerged close to Canterbury Gate and went into Oriel. Here there was a grand uproar in the quadrangle, the men threw out to the boys old hats (which were immediately used as footballs), biscuits were also thrown out and hot coppers, and the quadrangle echoed with shouting and laughter and the whole place was filled with uproar, scramble and general licence and confusion. Knox could scarcely get his boys under control again, but at length we went out the hall steps, down through the cloisters into the kitchen precincts where there was a Hogarthian scene with a laughable scrimmage with the young flat-white-capped cooks that might have furnished a picture for the Idle Apprentice. The procession passed next up Oriel Lane and here we left them.

ed. William Palmer, *Kilvert's Diary*, 1977

The friendly banter and water-throwing sometimes developed into actual fighting:

... some of the parishes made it an occasion for a regular battle; especially was this the case between St Ebbe's and St Roll's, as St. Aldate's parish was then called.

The fighting took place in Brewer's Street, at the cross that divided the two parishes, but not with fists, like town and gown, but sticks, some of which were formidable weapons, and much punishment was inflicted on both sides. The battle was kept up for several days, and then gradually ceased.

'An Old Freeman', *Early Recollections of Oxford*, 1900

This sounds most irreligious, and it cannot have been condoned by the respective vicars who should have been in charge of the proceedings! St Ebbe's was a relatively poor area of Oxford.

By the early 20th century the custom was not necessarily practised by every parish each year. The Oxfordshire Archaeological Society Reports for 1905 comment that the bounds of the parish of St Mary Magdalen were beaten every third year on Ascension Day by the Vicar, accompanied by the churchwardens and choirboys armed with willow wands:

These are carried by all in the procession. The ceremony begins in the Church as 2 p.m. and after the perambulations, which include some remarkable feats in climbing walls and getting through holes, there is a tea for the youngsters, which has now taken the place of the cakes and ale of earlier days.

The custom declined, and according to Christina Hole, was revived in 1949 by the Rev. Colin Stephenson, and performed bi-annually. The parishioners of St Michael-at-the-Northgate continued during the the Second World War:

Despite the war, the choristers of St Michael-at-the-North Gate held their traditional meal – the elders with their accompaniment of ground ivy ale – after beating the bounds of the parish today.

Ordinarily the lunch is held in the hall of Lincoln College, but this year as the College has been taken over by the Government this could not be held – nor the traditional scrambling for hot pennies in the quad.

The little party, however, went round the parish, marking the boundary in Lincoln, and had their lunch in the new 'Roebuck' snack-bar in Market-street.

Here, underneath a carpet in the private bar, is a stone marking a boundary of two parishes – St Michael's and St Martin's. The Rev. R. R. Marton, the Vicar, led the procession.

*Oxford Mail*, 1st May, 1940

In 1951 there was a mix-up over dates, and the ground ivy required to make the beer was only gathered at the very last minute by Ken Carter, who nevertheless succeeded in making over fifty pints, which butler Jack Clent poured into silver mugs for the parishioners. Three parishes were beating their bounds that year: St Martin, St Michael-at-the-North Gate and St Mary-the-Virgin – the latter parishioners had breakfast at All Souls. The traditional lunch was held at Lincoln College, with fruit drinks and buns for the youngsters and bread, cheese and spring onions for the adults. At the end of proceedings hot pennies were scattered for the youngsters by under-graduates from windows overlooking Brasenose Lane.

At one time all parishes would have beaten the bounds. Often it was only recorded when something went amiss, as in Appleford in 1673 when John and Katherine Whicheloe, according to the Presentiments to the Archdeacon of Berkshire by the Churchwardens, failed to provide two bushels of wheat to make into bread and a bushel of malt to make beer for Ascension Day for the perambulation: the two repented their fault and provided their dues.

At Bampton-in-the-Bush, according to Dr Giles in *History of Bampton* (1848), perambulations ceased after enclosure in 1818, but before that the procession covered the full extent of the tithing of Bampton, which took several days. On the Monday they went as far as Clanfield, breakfasting at the house of Mr Chiswell who farmed the tithes, on Tuesday to Haddon and Heart's Yat near Lew, again with various refreshments provided. On Wednesday they went to Aston, eating at Cote Hatch gate.

A vital member of the procession each day was a woman

Perambulating the Bounds. The Boundary Elm.

who had never been married who carried a paddle and cut deep crosses to mark the bounds. Each evening on their return home the party were provided with a barrel of beer and two bags of bread in the churchyard.

Sometimes coaches were provided in the 20th century to ease the proceedings, as in Banbury in 1952, but the parishioners still had to walk four-and-a-half miles. Twenty-two stakes were carried to hammer into the ground as boundary marks with a ceremonial mallet.

At Charlbury beating the bounds was done erratically after 1848, and revived in 1953 after a twenty-year break occasioned by the tragedy of two boys drowning in the River Evenlode during the procession. In 1953 it was done on 28th May instead of Ascension Day. The walk of about six miles started from the churchyard at 2.30, and the party stopped en route for a picnic.

At Cumnor the party had to cross the Thames by boat to touch the Oxfordshire bank (Cumnor was in Berkshire until 1974). The Eynsham ferryman brought six shillings and eight pence, the Swinford tithe, in a basin of water. The vicar removed the money and then sprinkled the water over the onlookers.

The route taken round the Forest Hill boundaries, as described in Ella Miller's *Forest Hill Village Book* (1933), sounds picturesque: 'Down Watery Lane, cut a cross in the turf, in at the gate below Pilfram [a little farm], over to Holton 'ood, up the Rattlin' Gutter, up the road by the Stone Pits, crossing over Red Hill, over Oxford Road, to the Cow 'us on Woodman's Hill where bread and cheese were served, on past a limekiln, across the road to Bayswater (where a boy was often thrown into the brook) and then home.'

Beating the Bounds was mentioned in Fritwell parish records in 1641 and in various other years up to 1699, then lapsed for a while. J. C. Blomfield in his *History of Fritwell* (1893) wrote that it had not been done in living

In towns boundaries were often marked by plaques, but in the country local landmarks such as this boundary elm were often used.

Illustration from John Brand and Henry Ellis, 'Observations on Popular Antiquities', 1841.

memory, but he recorded a description written by W. Vaughan, the vicar in 1743, who described some lands as having been given to the parish to encourage the parishioners to go 'Possessioning or Processioning'. The rent from this land was to be spent at the discretion of the minister, and the procession should take place around Ascension Day. He went on:

> This custom had for some time been omitted, but was reviv'd, and a piece of ground in Clifton meadow at the South end next to mean lands (the true bounds whereof were unknown to ye oldest man in the parish), properly laid out and mark'd with Holes and posts, one close to ye bank of the Cherwell, the other on the Bank of ye opposite stream dividing it from Bedmoor, and running in a line from the South end of Mr Gough's spinney ...

At Kiddington a Procession Way followed part of the parish boundary between Kiddington and Glympton Fields. In 1704 the Clerk, Thomas Slymaker, encouraged the Rector to organise a procession before all knowledge of the Way disappeared. This was done, and the Procession Way was found to have been ploughed up, so the landowner, Sir Thomas Wheel, agreed to restore it. However when the bounds were beaten in 1708, the way was hindered with brakes and large bushes so the people were forced to trample down some of the corn. To preserve what they could, the parish council passed a resolution: 'that care be taken hereafter that a Cross be made to point at the Procession-way which was not made this Ascension Day 1708 on pretence of bushes and thorns having grown up in the place where the Cross was usually made in former times, and besides the Cross meer-stones must be contrived to make the Procession-way distinct when the turning of the corn into sanfoyn breeds confusion.' (Rev.John Cudworth, quoted in R. P. Norwood, *History of Kiddington*, 1930.)

At Standlake the Beating of the Bounds included a special sermon, mentioned by Dr Robert Plot in 1677:

> I cannot but note an odd custom at Standlake, where the parson in the procession about Holy Thursday reads a gospel at a barrel's head in the cellar of the Chequers Inn, where some say there was formerly a hermitage, others that there was anciently a cross, at which they read a gospel in former times, over which now the house, and particularly the cellar being built, they are forced to perform it in the manner as above.

*Natural History of Oxfordshire*

The custom had died out by 1875, when Rev. Tuckwell was Rector, but he commented that '... another prettier custom still prevails and on the same festival out of a fund which has existed for many years is granted a sufficient sum to provide for each school child in attendance a penny loaf.' (Rev. L. S. Tuckwell, *Some Reminiscences of Thirty Happy Years of Clerical Work in the Parish of Standlake*, 1918.)

The boundaries of Stonesfield were beaten on 8th May 1807, and the churchwardens recorded the positions of the nineteen crosses and who held the rights of using water from wells situated on the boundaries. The details can be found in G. H. Powell's *Stonesfield through Two Centuries*.

## Inspecting the City Walls

Sometimes boundaries were beaten for secular rather than ecclesiastical purposes. In 1879 Richard II granted William of Wykeham, the founder of New College, permission to acquire the land upon which the college was built, which included a section of the city wall. Since then this section has been inspected regularly, currently every three years, by the city council. The inspection is usually carried out by the chief constable, the mayor (and sometimes the mayoress), the sheriff, town clerk, aldermen and councillors, dressed in their official robes. They process along the High Street to the gate in Queen's Lane, where the mace bearer demands entry. The original purpose was to ensure that the walls were in good condition for the defence and safety of the city.

## Riding the Franchise

Another version of beating the bounds in Oxford, known as Riding the Franchise, has taken place at least since 1391-2, and was held regularly until 1901, particularly whenever a mayor of Oxford held office for the first time. It usually took place in late summer or early autumn. The custom had a practical function in familiarising the mayor with the city boundaries and free waters, and enabling councillors of newly incorporated areas to meet their new colleagues and feel part of the larger unit. Civic ceremonies such as this can give a personal touch to rather impersonal local government, while the ceremonial aspect gives dignity and formality to events such as boundary changes which might otherwise pass almost unnoticed. It also imparts a sense of continuity in government.

Mace bearer, Riding the Franchise, Oxford, 1991.

In the Victorian period they tended to be light-hearted occasions (often with musical accompaniment from military bands or the City Waits, or more recently fifers and drummers) much enjoyed by the freemen and involving some horseplay. Each boundary stone was marked by the City Mace and flag being placed on it and the playing of part of the National Anthem. Refreshments of beer, cheese and cakes were supplied to participants at traditional halting places, and they were feasted by the mayor and his party at Godstow.

The ceremony took a whole day, for the city bounds had to be perambulated partly on foot, partly by boat – which could be hazardous, as on at least one occasion the Mayor's punt sank, and he, the Sheriff and the mace had to be rescued from the River Cherwell. On another occasion his punt ran aground and he only escaped wet feet by stepping across the backs of half a dozen men kneeling in the mud. Planks were carried for crossing ditches. In 1892 there was a minor battle when the residents of

Riding the Franchise at North Hinksey in 1872.

Oxfordshire Photogrqaphic Archive.

Wolvercote claimed that the boundary mark was in the wrong place, encroaching on their land.

The council changed the proceedings in 1837, excluding the city drummer and the freemen, making the occasion more decorous. However this new Puritan attitude did not last long and in 1840 the drummer was reinstated. The party were greeted at the Free Water Stone by the 'King of the Sclavonians', an elderly freeman who, according to ancient custom, greeted the mayor, and at Hogacre Ditch claimed a toll 'for the benefit of old and decayed freemen'. The role of 'King of the Sclavonians' was a sort of mock-mayor, but he and his court had an important role detecting non-freemen trying to vote illegally, and imposed fines on them, or pumped cold water up their sleeves if they refused to pay.

In 1901 the party met the mock-mayor of Summertown, wearing his insignia of a bicycle chain and large plated cycle chain wheel, with a crutch as a mace. He greeted the mayor:

So seldom are the Officers and Burghers of our Salubrious Borough visited by the high Officials of the City of Oxford, otherwise than for the collection of our tributary rates, that We, on this auspicious occasion, desire to extend to your Worshipful sirs our most hearty welcome, the more especially do being mindful of the fact that on a former visit connected with a ceremony similar to that which occasions your visit today, your right Worshipful Predecessor so nearly left us the precious emblems of your civic dignity.

Quoted in David Steel, *Riding the Franchise*, 1991

As usual the mayor provided bread and cheese at Godstow. However the custom was now only held

Riding the Franchise: Lord Mayor of Oxford, Councillor Alan Pope, unveiling a boundary mark close to the Sainsbury's superstore at Heyford Hill, 1991.

Photograph: Christine Bloxham

every three years, so it lost its traditional function of teaching the mayor the boundaries.

As Oxford City has taken in more suburbs it has become impractical to go round the whole boundary, so in on 7th September 1991 the Riding was confined to the new areas being included: Old Marston, Risinghurst, Sandhills and Littlemore. The mayor that year was Alan Pope, who was accompanied by his sheriff, John Power and a civic party. Music was provided by the City Waits. The party set out at 9 a.m. from the Town Hall, led by the mace bearer carrying the heavy mace, made in the reign of Charles II, followed by the mayor and lady mayoress in robes and chains of office, civic party and guests and proceeded to Folly Bridge to travel on a Salter's steamer to Iffley Lock. The party disembarked to walk along the ring road towards Sainsbury's at Heyford Hill. where they were met by Littlemore parish councillors who accompanied them to the grounds of Sainsbury's where a new boundary stone was unveiled.

The party walked on towards Blackbird Leys Parish and Minchery Farm Country Club, with a refreshment stop at the George Inn, Littlemore. At

the boundary of Blackbird Leys the party was met by the local parish coun-
cillors and all walked along the route of the new city boundary to
Watlington Road. A boundary stone in this area, donated by Sharp
Industries, was unveiled at a later date. On reaching the centre of Blackbird
Leys the party met Andrew Smith, Member of Parliament for Oxford East,
who was fortuitously inaugurating a balloon festival in the square.

The party then boarded a bus to the Marston slip road on the A40 near
the Elsfield flyover, and walked the new boundary to the Victoria Arms,
where lunch was provided. The busy Lord Mayor only had time to grab a
brief bite as he rushed off to attend another function while the rest of his
party lunched. After his return the party headed by bus to Risinghurst, and
after being welcomed by the Risinghurst councillors, walked up Kiln Lane
to the parish hall for tea. The final stretch was a walk back down Kiln Lane
round the side of Nielsen's to Thornhill Park and Ride, and across the A40.

## Beating the Bounds: Other Civil Functions

In Woodstock too the civil bounds were beaten. The beating in 1910
was led by Mayor Mr Haynes of Manor Farm, with his macebearer Mr
Miles, Mr Henman, Mr Pratt, the curate Rev. Randle and many youngsters. They had to climb a ladder and a stile to go into old Woodstock and
came back via the water meadow. The ceremony was not repeated until
1957, when it was reported in the *Oxford Mail* of 31st May:

> On Ascension Day, 1957, the bounds of the Borough of Woodstock were beaten
> again after a lapse of forty-seven years. This was a secular, not an ecclesiastical,
> bound-beating, which it is now proposed to repeat every five or ten years. About
> fifty people, led by the Mayor, the Mayoress, and the Vicar, including boys armed
> with wands walked round the borough limits as laid down in the incorporation
> charter of 1886. The distance is about two and a half miles. During the
> perambulation the River Glyme was crossed by a temporary bridge, and a ten foot
> wall was scaled with the help of two ladders. Afterwards, the Mayor distributed
> newly minted threepenny pieces and autographed copies of the Borough Guide to
> the children who took part. These gifts replaced the hot pennies formerly
> scrambled for on the rare occasions (twice only in the last ninety-five years) when
> the bounds have been beaten.

# Holy Thursday Spring Celebrations

On Ascension Day in the 17th century the New College fellows went to
St Bartholomew's Well off the Cowley Road to welcome the spring. This
replaced singing on their college tower like the Magdalen men on May 1st,
which had led to clashes. Anthony Wood described the occasion:

> ... the fellows of New College after their grave and wonted manner early in the
> morning used to walk towards this place, where they entered the chappell (being
> ready deckt and adorned with the seasonable fruits of the year): being seated, the
> chaplain of their place after some respite did use more sentiently to read a psalm
> and chapter allotted for the day. That being ended, the said fellows of New College

61

sung a himne or anthem of five or six parts. Then the second lesson was read. After that another was sung, or else a collect for the day, consisting of as many parts. Then the fellows one by one went up to the altar where stood a certaine vessell deckt with Inttyes [nosegays], and therin offered a piece of silver which is afterwards divided among the poore men [almsmen of the St Bartholomew's Hospital]. This ceremony ended in the chappell, they walked from thence to a well called Strowell at the upper end of the grove adjoining (Which with the way from the chappell thereto used antiently to be strewed with flowers). Where being fixt (after an epistle and gospel as was sometimes used) they in the open place like the ancient Druids the Appollonia of Spring, eccho'd and warbled out from the shady arbours harmonious melody consisting of several parts then most in fashion. Which being ended, each man departed home.

ed. A. Clark, City of Oxford, vol. II

This is the nearest thing Oxfordshire has to well dressing. Wood queried whether this essentially religious service could be connected with the Bringing in the Fly by the cooks, which took place at Whitsun (of which more later).

The Restoration to the throne of Charles II in 1660 saw a revival in spring festivities, in defiance of the ousted Puritans who had banned all such entertainments, so on 31st May, two days after his arrival in London, maypoles were erected, and there were no references to beating the bounds:

31.May 1660. This Holy Thursday the people of Oxon were soe violent for Maypoles in opposition to the Puritans that there was numbered twelve Maypoles besides three or four morises etc. But no opposition appearing afterwards, the rabble flagged in their zeal, and seldom after above one or two in a year.

Andrew Clark, The Life and Times of Anthony Wood, vol. I, 1891

Another Holy Thursday custom, recorded in *Reliquiae Hearnianae* in 1724-5, was for the parishioners of St Aldate's parish to eat sugar sopps out of the church font. No explanation is given as to why.

At Bloxham for the last two hundred years the primary school children have gone to church that day for a service, after which the children in the top class were permitted to walk onto the leads of the church roof. Minster Lovell children also went to church and then home to dinner. Afterwards they took their mugs up to the ruins of Minster Lovell Hall for 'Scrambles' – scrambling for sweets provided by the Vicar.

Witney children attending St Mary's Infants' School and the Batt Junior School brought eggs to church which were taken to the altar to be blessed, then distributed to the elderly living in the flats and almshouses in the town. The custom was recorded in the *Oxford Mail* of 1976 and was said to go back some years, although the origin was unknown.

# The Merry Month of May

Crouch Hill, to the west of Banbury, where boys used to greet May morning by blowing cows' horns.

Illustration from A. Beesley, *History of Banbury*, 1843

We've been rambling all the night,
And sometime of this day;
And now returning back again,
We bring a garland gay.

A garland gay we bring you here;
And at your door we stand,
It is a sprout well budded out,
The work of Our Lord's hand.

Verse from Abingdon, quoted in J. G. Frazer, *The Golden Bough*, 1967

**The first of May, which heralds the beginning of summer, has been** celebrated enthusiastically for centuries. It is a prime example of how customs have changed and adapted over the centuries as beliefs and interests have changed.

May celebrations were obviously rife in 1250, as the Chancellor of Oxford University forbade 'alike in churches, all dancing in masks or with disorderly noises, and all processions of men wearing wreaths and garlands made of leaves of trees or flowers or what not.' (Percy Manning, MS Top Oxon d. 200).

Oxford girls in the 17th century made garlands of flowers, which they carried round the streets and then placed in the churches. The making of garlands continued until the early 20th century, but certainly from the 19th century and possibly before, they were carried round the streets as the girls begged for money rather than being taken into church. Many garlands were elaborately made with crossed hoops decorated with greenery and flowers by girls, who went round in groups of three or four, one wearing a white veil and another with a blackened face. A feature of Oxford garlands was the use of cuckoo flowers, considered unlucky elsewhere. Girls also made floral crosses.

However girls did not have a monopoly on the fun: boys used to blow cows' horns or hollow canes in the early hours of May morning to welcome summer. It was recorded in Shepilinda's *Memoirs of the City and University of Oxford* (1737):

In the City of Oxford there is a custom on May Day for all the boys in town to blow horns, which that they might be perfect in, they begin to blow from the first of April, but of the particular morning they begin by 2 o'clock. The tradition of this is, that once upon a time the Tradesmen of this City went all out a gathering May in a Morning, in which Time their Wives made them all Cuckolds, so to warn all honest Mechanical Husbands to keep from May Frolics, and take care of their Spouses at home.

The explanation for the custom seems a little outlandish! Hearne commented on horn-blowing in the 18th century, by which times the horns were being used as drinking vessels as well as instruments. By 1847 the horn-blowing was actively encouraged, with stalls selling them:

Hosts of boys are there too, with tin trumpets, and stalls fitted out for the sale of them, and sweetmeats and as soon as the singers cease, the bells peal forth their merry sound in joyful welcome of the new months; and the boys, who have been impatiently waiting for the conclusion of the matins, now blow their trumpets lustily and performing such a chorus as few can imagine and none forget, start off in all directions and scour the fields and lanes, and make the woods re-echo to their sounds, in search of flowers.

L. Jewitt, *Literary Gazette*, May 1847

It was recorded in *Notes and Queries*, 4th series Vol VII, that workhouse children were permitted to participate in the horn-blowing and treated to a good meal by a local alderman. Later it was recorded as being to 'call up the old maids', in similar vein to the Banbury tradition:

...the boys of Banbury ... resort on the morning of May Day to Crouch Hill, a hill about a mile from the town, with horns to greet the rising sun, after which they return to serenade the old ladies of the town.

*Oxfordshire Archaeological Society Reports*, 1904

In the Middle Ages a highlight of the festivities was the adults going on May Eve to collect hawthorn boughs, returning at dawn to decorate the door of each house. Bishop Robert Grosseteste of Lincoln complained about priests participating in these pagan ceremonies around 1240. Geoffrey Chaucer referred to this maying in the Knight's Tale of the *Canterbury Tales*, where the knight makes a garland of hawthorn and wood-bine, and in Court of Love where:

Forth goeth all the Court, both most and least
To fetch the flowers fresh and branch and bloom.

In the 17th century green boughs were used to decorate Oxford churches, as according to manuscript Diocesan Papers (c27 f46 in the County Record Office) in 1634 there was a brawl at St Peter le Bailey, when parishioners brought a garland of flowers into the church after morning prayers to hang on the screen before ringing the church bells. Some Puritans attacked them to prevent them doing it. One Puritan, John Woodgoose, shouted: 'Oh impudent wicked people, God no doubt will revenge himself on you if there be any God at all.' He demanded that the churchwarden 'throw that toy or bauble … out of the church'.

A tailor's apprentice who was trying to hang up the May garland was attacked by another Puritan, John Eastbrooke, a Master of Arts of New Inn Hall Street, who was later hauled before the vice chancellor's court with Nathaniel Stanyforth and George Kendall, Bachelors of Arts, accused of causing a riot by attempting to stop lawful May Day junketings. Eastbrooke responded ingeniously that he was not guilty, as he had just told the man to keep the dirt from his shoes off the seat, but all three were found guilty and sentenced to stand before the clergy, churchwardens and congregation after morning prayer and make a public apology. (Information from David Vaisey, Anthony Wood Column, *Oxford Mail*, 30 April 1976.)

A few years later the Puritans triumphed:

1648 May 1. This day the Visitors, Mayor, and the chief officer of the well-affected of the University and City spent in zealous persecuting the young people that followed May-Games, by breaking of Garlands, taking away fiddles from Musicians, dispersing Morrice-Dancers, and by not suffering a green bough to be worn in a hat or stuck up at any door, esteeming it a superstition or rather an heathenish custom.

Anthony Wood, *History and Antiquities of the University of Oxford*

It was considered important to attach a green bough to each house, as it represented good luck and fertility for the coming year. In Woodstock Park, according to Aubrey writing in the 1680s, on May Eve they 'goe into the parks and fetch away a number of hawthorn trees which they set about their dores; 'tis pity that they make such a destruction of so fine a tree.'

Such activities were greatly disapproved of by the prudish Puritans, who felt that it led to loose morals and lasciviousness:

Bringing in the Maypole.

Ilustration from John Brand and Henry Ellis, *Observations on Popular Antiquities*, 1841.

Bringing in the May-Pole.

Against May, Whitsonday, or other times, all the young men and maides, olde men and wives, run gadding over night to the woods, groves, hils, and mountains, where they spend all the night in pleasant pastimes; and in the morning they return, bringing with them birch and branches of trees, to deck their assemblies withall. And no mervaile, for there is a great Lord present among them, as superintendent and Lord over their pastimes and sportes, namely Sathan, prince of hel. But the chiefest jewel they bring from thence is their May-pole, which they bring home with great veneration, as thus. They have twenty or forty yoke of oxen, everyone having a sweet nose-gay of flowers placed on the tip of his hornes, and these oxen drawe home this May-pole (this stynkyng ydol, rather), which is covered all over with floures and hearbs, bound round about with strings, from the top to the bottome, and sometime painted with variable colours, with two or three hundred men, women and children following it with great devotion. And thus being reared up, with hand kerchiefs and flags hovering on the top, they strew the ground round about, bind green boughs about it, set up summer hauls, bowers and arbours hard by it. And then fall they to dance about it, like as the heathen people did at the dedication of the idols, whereof this is a perfect pattern, or rather the thing itself. I have heard it credibly reported (and that viva voce) by men of great gravity and reputation, that of forty, three score, or a hundred maidens going to the wood over night, there have scarcely the third part of them returned home again undefiled.

Philip Stubbes, *Anatomy of Abuses*, 1563

The maypole described by Stubbes was probably exaggerated in size, but in some places large trees were used. Sometimes permanent maypoles were erected, sometimes new ones were put up each year and decorated with fresh greenery, flowers, and sometimes ribbons, but the dancers round them did not use the ribbons to plait round the pole as they do today. The stubby maypole with long ribbons was introduced from Europe in the late 19th century. This was the type Percy Manning described being used in Shipton-under-Wychwood, although this was seventeen feet high, with two different sized revolving rings at the top to which were attached alternating red and blue braids one and a quarter inches wide and twenty four feet long, eight for use by the girls, eight for the boys. At a given signal each boy rushed in and grabbed two braids, one for himself and the other for his partner on his left. They danced to various tunes including 'The White Cockade', making patterns with the braid.

May Day games. Illustration from John Brand and Henry Ellis, *Observations on Popular Antiquities*, 1841.

The traditional maypole was a great source of controversy in Banbury in 1589 and 1590, when Richard Wheatley, the Constable of Banbury, who must have had Puritan leanings in the notoriously Puritan town, ordered William Long, Constable of Neithrop and Calthorpe, to take down all maypoles in his district, and ensure that he suppressed all entertainments such as May Games, Whitsun ales, morris dancing, wakes and fairs. John Danvers, the Sheriff, heard what was happening and wrote to the Lord Chancellor that he had informed the Archbishop of Canterbury that Anthony Cope of Hanwell Castle and other Banburians

May-Day Games.

were using religion as an excuse for banning pastimes, and that the local people were not pleased, causing disorder. He wanted the matter taken up by Queen Elizabeth's Council.

Anthony Cope claimed that Mr Danvers was being malicious and that restraint of Whitsun ales and morris dancing was not only nothing to do with him, but that any disorder in Banbury was engineered by Mr Danvers. The Council duly considered the matter and wrote to Lord Norris, saying that it had heard about the disorder in Banbury caused by the destruction of the maypoles and condemnation of their pastimes, and could find no objection to the pastimes, as long as they were not used as an excuse for unlawful meetings. The Sheriff wrote:

John Danvers, Sheriff of Oxford, to all Justices of the Peace and other officers in that County. Order to repress all riots and tumults that may be raised under pretence of taking down may-poles, which being well used, and the time of Divine Service duly observed, were lawful to be kept.

Notes in the William Potts Collection, Banbury Library

Although the use of maypoles was banned under Cromwell, it was brought back with great enthusiasm after the restoration of Charles II. Anthony Wood commented that in 1693 that there were as many maypoles as there had been in 1660, but to him they then seemed less relevant.

In 1702 the women of Ewelme wanted to erect a maypole to celebrate the accession of Queen Anne; their activities were recorded in a pamphlet entitled *The History of the Famous Maypole at Ewelm in Oxfordshire or a True and Exact Relation, How it was first Begg'd, then brought Home; How it was Set Up, and how immediately it Fell down again with some very remarkable Circumstances that followed at its fall.*

The villagers went to Brightwell to beg a maypole from a local gentleman, but the lady of the manor insisted that the pole, instead of being put up in its usual place, should be where she could see it from her house. The pole was brought back in great splendour:

The Farmer had his horses deck't in a most splendid fashion;
With Ribbands, Bells and Feathers Fine as any in the Nation.
The Carter his best Shoes put on,
White Frock and Castour too,
Which was most gloriously adorn'd
With Favours Red and Blew.

However the lady had sent her own coachman to collect the maypole and the two parties argued over it, which ended with both sets of horses being unhitched and the village women hauling the pole home themselves. The irate lady initiated a court case to get the maypole back. The story continues:

Within two days the First of May
Comes on, and then this tall thing
Must be set up, with Garland deckt,

67

And all Daunce round in a Ring;
A Garland with gay Ribbands, and
Fine feathers too set forth,
Which once the Lady did adorn,
And therefore of great worth.

The lady planned to either walk along a carpet from her house to the maypole, or be brought in her coach. However disaster struck as the pole fell down. There was no time to put it back, so a substitute was used:

I'th Same Close then, where May Pole stood,
Was plac'd a good tall Ladder.
On top of this the Garland set;
And lest they should grow Sadder,
The Drum it beat, the Fiddle play'd,
And so they Danc'd about.

The maypole was re-erected that evening, and the lady, now mollified, treated the villagers to cakes and ale and a punch bowl. However the controversy was not over, as the Ewelme women wanted the pole to stay in position for the whole of Queen Anne's reign, but the wayward lady became bored with it and took it down.

The villagers, who did not support the lady's politics, decided to celebrate their own May Day without her and danced to tunes such as 'White-Hall', 'Queen's Delight' and 'Royal Standard', and the fiddler played dance tunes 'Hey Boys', 'Up We Go' and 'The Willing Lass'.

The tall Longcot maypole, still standing proudly in the village in the early 19th century, was much envied by the inhabitants of other villages in the Vale. One night it was stolen by thirty lads from Ashbury who erected it in front of the Crown Inn. It was stolen from them by the men of Uffington, and stolen again by Lambourn men who got into a fight, in which the Uffington men used boiling water as a weapon, and won the day.

Parson Watts of Uffington was horrified by the whole proceedings, and afraid there would be more fighting, so he ordered that the pole should be cut up into small pieces and given to the poor at Christmas for fuel. And that was the end of the Longcot maypole. The theft of maypoles was not unusual: the one Thomas Martin brought to Blewbury in the late 18th century to form the focus of Whitsun sports was said to have been stolen from another village.

The Chalgrove maypole was apparently engraved with a large letter 'M', but it fell into disuse around 1805 and was incorporated into the rafters of a barn.

# May Day in the 18th century

The Puritans tried to put an end to the spring festivities of May Day, and formal celebrations and maypoles were officially banned. However some people must have carried on with them, even if they had to do it surreptitiously, and with the Restoration of Charles II to the throne in 1660 many people participated in May festivities with renewed fervour

Gradually during the 18th century the adult celebrations changed, and fewer people went out into the countryside to collect green branches, and instead activities such as milkmaids' processions and sweeps' processions appeared, concentrated in towns. However, lively May games were recorded at Long Combe and elsewhere in the late 18th century.

## Combe May Games

Special May Games were held in a barn at Combe (earlier known as Long Combe) organised around 1774 by some wealthy farmers, described in Walford's *Antiquarian*, quoted by Percy Manning (MS Top Oxon d.199). A bower and maypole were erected and several barrels of specially brewed ale were stored in the barn, which was decorated with ribbons and entitled the 'Lord's Mansion'. Sale of the ale covered the cost of the games.

An active handsome man was chosen as Lord and the pretty daughter of a respectable farmer as Lady. She was assigned a new pair of shoes each day and twenty yards of ribbon, and was presented with a guinea at the end of the games. (The practice of giving new shoes to the Lady each day also applied in the Lamb Ales.) She carried a floral mace, and the Lord held the other end of her ribbon.

Their attendants, the Lord's footman and the Lady's Maid went round selling ribbons. The Lady's Maid was armed with her 'mace of mischief' containing prickly pins and briars, which she used to 'tickle' the noses of her admirers. The squire dressed in a mixture of mime costumes such as harlequin and scaramouche. He carried a stick with a soft leather sand bag at one end and a dried oxtail at the other, with which he belaboured anyone hindering the progress of the Lord and Lady. (He has great similarities with the Fool of the Morris men.)

Early on May morning the Lord and Lady stood by the maypole to welcome visitors, then proceeded to their bower and mansion, where the visitors were told the regulations for the games and shown some curiosities: a flail (two sticks joined with an eel-skin joint used for threshing the ears of wheat off the corn), which was known as 'my lord's organ', a portrait of a lion ('my lady's lapdog') and an owl (her 'parrot'). Onlookers were asked the names of these curiosities, and if they got them wrong were expected to pay a fine of sixpence or a forfeit. Any offender refusing to pay had to ride 'My Lord's Horse', a wooden machine four feet high set on poles which had the head of a horse with a bridle. The Lady sat side-saddle on it holding the reins with the offender behind her and they were carried by two men round the maypole. Many men deliberately got the name wrong to have the excuse of sitting behind the Lady!

The Morris dancers provided entertainment, and refreshments were available. This custom has a lot in common with the Whitsun Ales such as those held at nearby Woodstock, of which more later.

## May Day in the Nineteenth Century

The role of the children came to the fore in the 19th century. It was generally the poorer children, often from the families of farm labourers, who tended to be impoverished by the ever-growing enclosure movement, who made their own May garlands and went round in small groups singing May songs and begging for pennies, as they begged at every opportunity to earn the pocket money their parents could not afford to give them.

During the Victorian era education was encouraged and primary schools set up, so children who might not have received education before now had to attend school. This brought about a change in May Day festivities. Many village schools were set up by the Church of England, and the vicars disapproved of the children begging, so May Day was formally organised by the schools, and the money collected usually provided a special tea for the children, or in some cases was divided between them. Obviously customs did not change overnight, and some children carried on making their own garlands and going from house to house.

The practice varied from place to place – sometimes children wandered around in little informal groups, sometimes a lord and lady or king and queen were elected, sometimes other characters formed an integral part of the festivities.

The May songs varied too – one basic song beginning 'Good morning ladies and gentlemen…' has been adapted in many ways in different villages, and over the Victorian period many other songs, presumably taught at school, were added to the repertoire. As the songs were largely passed down by word of mouth over many generations, often not being written down until the late 19th or early 20th centuries, it is hardly surprising that there are so many variants, or that in some cases elements of several songs have been condensed into one. The garlands varied in shape from double crossed hoops decorated with flowers to the more unusual bell and pyramid shapes. Most but not all garlands contained dolls.

The custom waxed and waned: there was a decline at the end of the 19th and early 20th centuries, and in some schools the custom died out altogether. However in many schools May Day is still an important annual event, as witnessed by the number of May Day photographs found each year in local newspapers such as the *Oxford Mail* and *Oxford Times*. Sometimes national events such as the Festival of Britain in 1951 triggered a revival, as in Iffley.

## May Day at Magdalen College, Oxford

The Magdalen College ceremony is now unique, although in the 16th and 17th centuries several colleges celebrated May Morning. Again, the custom has changed drastically over the years, and it was only in the 20th century that it became the true town and gown festival it is today. The most complete description of the changes can be found in Roy Judge's article 'May Morning and Magdalen College, Oxford' (*Folklore* Volume 97, 1986, i).

In the early 17th century there was also singing from the top of New College tower, followed by a procession to St Bartholomew's Hospital on the Cowley Road 'with their lords and ladyes, garlands, fifs, flutes and drumms to salute the great goddess Flora and to attribute her all prais with dancing and music,' as Anthony Wood wrote. He added that this was changed to Ascension 'because Magdalen College men and the rabble of the towns came on May Day to their disturbance.'

The origins of the Magdalen custom are obscure. Some suggest that it welcomed the spring, others that it has an ecclesiastical origin – perhaps the ecclesiastical attributes hijacked the other? So much time has passed, and the sources are incomplete, so we shall perhaps never fully understand. It may have begun as a celebraton of the completion of Magdalen tower in 1509, and as Henry VII had died on April 21st that year, the day could have been chosen for a solemn service in the chapel to commemorate him both as late king and as benefactor of the college. At the Reformation 1st May was chosen as a Commemoration Day for Henry VII, replacing the previous annual requiem mass – it is highly unlikely that this would have been said on top of the college tower, and this theory probably arose from a misreading of John Pointer:

> Another remarkable Custom is their having a Concert of Music upon the Top of the Tower, every May-Day, at four o'clock in the morning, in commemoration of King Henry VII the Founder of the Tower, being at first a Mass of Requiem, or Mass sung for the Rest of his Soul.... But now it is a merry concert of both Vocal and Instrumental Music, consisting of several merry Ketches, and lasting almost two Hours, and is concluded with Ringing the Bells. The Clerks and Choristers with the rest of the Performers, are for their Pains allow'd a Side of Lamb, etc. for their Breakfast.
>
> *Oxoniensis Academia, 1749*

The ecclesiastical connection was reinforced in the late 17th century when Richard Parsons wrote 'there is £10 per annum to be pd by ye Rector to Magd Coll Oxon to keep up ye vocall and instrumentall from the top off ye Coll. Tower.' (*A Parochial Visitation of the Diocese of Gloucester*, Bodleian Library, MS Rawlinson B. 323. f.86.)

The rector in question held the living at Slimbridge the advowson of which had been given to the college by William, Lord Berkeley and Earl of Nottingham in 1484, while he gave the manor to Henry VII, who in turn allowed the college to retain the advowson.

Anthony Wood refered to May morning in 1674:

> .. the choral ministers of Magdalen College do, according to an ancient custom, salute Flora every year on the first of May, at 4 o'clock in the morning, with vocal music of several parts, which, having been sometimes well performed, hath given great satisfaction to the neighbourhood and auditors underneath.
>
> Quoted from John Gutch, *The History and Antiquities of the Colleges and Halls in the University*, 1786 p 350

This suggests a joyful secular rather than ecclesiastical festival. However only two years later, in 1688, Wood commented :

... whereas on every May-day morning about 4 of the clock, the choristers and clerks of Magd. Coll. used to sing on their Tower (which hath been constantly kept since the King's returne) was this morn. neglected for want of choristers and clerks.

Andrew Clark, *The Life and Times of Anthony Wood*, vol. III, Oxford 1894

A feature of the festivities which was probably introduced at the beginning of the 19th century (although the music was written much earlier by Benjamin Rogers, college organist and choirmaster from 1665-86) is the hymn 'Te Deum patrem colimus', which was written as a college grace. The words were probably written by Thomas Smith, a Fellow of Magdalen from 1666 to 1692. The name 'Hymnus Eucharisticus' originally referred to another piece by Rogers, with words by Nathaniel Ingelo to commemorate the Restoration, but by 1810 'Te Deum Colimus' was entitled 'Hymnus Eucharistcus' in print by John Clarke, and the name has firmly stuck. The words are:

| | |
|---|---|
| Te deum Patrem colimus | Father and God we worship Thee |
| Te laudibus prosequimur, | And praise and bless, on bended knee, |
| Qui corpus abo reficis, | With food Thou'rt to our bodies kind |
| Celesti mentem gratia. | With heavenly grace dost cheer the mind. |
| | |
| Te adoramus, O Jesu, | O Jesus, only Son of God! |
| Te Fili ungenite, | Thee we adore, and praise, and laud: |
| Te qui non dedignatus es | Thy love didst not disdain the gloom |
| Subire claustra Virginis. | Of a pure Virgin's holy womb. |
| Actus in crucem, factus es | Nail'd to the cross, a victim made, |
| Prato Deo victima | On Thee the wrath of God was laid: |
| Per te, Salvator unice | Our only Saviour, now by Thee |
| Vita ce spes nobis rediit. | Immortal life we hope to see. |
| | |
| Tibi aeterne Spiritus | To Thee, Eternal Spirit, rise, |
| Cujus afflatu peperit | Unceasing praise, for earth and skies: |
| Infantem Deum Maria, | Thy breath awoke the heavenly Child, |
| Aeternum benedicimus. | And gave him to his Mother mild. |
| | |
| Triune Deus, hominum, | To Thee, the Triune God, be paid - |
| Salutis auctor optime | To Thee, who our redemption made, |
| Immensum hoc mysterium | All honour, thanks and praise divine, |
| Ovante lingua canimus. | For this great mystery of Thine. |

Percy Manning, *Seasonal Customs*, MS Top Oxon d.199

According to Dr Routh, President of Magdalen from 1791 to 1854, the hymn was first sung one extremely wet May morning when only the organist and choristers turned out and the organist got them to sing it. It is now a constant feature of the ceremony.

During the 19th century it was generally believed that the celebration had an ecclesiastical basis, as epitomised in an account given by William Wade in *Walks in Oxford* (1817):

MAY MORNING ON MAGDALEN TOWER

Postcard showing earnest looking choirboys on Magdalen Tower. Courtesy of the Oxford Stamp Centre.

At the hour of five in the morning of May-Day, the choristers of the College assemble on the top of this tower, and sing the following hymn: Hymnus Eucharisticus Deo Tri-Uni ... This is done in lieu of a requiem, which, before the Reformation, was performed in the same place for the sould of Henry VII. The rectory of Slimbridge in Gloucestershire is charged with an annual payment of ten pounds for the performance of this service.

This mentions a later hour – five instead of four in the morning for the singing. Gradually the ceremony declined, being treated with indifference and irreverence which brought it into disrepute, but this was rectified through the influence of John Rouse Bloxam, Fellow of Magdalen from 1835 to 1863, a proponent of the Oxford Movement and an enthusiastic antiquary. In 1844 he determined to improve the May Day ceremony. He did not mince his words in describing the laxities of the past, due in part to two previous choirmasters, one of whom was allegedly ineffective and the other drunken:

There are some now living who remember the mode of singing the hymn at an early period of the century as irreverent, and more like a Bacchanalian song than a sacred hymn. The choirmen and choristers went up the Tower in their usual garb and kept their hats and caps on during the singing. The principal function of the choristers seemed to be to throw down rotten eggs on the people below. Old Munday, the principal Porter, tried to remedy this, by standing at the bottom of the Tower staircase and tapping the pockets of the choristers, as they passed with the Tower key. Few if any persons from other colleges ever attended, but in 1843 Dr Barrow, Fellow of Queens, made his appearance on the tower, and when the Hymn commenced, shamed the solitary Fellow then present, by uncovering his head. This led to an important change in the following year. Instructions were given, afterwards confirmed by the President, Dr. Routh, 1st.

The twentieth century saw May morning becoming much more of a town and gown ceremony, with increasingly large crowds gathering on Magdalen Bridge in the early morning to hear the May singing. Oxford Photographic Archive

May Day at Magdalen College: Postcard dating from around 1910 illustrating the choirboys on top of Magdalen Tower.

That the Choir should wear their surplices. 2. That they should uncover when the hymn commenced. 3. That they should turn to the East towards the sun, which usually rose at just that time.

When this more orderly and reverent mode was adopted the attraction to the ceremony became great. Fellows from other colleges and strangers of note, and even a vice-chancellor, were seen there. Isaac Williams of Trinity College, and John Brande of Exeter, appeared there, and afterwards recorded the effect produced upon them in verse.

MS note by Bloxam in his copy of Ingram's *Memorials of Oxford: St Mary Magdalen College*, Magdalen College Archives
MS 723

Rev. Bloxam was modest about his contributionto the changes, which were on his initiative, and had a lasting impact in rehabilitating the ceremony. Some changes, such as ordaining the wearing of surplices, were less innovations than reinforcements of previous practices which had lapsed. He had leaflets printed including extracts from poems, specially commissioned pieces and a translation of the Latin hymn.

Another influential figure was Frederic Bulley, President from 1854 to 1885, who, with his successor Herbert Warren, encouraged a more genteel atmosphere. In 1861 a further element was added – 1st May became a reunion day for old Magdalen scholars. By 1869 the occasion was thoroughly reinstated, with 200 on the tower. Later distinguished visitors included Prince Hassan of Egypt (1872), Prince Leopold, fourth son of Queen Victoria (1873), Lord Rosebery (1898) and the Prince of Wales (1914).

Oxford citizens gradually became involved in the college ceremony. The rotten eggs taken up by the choristers to drop down the Tower were to antagonise the citizens below, who in turn annoyed the choristers by blowing horns from about 1800 to try to drown them out. As the century wore on, horn-blowing gradually declined. By about 1900 the Magdalen College ceremony was only one aspect of the general festivities, as described in the *Oxford Times* of 8th May 1909:

On Saturday the choir of Magdalen saluted the advent of the 'Month of Flowers' from the summit of the tower with the chanting of the Hymnus Eucharisticus. A warm blush in the eastern sky, and the transformation into pink of a few downy clouds, heralded the strains of the Latin chant which were wafted to the crowd gathered on the bridge below and in river-craft. As the music died to silence the discordant note of the May-horns rose from the street as the contribution of the populace to the general rejoicing, but the tuneful bells rang out and drowned the discord with their melody.

May garlands were carried from door to door by children, and a Jack-in-the-Green, who danced to the accompaniment of a barrel-organ, was also to be seen in the streets. There was also the usual parade of gaily bedecked horses and vans. The turn-out of the Oxford Sanitary Steam Laundry Co. was headed by a large double van with a pair of horses, which was followed by three simple vans, and a pony trap. They traversed the principal streets of the city travelling from Magdalen Street up High Street to Carfax about 10.30.

Messrs Stevens and Co., coal merchants, held their annual parade of horses at 8.30, the route taken being from the L.&N.W.R.-wharf via Hythe Bridge-street, Beaumont-street, Woodstock-road, North Parade, and Banbury-road. There were ten entries, and prizes were awarded to J. Busby and W. Hook. Hall's Oxford Brewery Ltd. also had a parade and competition.

In some places children went from house to house in groups of three – two holding a garland of flowers between them suspended on a stick, a third having a box for the reception of coins. When they had posted themselves outside the front door they sang in chorus the following words:

'*A bunch of May I've brought you, and at your door I stand;*
*It's but a bit, it will spread about the work of our Lord's hand;*
*Good morning ladies and gentlemen, I wish you a Merry May;*
*I've come to show you my garland, because it is so gay.*'

The garlands were certainly gay, and were arranged in different styles, according to the individual tastes of the children or their parents, but the May blossom, as far as we could observe, was absent. The sprig of May left at each house was supposed in ancient times to confer good luck on the occupants, and cause good crops and general fertility. This is what is meant by the phrase 'It will spread about the work of our Lord's hand.' Again it was usual for the girls to hold the garland and distribute the May blossom, while they were followed by a boy and girl called the 'Lord' and 'Lady' respectively, who were connected by a handkerchief, which they held at each end, and, on receiving food or money from the house-wife, the Lord would embrace his Lady and kiss her.

The local businesses organised parades of their vans, their horses gaily decorated with brasses, which had the secondary advantage of providing good advertising, and the children carried on the long tradition of making garlands

May Morning, Oxford. The brewers' drays used to process round the town on May Day. Here they are shown in 1912 crossing Magdalen Bridge and heading up the Cowley Road.

Oxfordshire Photographic Archive

and raising some extra pocket money. The Jack-in-the-Green seems to have become separated from the sweeps' procession – more of him later.

During the 20th century the 'town' aspect increased, although the college maintained its separateness, even cancelling the performance in 1913 when 1st May coincided with Ascension Day and it was claimed that the choristers were required for 8 o'clock communion in the chapel instead, much to the dismay of the city. The college added a second May carol after the 'Hymus Eucharisticus' for a few years from 1922, and from 1952. Several aspects have disappeared, notably the garlands, people picking flowers (in 1936 the *Oxford Mail* journalist commented that many people carried bunches of primroses and cowslips), and numerous cyclists. For a while they were replaced by picnicking punters breakfasting on the river. Since 1923 morris dancing has formed an indispensable element, and from 1948 until 1982 there was a version of a processional dance up the High Street. In 1940, during the Second World War, there were many evacuees attending the ceremony, and more children than usual.

Numbers attending have grown drastically from about 2000 in 1948. Televising the event in 1952 raised the number to 2500, and the momentum gradually built up to about 5000 people in 1968, 10,000 in 1974. The granting of a May Day bank holiday in 1978 added to this and now over 15,000 is common. As it has grown additional entertainments such as various types of music have spread through the town, catering establishments open to offer refreshments, and recently the crush of people has been so great, and the instances of drunken revellers jumping over Magdalen Bridge greater (one unfortunate man ended up in a wheelchair

77

as a result of this exploit), that the bridge has been thought to be in danger of collapse and consequently closed to revellers. A May Ball has been set up at Milton Common to entertain the better-off revellers on May Eve, with everyone coming down to Oxford in time for May singing.

The occasion has evolved, and people's thoughts about it have changed, so what was originally probably a happy and uncomplicated greeting to the spring from the newly built tower was given a possibly spurious religious significance, which in itself gave a different character to the ceremony, accentuated by the development of the Oxford Movement and the influence of Rev. Bloxam in the 19th century, and by the beginning of the 21st century, with a decline in church-going, it has perhaps reverted to the joyful secular entertainment of the past, which now involves thousands of people, maintaining its character as a unique event.

As a small afterword, there was said to be a belief that if May Day was not celebrated at Magdalen the college would lose its lands, but this has not been borne out after the cancellation of the 1913 performance!

The Oxford City morris men entertaining the crowds outside the Bodleian in 1990 shortly after the May singing. Photograph: Christine Bloxham.

## Jack-in-the-Green and the Sweeps' Procession

The Jack-in-the-Green, despite his pagan age-old appearance, seems to have appeared first in the sweeps' processions in the 18th century. He has been studied in depth by Roy Judge in *The Jack in the Green* (Brewer, 1979). Early May marked the end of the main chimney sweeping season, so the sweeps used May Day as a good excuse to go out and earn some extra money. J. Strutt described a London procession in *Sports and Pastimes of the People of England* (1801):

The Sweep's Procession with Jack in the Green, photographed by Henry Taunt outside Balliol College in 1886. The Lady is played by a boy, Lewis Bentley; the Lord (Robert Bensley) and the fool (Henry Bensley) with his bladder on a string, money collectors (Dave and Robert Hathaway), the fiddler (John Hathaway) and the man playing shovel and poker as a musical instrument (Henry Hathaway) have their faces blackened. The Jack-in-the-Green (John Hathaway) is encased in a wicker framework decorated with leaves and laurel with a few flowers. Photograph courtesy of Oxford Stamp Centre.

Their dresses are usually decorated with gilt paper, and other mock fineries; they have their shovels and brushes in their hands, which they rattle one upon the other; and to this rough music they jump about in imitation of dancing. Some of the large companies have a fiddler with them, and a Jack-in-the-Green, as well as a Lord and Lady of the May, who follow the minstrel with great stateliness, and dance as occasion requires. The Jack-in-the-Green is a piece of pageantry consisting of a hollow frame of wood or wicker-work, made in the form of a sugarloaf, but open at the bottom, and sufficiently large and high to receive a man. The frame is covered with green leaves and bunches of flowers interwoven with each other, so that the man within may be completely concealed, who dances with companions, and the populace are mightily pleased with the oddity of the moving pyramid.

This could have been a description of the sweeps' processions in Oxford, which were very similar in character. They were well established in Oxford by 1836, when the procession was referred to in passing one windy May morning in *Jackson's Oxford Journal*: 'The horses in the Tantivy coach coming into St Giles's ... took fright at some sweeps in their May-day finery...' (7 May 1836). In 1865 the same newspaper mentions that 'several sweeps made their appearance in the costume of Jack-in-the-Green' (6 May 1865).

However the sweeps' procession became notorious for drunkenness and begging, which the police tried to prevent:

Oxford City Court, Friday (Mat 5th). William Moore, sweep, was ordered to pay 6s for being drunk on May Day. He admitted the offence and pleaded the Sweeps' Festival in extenuation.

*Jackson's Oxford Journal*, 6th May 1871

Soon after that the custom declined, although several sweeps were seen in 1884, to be revived by the Hathaway family in 1886 to public acclamation: 'The most amusing, and one creating a great deal of mirth, was the revival of a very old custom which has not been seen in Oxford for many years, viz., 'Jack-in-the-Green', excellently got up by Messrs Hathaway, chimney sweepers'. (*Jackson's Oxford Journal*, 8th May 1886.)

Henry Hathaway was a chimney-sweep and horse-slaughterer from St. Ebbes. The fame of the procession was augmented by the fact that noted local photographer Henry Taunt took a picture of the Hathaway procession, used in *Reviving Merrie England: May-Day Ceremonies*, a supplement he wrote and illustrated for *The Sphere* in 1908. He described the Jack-in-the Green's costume as being made from a wicker framework decorated largely with green leaves and laurel, with a few flowers interspersed.

The procession that year consisted of Jack-in-the-Green (John Hathaway), the Lord (Robert Bensley) carrying a frying pan and the Lady – a man in woman's costume (Lewis Bensley) – carrying a ladle, both figures in white costumes decorated with ribbons, a fantastically dressed Fool (Henry Bensley) carrying a bladder on a string, used to belabour the crowd, a Fiddler (John Hathaway), and a man carrying a shovel and poker which he used as musical instruments (Henry Hathaway). All the above, except the Lady, had blackened faces and were decked with ribbons and flowers. They were followed by two men carrying money boxes (Thomas Dane and Robert Hathaway). They sang:

'Please to remember the chimney-sweeps.
Please, kind Sir, don't pass us by,
We're old sweeps, and want a living,
Spare us a copper, as in olden time,'

Percy Manning, *Folklore*, vol. 14, 1903

The Jack twisted first one way, then the other, while the other characters danced round him, clanging the frying pan and ladle and shovel and poker, while the Fiddler played English dance tunes. In 1888 one sweep's boy wore a college cap and carried a sweep's brush and shovel. In 1894 it was made very clear that the main purpose of the activity was 'an excuse for begging from passers-by and from houses.' In the 1890s the custom declined again, and when revived in 1907 had a very different character:

About noon in St Giles – a sweep's brush arose above the Jack-in-the-Green and the faces of his companions confirmed the conjecture that these were sweeps making holiday, which they did very gaily, dancing and prancing around to the music of an instrument on wheels. One of the revellers had unblushingly donned the cap and gown of a B.A., and when he pranced he waved his sleeves in a fashion which was exceedingly droll. Another wore a riding suit with a green velvet coat, a third was dressed to represent a woman in a white skirt and a pink bodice and the fourth was of a nondescript sex in a kind of Japanese Kimono. The B.A. carried the collecting box and it seemed to receive many contributions. The sweep's piano was covered with a white flag bearing a red cross like the coat in which King Richard appears from the Crusades in Robin Hood.

*Jackson's Oxford Journal*, 4th May 1907

Occasional Jack-in-the-Greens were seen after that, but the hey-day of the sweeps was over. In 1912 a very different Jack appeared, organised by the Royal Ancient Order of Buffaloes who traversed the city collecting for the children's tea and entertainment fund.

Ivy North told John Forrest that her father Henry Stroud (1873-1953), a pavior and ratcatcher, performed the role of Jack-in-the-Green from 1898 or before until 1914. Apparently the role was shared by four people because it was so arduous. Ivy North recalled Butcher Long dancing using a shovel as a 'hobby-horse', accompanied by a fool wearing top-hat and tails and wielding a bladder. After their musician died about 1900, they hired the local barrel organ grinder to play and later the publican of the Duke of York, Mr. Rose, played his concertina. Other Jacks were Mr. Boswell and Jimmy Acres. Their costume included a one-legged stool so that Jack could occasionally sit down. She couldn't remember the route because they danced all day but she knew that they would spend midday in Jericho. (Information from John Forrest's notes, quoted in Roy Judge, *The Jack in the Green*, Brewer, 1979).

The Duke of York pub had a pivotal role in the ceremonies, as Jack used to don his costume there, and the proceeds were shared out there afterwards. The advent of the First World War brought an end to regular performances, although there may have been odd attempts to carry on. The Jack reappeared in 1951, this time not with the sweeps, but as an adjunct to the Oxford University Morris Men. He is still part of the festivities and it is traditional for the morris men to dance round him while performing the opening dance, 'The Bonny Green' (Bucknell) in Radcliffe Square. Tom Hassall, formerly Director of the Oxford Archaeological Unit, who is tall and strong performed as the Jack, and recalled how arduous it was to caper around in the heavy costume – it made the performer very thirsty, and he said that once again the role was shared by several people.

## May Day at Charlton-on-Otmoor

The way May Day is celebrated in Charlton-on-Otmoor, where an evergreen garland in the stylised cruciform shape of a woman is kept on the church rood screen throughout the year, is unique in Oxfordshire, although there may once have been a similar practice in St Michael's church in Oxford, where the churchwardens accounts record buying hoops for a garland. Rev. Crusha wrote in 1977 that the festival could have pagan origins:

We have to go back to pagan times. It would seem that in Celtic days a spring festival, presumably in honour of a mother-goddess, was held here and included a

perambulation round the neighbouring marshy tract of Otmoor (which perhaps may have been a breeding ground for geese, a bird sacred to the Celts). But we can only argue this on general principles, not on direct local recorded evidence.

With the coming of Christianity the missionaries had two choices with this, as with other customs – they could suppress it or adapt it. It would seem that they adopted the second course. It was clearly impossible to continue a pagan spring festival, so that ended; instead a Christian festival was held in honour of the Blessed Virgin Mary. This was, or became, associated with the figure on the rood in the church, representing the Lord's Mother. With the coming of Christianity, therefore, the pagan mother-goddess was no longer worshipped. That chapter closed, and a new one opened.

E. H. W. Crusha, leaflet, *May Day at Charlton-on-Otmoor*, 1977

Unfortunately there is no information about whether or how May Day was celebrated at Charlton-on-Otmoor in the Middle Ages, and another origin has been suggested for the custom (although this in turn may be no more than an attempt to explain an earlier custom, if it existed): this postulates that it began at the Reformation when the statues of St John the Evangelist and the Virgin Mary stood on either side of a crucifix or the figure of Christ on the top of the rood screen. These were destroyed by Puritans, after the 1548 edict to destroy rood screen statues, to the dismay of the parishioners. However they realised that if they replaced the statues as they had been, the replacements would be destroyed. Not wanting to abandon them altogether, they made two garlands in human form, based on

May Day at Charlton-on-Otmoor: The wicker figures of the Virgin Mary and St John the Evangelist were said to be replacements for real statues destroyed at the Reformation. They were redecked with evergreens each May Day and for the church patronal festival in September. On May Day they were carried round Otmoor, then replaced on the rood screen.

Illustration from J. Dunkin's *History of Bicester*, 1816, courtesy of David Watts

During the 19th century the figure of St John disappeared, and only the 'Virgin' was left. A drawing of it in 1846 was used in Percy Manning's 'Stray Notes on Oxfordshire Folklore', *Folklore*, vol. XIV.

a wicker framework decorated with evergreens, which were placed on the rood screen. These were illustrated in 1823 in Dunkin's *History of Bicester*, in which he wrote:

The roodloft shows two large hooped garlands of flowers, appropriately surmounted with crosses, conveying a faint impression of its former appearance when decorated with its massive crucifix and the attendant figures...

These garlands were redecorated with evergreens each May Day and for the church's patronal festival on 19th September. On May morning the garlands were taken down, and the figure of Christ or St John (it is not entirely clear which was represented, although Christ is the more probable), was carried by the men and that of the Virgin by the women. The figures were paraded round Otmoor, accompanied by the morris men, a piper, a clown carrying a money box followed by the villagers. On their return to Charlton-on-Otmoor in the evening the figures were set up in the churchyard for people to dance round, then replaced on the rood screen. Tom Hall of Islip played the pipe for the dancers for many years in the 19th century, and later Frank Cummins of Marston played the fiddle for them. Processions round Otmoor ceased around 1860, but the garland continued to be decorated.

By 1840, when J. H. Parker's *Glossary of Architecture* was published, one garland had been removed, leaving just the Virgin. This garland was carried round Otmoor, being taken in alternate years to Beckley or Horton-cum-Studley; at Studley Prior Lady Croke used to give the bearers ten shillings. Other sources suggest that it was carried by four strong women or two men. That garland fell into disfavour in 1854 when the vicar, the Rev. George Riggs, had it removed, but as soon as he left the village 'Our Lady' was replaced.

The *Oxford Times* of 9th May 1891 contained a letter written by A. W. B. Evritt of Exeter College, who described the custom in detail, and commented that that year it had not been celebrated as usual:

May I be permitted ... to draw attention to an old May Day custom at Charlton-on-Otmoor, which has been dropped this year, for the first time (with perhaps one exception), since its institution.

Everyone who has visited Charlton's Church must have observed over its beautiful rood screen a cross decorated with evergreens. This cross, or garland as the villagers call it, is kept there all through the year. It has always been the custom, so far, for the village lasses to decorate it afresh each first of May. It was then carried round in procession to Merton, and one or two other villages, and, when brought back, replaced on the screen till the following year. The ceremony hardly resembled a religious one in any way, except that there was a collection.

The reason why it was not kept up this year is said to be on account of the scarcity of flowers. This is to some extent true, but the custom has been gradually dying out for a long while, and if not actually knocked on the head bids fair to survive but a very short time. There are several reasons for this. The cross there now used is not the one originally used, and is comparatively small. It is but a few years old. The former one was as tall as any man, but got at last too decayed to be used. The boys and girls of the old regime, who carried it, have all gone out into business or service, and their representatives hardly seem to take the same enthusiasm in the modern usurper. Then, again, Charlton has a Club Feast on the first Thursday of every May, and in the struggle for the survival of the fittest, the Club Feast appears to have got the best of it. Last year it happened that the 1st of May was on a Thursday, and the two ceremonies were amalgamated. The result is that grand preparations were made at the 'Crown' for the 7th of this month, while on the 1st the garland stood forgotten and untouched, unless some kind hand put a few flowers on it for 'Auld Lang Syne'.

So far as I know, the origin of this May cross procession is unknown. Some say it was instituted as a charity. The church is dedicated to the Blessed Virgin, and so others would attribute the festival to this fact, seeing some connection between Mary and May. The date of its institution is, I believe, undiscovered. I was kindly told at the vicarage that probably there were originally three crosses on the screen to represent Calvary. One old man in the village told me he remembered two. The smaller one was carried by the children, and the larger one by the young men and women. The ceremony in former times, within the recollection of many living, was that for at least a week beforehand the village children went out into the country round, gathering flowers. On the last day of

April the cross was taken down, and carried to a house, where busy maidens decorated it in the most beautiful manner possible. About 9a.m., or so, on May Day, the procession started, accompanied by morris dancers, well dressed up, and wearing bells tied round their legs just above the knee. The girls were dressed in white. They proceeded to the vicarage, and through their own village first, and then to Merton and other places near, as already mentioned. The cross was carried lengthways by two of the procession. When they came to a house where they were likely to get any money (that was perhaps at nearly every house in the village), the cross was held upright in front of the door and a hymn sung. I have procured this with some difficulty, as now being apparently forgotten, and a new one taking its place:

THE MAY CROSS SONG.
A bunch of May I have brought you,
And at your door it stands.
It is well set out, and it's well set about,
By the works of our Lord's hands.

Then take a Bible in your hand,
And read a chapter through;
When the Day of Judgement comes,
You'll find it very true.

Oh! man, your life is but a span,
It withers like a flower,
It's here to-day, and it's gone tomorrow,
And it's all cut down in an hour.

And now I've sung my little song,
I can no longer stay.
I wish you all a good morning,
And a merry month of May.

The money collected was always spent, so far as is known, in a public tea, and any surplus was divided among the children. No doubt the usual May Day games and dances followed. Such was this pretty and interesting custom. An aged inhabitant of the village informed me that for the last seventy years he had known the garland go round, and this was the first year it had been neglected. I was told, however, by someone else that there had been one other year in which it was forgotten, but only one.

I am glad to be able to state that even this May there were two little girls, who accompanied by a faithful few, in the shape of infants from the school, kept up part of the old custom. They made a couple of crosses, decorated them very prettily, and went boldly round on their own account, holding up their garlands before each door, and singing. Before 9.30 in the morning I asked one of them how much she had collected, and she replied, 'Two and seven-pence, and three half-pence.' One of the parties sang the old song given above, and the other the new one, commencing:

See our garland gay we're bringing,
For it is the 1st of May,
And the little birds are singing,
Singing sweet on every spray.
*Chorus*: 'Tis the merry month of May,
Come on and see our garlands gay.

...I would I could restore to the Charlton May Cross a vitality such as is possessed by the Latin Hymn sung on Magdalen Tower.

Fortunately Charlton-on-Otmoor May Day was not in the terminal decline suggested. It is interesting to note how it had become enmeshed in the Club Feast, a newer occasion. However, the Vicar was evidently determined that the venerable May custom should not die out, as a note was put in the *Charlton Church Monthly* in June:

May Day, marked hitherto in Charlton from time immemorial by the decking of the Rood Cross, was this year, through an infinite want of organisation, shorn of its accustomed honour. What was nobody's business in particular had till now always found somebody to do it unbidden. In future – for a custom now so unique and all our own must not be allowed to die out – definite arrangements will need to be made to secure that the old tradition shall live on. How shall we best contrive that the honour of dressing the Cross fall into the worthiest hands?

It was not until the custom suffered neglect that the community realised how important it was to them, and made deliberate plans to keep up the continuity. The Vicar's plea was answered, and in the parish magazine the following June was a satisfied little note:

The time-honoured decking of the Rood Cross was not wanting on the 1st of May, and helped the old folks, doubtless, to live over again a little of their youth.

The making of the garland became an important process. It was described in detail in the *Oxfordshire Archaeological Society Reports* for 1903:

The large cross made of wood, with a circular base, which stands on the rood-screen, is known locally as 'The Garland'. It is completely covered with spring flowers or evergreens, and placed on the screen on the first of May. The old woman who has lately superintended the dressing of 'The Garland' speaks of it as 'My Lady', talks about 'giving her a waist', and calls the flowers down the front 'buttons'. The arms of the cross are 'her arms'...children sometimes carry about little crosses decked with flowers and sing a May Day song, but compulsory school attendance had nearly put an end to this custom.

The 'old woman' referred to was Caroline Smith (1817-1914) who lived much of her life in Charlton. The May song recorded that year was a newer version than the one recorded by A. W. B. Evritt:

See, our garlands gay we're bringing,
For it is the First of May,
Hark the little birds are singing,
Singing sweet on every spray.
*Chorus*: 'Tis the merry month of May,
Come out and see our garlands gay.

Now the pretty flowers are springing,
April showers have passed away,
So good-bye to grief and sadness,
Let us all rejoice today.
*Chorus.*

Now the bees are humming gaily,
On ev'ry flower that honey gives,
Teaching us that we should daily
Do our duty while we live.
*Chorus.*

The Charlton-on-Otmoor garland photographed in 1980. The woman who dressed the garland for many years from the early 20th century talked about giving the 'lady' a waist and putting 'buttons' of wild flowers down her bodice.

Photograph: Christine Bloxham

The churchwardens organise the redecoration of the garland each year for May Day. R. E. Busher, the daughter of one Rector, said in 1954 that the children carried small crosses decorated with flowers round from house to house on May morning, singing:

A Cross of May, a Cross of May,
And at your door I stand.
'Tis but a bit, but it smells very sweet,
And it comes from the Lord's right hand.

Good morning, ladies and gentlemen,
We wish you a happy May.
We've come to bring our May Garland
Because it is the First of May.

Christina Hole Collection

This song was later changed to:

A May garland we have brought you
Before your door we stand
It is but a bit and it smells very sweet
And it comes from the Lord's right hand.
Good morning ladies and gentlemen
We wish you a happy day
We've come to show our May garland
Because it's the first of May.

E. H. W. Crusha, op. cit.

The children stopped coming from house to house in 1962, because in 1963 the primary school became involved, and the children now make a

Now the primary school children make a garland consisting of bosses of flowers linked by evergreen swags, which they carry in procession from the school to the church where it is carefully placed on the rood screen.

This and the following series of photographs were taken by the author in 1988.

long 'garland' of evergreen swags joined by bosses of flowers which is carried in procession from the school to the church, blessed at the church door then placed on the rood screen. The children not carrying the garland make little wooden crosses, covered with silver foil and then decorated with flowers which are placed at the base of the rood screen and on the windowsills of the church. A short church service is then held in the packed church. In 1989 this included the hymn 'O Lord my God, when I in awe-struck wonder...', followed by a prayer for May Day, the Lord's Prayer, a May Song sung by the school, a reading, the hymn 'The winter's sleep was long and deep', an address and then the May Carol, obviously written for Otmoor:

The school garland is hung just below the 'Lady', which is redecorated for the occasion by the churchwardens or their appointees.

The happy birds Te Deums sing for Jesus lives again!
His smile turns winter into spring and sun comes after rain,
And there's a fragrance in the air, and bells their music ring;
And oh, the world is bright and fair, for Jesus rose in spring.

And Jesus' people share His joy, a life made bright and new
For every girl and every boy, for them and me and you!
Like Mary, Jesus' mother dear, we sing the Father's praise,
Who sent his Son to join us here and lead us all our days.

All over Otmoor comes again the merry month of May,
And every field and farm and lane is bright with colours gay.

The children not carrying the garland make small wooden crosses which they cover with silver foil and decorate with flowers.

After the service the children entertain the congregation with country dancing in the village street.

With Mary let us raise our song and greet the world as friend:
For all who to our God belong the Spring will never end.

This was followed by notices, and the offertory hymn, 'All things bright and beautiful', then the service ended with a blessing.

After the service there was maypole dancing in the street. The whole ceremony was performed with great enthusiasm and is thankfully still thriving.

# May Day at Cottisford

Flora Thompson immortalised May Day at Cottisford in her trilogy *Lark Rise to Candleford*. She was brought up in the small hamlet of Juniper Hill, just south of Brackley, and attended school in Cottisford in the 1880s. In her later middle age she wrote evocatively about her childhood experiences, and her chapter on May Day is not only exceptionally vivid, but perhaps the most complete evocation of an Oxfordshire village May Day, although as it was written many years after she actually experienced it, she may have idealised it to a certain extent. By the 1880s May Day was firmly entrenched as a school occasion, and the period around May Day formed the highlight of the school year.

She described how at the end of April the children collected all the flowers they could find in the fields and hedgerows and the cottage gardens: violets, cowslips, wallflowers, oxlips and sprays of redcurrant, with greenery from the sweetbriar hedge in the schoolmistress' garden. The Sunday before the boys walked about eight miles to collect primroses from a wood. A lot of flowers were needed for the garland, because unlike most Oxfordshire garlands, made from crossed hoops, the one at Cottisford was a bell shape, about four feet high. It took so many flowers to cover it that the local supply often ran out, even after fresh supplies had been begged from all the nearby Cottisford houses including the rectory, manor house and farms, so that the back of the garland had to be completed using evergreens. The 'top-knot' was made from a bunch of yellow and brown crown imperials.

At six o'clock on May morning the garland was completed:

Then a large china doll in a blue frock was brought forth from the depths of the school needlework chest and arranged in a sitting position on a little ledge in the centre front of the garland. This doll was known as 'the lady', and a doll of some kind was considered essential. Even in those parishes where the garland had degenerated into a shabby nosegay carried aloft at the top of a stick, some dollish image was mixed in with the flowers. The attitude of the children to the lady is interesting. It was understood that the garland was her garland, carried in her honour. The lady must never be roughly handled. If the garland turned turtle, as it was apt to do later in the day, when the road was rough and the bearers were

May Day in Cottisford. The celebration of May Day here was beautifully evoked by Flora Thompson in *Lark Rise to Candleford*. She described a pyramid-shaped garland, not the most common shape in Oxfordshire, with a doll perched in the centre. In her era the doll was covered by a veil, which was only lifted when the onlookers paid a penny. Another penny could often be obtained by the king lifting the queen's veil and giving her a kiss. The Cottisford group shown here was photographed at Shelswell Park.

Photo courtesy of Baroness von Maltzahn

growing weary, the first question was always 'Is the lady all right?' (Is it possible that the lady was once 'Our Lady', she having in her turn, perhaps, replaced an earlier effigy of some pagan spirit of the newly decked earth?)

The lady was hidden underneath a muslin veil, then a stick was pushed between the hoops to make it easier for two children to carry. The children dressed in white or light dresses if possible, plus white veils and gloves if they could obtain them, and wore sashes round their waists decorated with bright ribbon knots and bows. The boys wore similarly decorated sashes crosswise over one shoulder.

The May Queen wore a white veil and a daisy crown (daisies once had magic significance) and gloves which were often much too big for her, but as Flora remarked: 'The empty finger ends came in handy to suck in a bashful mood when, later on, the kissing began.'

The children set out in procession, led by a boy carrying a flag and a girl bearing a money box, then the garland with its two bearers, followed by the king and queen, two maids of honour, a Lord and Lady, two more maids of honour, the footman and his lady followed by the rank and file in a croc-odile, with the girl known as 'Mother' and the Ragman walking together in the rear. The 'Mother', one of the older girls, took responsibility for the children's behaviour and carried a basket with lunches for the principal performers. The Ragman carried the coats in case it rained. (Perhaps Flora Thompson has combined memories from different villages here, as there are no other recorded examples of both a king and queen and a lord and lady being found together – generally either one pair or the other was chosen, and which was chosen could vary over the years.)

The May songs were chosen to suit the house at which the children stopped. The procession first visited the Rectory, where they sang a tradi-tional song:

> A bunch of May I have brought you
> And at your door it stands,
> It is but a sprout, but it's well put about
> By the Lord Almighty's hands.
>
> God bless the master of this house
> God bless the mistress too,
> And all the little children
> That round the table go.
>
> And now I've sung my short little song
> I must no longer stay.
> God bless you all, both great and small,
> And send you a happy May Day.

The Rector leaned out of the window, covered in shaving foam, to see the garland, and his daughter came to the door to see the veil lifted to reveal the doll, then she put her silver coin into the collecting box. The children then walked across the road to Cottisford House to be admired by the squire's lady. If there were any grandchildren staying, the doll was actually removed from the garland to be held up to the nursery window. Often the squire himself came up and gave the children five shillings. A newer song was selected for them, such as:

> All hail gentle spring
> With thy sunshine and showers,
> And welcome the sweet buds
> That burst in the bowers;
> Again we rejoice as thy light step and free
> Brings leaves to the woodland and flowers to the bee,
> Bounding, bounding, bounding, bounding,
> Joyful and gay,
> Light and airy, like a fairy,
> Come, come away.

If the song referred to varieties of flowers, as in the verse below, the children would point to the flower in question on the garland as they sang:

> Come see our new garland, so green and so gay;
> 'Tis the firstfruits of spring and the glory of May.
> Here are cowslips and daisies and hyacinths blue,
> Here are buttercups bright and anemones too.

The children visited the other houses in Cottisford, then set off along the roads and footpaths to nearby country houses and villages. Sometimes they encountered a procession from another village, and the groups stuck out their tongues at each other, or chanted rude rhymes:

> Old Hardwick skags!
> Come to Fordlow to pick up rags
> To mend their mother's pudding bags,
> Yah! Yah!

(Fordlow was Flora's name for Cottisford in her books, so presumably the original rhyme would have referred to Cottisford). When they came to country houses such as Tusmore Park and Shelswell Park they were greeted in the courtyard by the indoor and outdoor servants, who gently teased the children and urged the king and queen to kiss repeatedly. The children walked several miles, and the day did not always proceeded idyllically – sometimes squabbles broke out, or children got soaked in the rain. The Cottisford children's circuit included Cottisford, Juniper Hill, Tusmore, Shelswell and Fringford. At Cottisford the money collected was shared among the children, in other places it was often used for a special tea. Finally 'the lady' was carefully removed from the garland and tenderly stroked by the girls before she was placed back in her box and stored away until the next year.

May Day at Iffley in the 1890s. The May Queen's face is hidden by a veil and her king wears a patched outfit which looks as though it may have been decorated with gold braid. The central garland appears to contain a doll in a long dress.

Photograph by Henry Taunt, courtesy of the Oxford Stamp Centre

# Iffley May Day

Iffley May Day has been immortalised in the photographs of Henry Taunt, taken in the 1890s and early 20th century. In the first, the children look shabby, but an effort has been made to dress the king and queen – the latter having her face covered with a veil. The children carried two garlands, one which looks as though it has a doll, the other made of two large crossed hoops covered with evergreens.

A few years later, in 1907, the celebration had become more formal, with the queen in a white dress with a diagonal sash of glossy leaves and white lilies over her right shoulder and a hat, with her consort smartly dressed and wearing a similar sash over his left shoulder. The garland, about three feet high, was cone-shaped, with a stick through it to accommodate two bearers, and another square concoction decorated with flowers looks as a money box. The children wore clean pinafores and tunics and nine boys carried poles about six foot high decorated with flowers and leaves for the top two feet or so.

The May king and queen were elected by ballot among the elder children at school in April. However in about 1917 the girl chosen as queen quarrelled with her friend and was forbidden by her mother from taking part as punishment, so a replacement had to be found at the last moment, and to her surprise and delight Lily Pulker was chosen. At twelve she was two years older than most May queens. Lily told Gaby Porter of the Museum of Oxford:

> I remember my mother buying me some white shoes especially to wear with it [her white dress] ... We wore decorated hats with flowers, like a wreath on your head, and the king and queen carried a bouquet and even the king carried a bouquet and they got arum lilies in this bouquet and these arum lilies came from Hawkswell, home of Emlyns, he was the tailor in High Street, and we wore a chaplet of flowers across the chest... the flowers were sewn on white or brown paper and tied with a white ribbon... The boys carried poles, all done with flowers, high up, and a crown imperial on the top.

Tape of interview with Lily Dear in Oral History Collection, Centre for Oxfordshire Studies

May Day at Iffley in 1907, again photographed by Henry Taunt. This illustrates how quickly a custom can change. It has become far more organised, with young 'policemen' with their floral poles keeping the children in order. The King and Queen are obviously better off, with smart clothes, and their exotic lilies and laurel leaves come from the gardens of the wealthy.

Oxfordshire Photographic Archive

The children went to a church service first, as they went to the church school of St Philip and St James, then processed round Iffley. One boy, called the music master, selected and started the songs. A 'policeman' kept the children in order, walking two by two. Their circuit took them up Tree Lane to Rose Hill then down the Iffley Road to Freelands House, on to Brazil's old people's homes and St John's Home before walking back to Iffley for tea, often at someone's house. The year Lily was queen they were entertained at the home of the king, Gerald Pearman, whose father was Manciple at Keble College. The King and Queen had the positions of honour at the top of the table and the children consumed delights such as jellies, chocolate cakes and trifles, then played games in Iffley Park.

The traditional May Day ceremonies were written down by George David and Mary Parkes in *May Day at Iffley* (1934). They reinforced Lily Pulker's description of a ballot to select the king and queen – at one time a small girl would be chosen for the queen, but by the 1930s she was chosen from the older girls. The elder children taught the younger children the songs.

The garlands featured fritillary flowers, which were common locally, plus cultivated and hedgerow flowers. The queen traditionally carried a bouquet of lilies presented by the owners of one of the larger houses in the village. The procession was much as in Lily Pulker's day, and ended by them leaving their flowers at St Basil's Home before going back to the school for a tea financed by their collection.

The children sang a wide variety of songs, including:

The summer days are coming,
The blossoms deck the bough,
The bees are gaily humming,

May group at Iffley, 1907, photographed by Henry Taunt. The King and Queen stand proudly in the centre, with a pyramid shaped garland and a large square flower-decked money box, with the 'policemen' with their floral poles and the rest of the children around them.

Photograph courtesy of the Oxford Stamp Centre

And the birds are singing now.
We have had our May garlands,
We have crown'd our May Day Queen
With a coronal of roses
Set in leaves of brightest green;
But her reign is nearly over,
And spring is on the wane;
Oh haste ye, gentle summer,
To this pleasant land again.

The minstrel of the moonlight,
The lovelorn nightingale,
Hath sung his month of music
To the Rose Queen of the vale.
And what though he be silent
As the night comes slowly on,
We'll have dancing on the greensward
To sweet music of our own.
The summer days are coming,
The blossoms deck the bough,
The bees are gaily humming
And the birds are singing now.

We'll rise and hail these early,
Before the sun hath dried
The dewdrops that will sparkle
On the green hedge by our side.
And when the blaze of noonday

Glares upon the thirsty flowers,
We will seek the welcome cover
Of our jasmine-shaded towers.
The summer days etc.

Another song is:

The blossom's on the blackthorn,
The woods are full of song.
The wind steals o'er the flowers
And bear their sweets along. [or: 'and bear their sweetest song']
Like stars the bright-eyed daisies
Upon the meadows glow,
Then up and through the greenwood
A-maying let us go. [These two lines sung twice.]

And hark what thrilling music
Is that which sounds on high;
It is the gay lark soaring
With song into the sky.
Again it is the robin
Perched on the bending bough,
Then up and through ... [twice]

The bees are gaily humming,
While in the sun's warm glance
Cheered by the south wind's whisper,
The green leaves gaily dance,
All nature seems so happy,
Above, around, below,
Then up and through ... [twice].

Another song sounds little like a folk song:

A merry little maiden,
In the merry month of May,
Came tripping o'er the meadows,
As she sang this merry lay:
'I'm a merry little maiden,
My heart is light and gay,
and I love the sunny weather
In the merry month of May.

I love the little birdies
That sit upon the spray,
And sing me such a blithe song
In the merry month of May.
I love the pretty lambkins

That gently sport and play,
And make such frolic gambles
In the merry month of May.

I love the blooming flowers
That grow on bank and brae,
And with them weave my garland
In the merry month of May.
I love to see the green leaves,
The leaves that fall away,
Come back to clothe the hedges
In the merry month of May.

I love my little sisters
And brothers every day,
But I seem to love them better
In the merry month of May.
For winter now is over,
We run about and play,
And Nature seems to love us
In the merry month of May.

Another song features the joys of spring:

Hark the birds begin their lay,
Flow'rets deck the robe of May;
See the pretty lambkins bound
Playful o'er the clover ground.
Where the yellow cowslips grow,
Where the sportive heifers low,
And around us everywhere
Insect tribes disport the air.
Ev'ry heart with joy shall glow.
Royal [formerly rural] pleasures banish woe.
Bells shall ring and all be gay,
This is nature's holiday
For it is the first of May.

Now the nymphs and swains advance
O'er the lawn in cheerful dance,
Garlands from the hawthorn bough
Grace the happy shepherd's brow;
While the maidens in array
Crown the happy Queen of May,
Innocence, consent and love
Fill the meadow and the grove.

And finally, a spring song:

Welcome bright and sunny spring,
Oh what joy and light you bring!
Meadows sweet with pretty flowers,
Pleasant walks and happy hours;
First the pretty snowdrop seen
Droop her head so tenderly,
Then the crocus golden bright
Lifts its head into the light.

Hark the little birds they sing
'Welcome bright and sunny Spring',
And the little children's feet,
Patter down the village street.
In the woods and meadows fair
Primroses and violets there,
Some to pick and some to sing
'Welcome bright and joyous Spring'.

'The blossom's on the blackthorn' possibly harks back to the old tradition of collecting may in the woods with the chorus:

Then up and through the greenwood
A-maying let us go.

The custom lapsed for about ten years over the period of the Second World War, and was revived for the Festival of Britain in 1951, when about 30 children participated. The tradition has continued.

Edward Cordrey, in *Bygone Days at Iffley* (1956), commented that the sweeps used to come round the village:

About May Day we generally had a Jack-in-the-Green from Oxford, who used to come and parade through the village. Also with him a company of sweeps, and Maid Marion, who was a man dressed in woman's attire, and another man on a hobby horse, who used to delight us with his capers. How Jack got into the green or yet out we never could fathom, as nothing could be seen but a moving mass of greenery. The sweeps carried a money-box and collected as they came along the street.

The references to Maid Marion and the hobby horse are interesting, as the 'female' figure is usually identified as the 'queen', and the hobby horse is not mentioned elsewhere in connection with the Oxford sweeps, nor is it featured in local morris teams.

# Gazetteer of Some May Day Customs in Oxfordshire

It would be impossible to give every single reference to Oxfordshire May Days, as it would encompass several books, so this gazetteer aims to give a flavour of the customs. Just because a village is not mentioned, it does not mean that it never celebrated May Day – it has just not been well recorded. No attempt has been made to detail exactly where May Day is still celebrated in schools today. Where no sources have been given for information the material has often been received orally by the author from local organisations such as Women's Institutes.

## *Adderbury*

At Adderbury the May Day celebrations of 1897, the year of Queen Victoria's diamond jubilee, were combined into a pageant honouring the Queen:

The children assembled at the boy's school, and at half past two o'clock the procession commenced the parade of the village before entering the Vicarage grounds, where the fete was held. The royal standard, borne by two stalwart young lads, preceded the Queen of last year's May revels, Zilpah Hone, riding in a florally decorated car, and attended by gorgeously attired attendants. Next came the Bloxham brass band, playing lively airs, followed by a number of little boys and girls, the youthful maidens being prettily dressed alike in red, white and blue, and the lads as old time countrymen, their three-cornered hats and knee-breeches being decked with favours of the colours worn by their fair companions. 'Britannia' (Fanny Brown) and her court, including representatives of different nationalities, all appropriately costumed, filled the next carriage, and representatives of various trades walked behind. The Queen-elect (Emily Luckett) and her attendants also occupied another carriage which was prettily adorned with flowers and foliage, and the rear of the procession was formed by three florally-dressed wagons filled with children.

After passing round the green and visiting Adderbury West, the party proceeded to the pleasantly sited grounds at the Vicarage, at the entrance to which was a triumphal arch of greenery, flowers and flags. In the centre of the dais on the lawn, covered with Union Jacks, and the pot flowers and plants, was enthroned the Queen, surrounded by her Court: Emily Luckett having been proclaimed by one of the heralds Queen for the year, the young lady advanced to the throne, preceded by a page bearing on a cushion the crown of flowers which the ex-Queen placed upon the head of her successor to the throne, handing also to 'her Majesty' the sceptre of power. The new Queen took her place on the throne amid the cheers of her Court, the song 'Hurrah, hurrah for England' being sung by the children. This very pretty sight was followed by the old song of 'Joan to the May pole', and the may-pole dancers went through a number of very tastefully executed dances, to the strains of the band. The first part of the programme was concluded with a cantata 'Britannia; or who has made England great'.

Fanny Brown, trident in hand, seated on her throne as 'Britannia', received the homage of various representatives of her dependencies, the army and navy, arts, commerce, trades etc., several appropriate songs being introduced. The characters were: Scotland, Bessie Day; Ireland, Mabel Dale; Wales. Alice Wain; India, Zilpah Hone; Australia, Tom Stacey; Captain in the Army, Arthur Plackett; Captain in the Navy, Aubrey Finch; Music, Elsie Walton; Education, Alice Haynes; St George, John Silman; Commerce, Percy Banwell; Industry, Amy Lines and Annie Stanton; Hodge, Edgar Coombes; Postman, Fred Brooks; First Herald, Fred Plackett; Second Herald, Harry Nicholls; citizens, George Wallin, Wm. Elkerton, Wm. Stacey and George Stanton ...

After the cantata ... the company partook of an al fresco admirably served on the lawn, and there was subsequently a return to games, songs, may-pole dances etc., being given by the children in the afternoon.

*Jackson's Oxford Journal*, 29th May 1897

## Aston Rowant

The characters about 1924 included a girl dressed as the Spirit of Spring in a white dress, trimmed with green ribbons and primroses, with a primrose-decked sunbonnet and a wand of flowers, accompanied by four children in crepe paper costumes representing flowers, the four corners, or north, south, east and west.

## Aston Upthorpe and Aston Tirrold

The children toured both villages with their garlands with a doll in the centre, and the two children carrying the garland were usually given twopence and the little ones following behind with bunches of flowers tied on their decorated sticks received a halfpenny each. They had a special rhyme for the first of May:

On the first of May
Sooty bud day
Give me a penny
And send me away.

## Bampton-in-the-Bush

Percy Manning described how May Day was celebrated in the town of Bampton-in-the-Bush until around the 1850s. The children dressed in white, decorated with red, white and blue ribbons (the colours of the Bampton club as well as of the Union Jack). He went on:

A boy called the 'Lord' carried a stick dressed with ribbons and flowers, which was called the Sword, and a collecting box for pence.

Two girls, known as the 'Lady' and her 'Maid', carried on a stick between them the 'garland' which was made of two hoops crossed and covered with moss, flowers and ribbons. The 'Lady' also carried a 'Mace', or square piece of board mounted horizontally on a short staff, on the top of which were sweet-smelling herbs under a muslin cover, decorated with red, white and blue ribbons and rosettes. The 'Lord' and 'Lady' were accompanied by a 'Jack-in-the-Green'. From time to time the 'Lady' sang the following words:

Ladies and gentlemen,

I wish you a happy May;
Please smell my mace,
And kiss my face,
And then we'll shew our garland.

After the words 'kiss my face', it was the Lord's duty to kiss the Lady and then to hand round the money-box. The farmers and well-to-do people, so my informants say, used to give as many half-pence as possible, the fun of seeing the Lord kiss the Lady after the giving of every half-penny.

Percy Manning, 'Some Oxfordshire Seasonal Festivals', *Folklore*, Vol. 8, 1897

Many May activities were transferred to Whit Monday.

## Banbury

Young people congregated on Crouch Hill early on May morning, as immortalised in a poem entitled 'Crouch Hill', published in 1789:

And moving careless on, as suits the will,
Make our approach to Crouch the may-morn hill.

In 1885 the *Banbury Guardian* reported on the first display of May garlands and 'tastefully dressed' dolls in the Exchange Hall: fifty-six garlands and seventeen dolls were entered for the competitions.

The usual May festivities continued into the 20th century. Miss Bromley, talking to Dr. E. R. C. Brinkworth (*Cake and Cockhorse*, vol 5, no. 2, Spring 1972) remembered back to c. 1910-20, when children made garlands from two small hoops tied together and covered with flowers and greenery. A crowned doll called the Queen of the May perched in the middle, and the whole thing was covered with a cloth. If an onlooker paid a penny or two the sheet was lifted to reveal the doll.

Mary Stanton and Mr Humphris remembered children taking dolls round in prams decorated with flowers until about 1920, some asked for money, others just enjoyed the ritual, which was not accompanied by a song. Mr Humphris also remembered a garland in the shape of a flat open ring decorated with hawthorn and primroses.

## Middle Barton, Steeple Barton and Westcott Barton

In the late 19th century girls went round in groups of four, dressed in white with pink or blue sashes, carrying a garland with a doll in the centre. They sang:

Gentlemen and Ladies,
We wish you a happy May.
We've come to show our Garland
Because it is May-day.
This garland we have brought,
and at your door it stands.
'Tis but a sprout, but it is well put out
With the work of Our Lord's hands.

The children did not have to ask for money – people just offered it to them. Later the children gave their money to the organisers of a tea party.

The *Oxfordshire Archaeological Society Reports* for 1904 recorded another two songs from the Bartons:

> Come see our new garland so green and so gay.
> 'Tis the first fruits of Spring and the glory of May.
> Here are cowslips and daisies and hyacinths blue,
> Here are buttercups bright and anemones too.
> Here are pansies all varied and hawthorn so sweet,
> And violets fragrant together do meet.
> But yet there's no garland that we may entwine
> Like a garland of virtue unfading, divine.

The other also featured flowers:

> We have been seeking fresh flowers,
> White, yellow and blue,
> We twine this sweet garland, dear mother, for you.
> So bright is the sun,
> So hot is the day,
> So look my sweet garland is fading away.
>
> I smile, my dear child,
> But I could almost cry,
> The flowers that don't fade upon earth will not die.
> I smile, my dear child,
> But I know it is true,
> The flowers that don't fade upon earth will not die.

Mrs Boniface, born c. 1915, recalled another May song, which combined old and new elements:

> Maypole, Maypole, Trit, Trit, Trot.
> See what a Maypole I have got.
> Gentlemen and Ladies,
> I wish you a happy day.
> I've come to show my garland
> Because it is the day.
>
> I have a little garden,
> And every summer's day,
> I rake it well and dig it well,
> And throw the weeds away.
> I rake it well and dig it well,
> And throw the weeds away.

## Beckley

Many people went to Oxford for May morning, so breakfast was provided for their return at the Oddfellows Barn. Children carrying poles decorated with flowers went round collecting pennies, and cowslips were gathered for wine-making.

## Bicester

Dunkin wrote in his *History of Bicester* that in the early 18th century May Day was an important holiday in the Bicester area:

> Both parents and children felt highly interested in its pleasure, and parties vied with each other to produce the best garland of flowers. A little Lord and Lady, decked in gay ribbons, and accompanied by several attendants, with small instruments of music, called on their friends, and went in procession round the town and neighbourhood. The afternoon and evening were spent in the greatest hilarity, and generally concluded with a dance round the May-pole.

He noted that the custom had declined and was only followed by the children of the poor. An additional verse of the traditional 'Good morning' rhyme was used in the 20th century, as recorded by Sid Hedges in *Bicester wuz a little town* (1968):

> Good morning ladies and gentlemen,
> I wish you a merry May;
> I've come to show you my May garland
> Because it is May Day.
> A bunch of May I have brought you,
> Before your door I stand,
> It is but a sprout, but will spread about
> By the work of God's own hand.

> I have a purse in my pocket,
> All tied with a silken string,
> And all I want is some money
> To line it well within.
> But now I've done my merry song,
> I have no more to say;
> God bless you all, both great and small,
> And I wish you a merry May.

## Blackthorn

Percy Manning discovered (MS Top Oxon d.192) that Blackthorn children chose a Lord and Lady rather than a King and Queen, and carried a garland fixed to the top of a pole which they carried round Blackthorn and Ambrosden singing:

Good morrow, ladies and gentlemen,
I wish you a happy May,
I am come to show my garland,
Because it is the first of May.
You may smell my mace
And kiss my face
And then you have to pay.

Six couples went round in the late 19th century: the Lord and Lady carried maces of sweet smelling herbs which sound similar to the ones used in Bampton; a waiting man and maid opened the gates for them, two children carried the garland followed by three other couples.

## Bloxham

The children had an organised May Day from 1882; as recorded in *Jackson's Oxford Journal* on 10th May 1890:

When all was ready the queen with her maids of honour and fairies, walking beneath a canopy of red cloth, supported by maids, attended by Jack-o'-the-Green, came forth, followed by about 50 children, and perambulated the village singing some pretty verses appropriate to the occasion.

This sounds formal, with the canopy, and fairies were unusual participants. In 1893 something went wrong with the organisation and small groups went round again and *Jackson's Oxford Journal* (6th May 1893) commented that 'as a consequence the numerous groups of children parading the parish kept the door knockers in action until midday.'

## Bucknell

Bucknell's king and queen of the May dressed in their best clothes. The custom was organised from the school from about the 1880s: the children attended a short church service after which the Vicar and the schoolmaster accompanied the procession round the village. A maypole was introduced in 1893. Their song is another variant on the traditional rhyme:

A bunch of May I bring to you,
Before your door it stands.
It is but a sprout, but 'tis well spread about,
By the work of a mighty hand.
Arise, arise, pretty maidens all,
And take your garland in,
Or else next morning when you rise,
You'll say I brought you none.

Arise, arise, pretty maidens all,
And call on God for grace.
Repent, repent your former sins
Whilst you have time and space.

A man's but a man, his life but a span,
He flourishes like a flower.
He's here today and gone tomorrow,
Cut down all in one hour.

And when death strikes, it strikes so deep
It strikes us to the ground.
There's not a surgeon in all the land
Can cure the deadly wound.
So now I've sung my little May song,
No longer can I stay.
God bless you all, both great and small,
And bring you a merry month of May.

The reference to taking in the bunch of May resembles a Huntingdon divination, not recorded in Oxfordshire, in which young girls would hang some hawthorn on a high post on May eve, and next morning looked to see in which direction it had been blown, expecting their lover to come from there. If it had vanished or blown away, there would be no lover that year.

## Burcot

The rhyme recorded by Percy Manning shows yet another variant of the basic rhyme, here with references to birthdays and marriage:

Good morning ladies and gentlemen,
I wish you a happy day.
I am come to show my garland
Because it is the first of May.

The first of May is my birthday
The second of May is my wedding day.

A bunch of flowers I have brought you,
Before your door I stand.
'Twas made by him who made all things
And makes the world to stand.

## Charlbury

C. M. Pumphrey described the garland, around 1845-60, as being two crossed hoops with a gaily dressed doll in the centre, carried on a stick by two children. The attendants carried bunches of flowers on sticks and sang:

Gentlemen and ladies, I wish you a happy May,
I've come to shew my garland because it is May Day.
The cuckoo comes in April and sings a song in May,
Chasing through the shadows, in June he flies away.
Cuckoo! Cuckoo! Bravo! Sing on!

Gentlemen and ladies I wish you a happy May.
I've come to show my garland, because it is May Day.

Elsie Corbett quoted a song in *Folklore* (vol. 40, 1929):

Spring is coming, spring is coming,
Flowers are coming too,
Pansies, lilies, daffodillies,
All are coming through. etc.

Another song was 'Come Lasses and Lads'. When they had visited all
the houses they climbed aboard wagons lent by the farmers and were taken
for tea and games at Ditchley Park.

## Chiselhampton and Stadhampton

May Day declined towards the end of the 19th century, and was revived
in 1895. The *Oxford Times* reported that on May 8th schoolchildren from
the combined parishes assembled at the school and processed to
Chiselhampton Park. The May Queen was Sybil Shepherd, and the violin
was played by Mr Dover. There were sixteen dancers. Each child made a
garland and there was a competition for the best.

Characters in the festivities included Robin Hood and Jack-in-the-
Green. At the end they all sang the national anthem and each child was
given a bun and a packet of sweets. The following year *Jackson's Oxford
Journal* mentioned that Jack-in-the-Green participated.

## Coombe

In the 19th century, according to *Notes and Queries*, 3rd series, vol. VII:

Troupes of little girls dressed up fantastically parade the village, carrying
sticks, to the top of which are tied bunches of flowers, and singing: 'Gentlemen
and Ladies. We wish you a happy May...'

The primary school has enthusiastically taken on the role of organising
May celebrations in the 20th century, with a King and Queen. In the 1970s
the royal pair progressed round the village in a carriage, accompanied by a
collecting box. The mothers participated too and in the evening maypole
dancing was enjoyed on the green.

## Deddington

The children began a combined May Day in 1857, organised by the
National Schools. A large garland was carried in procession by two children, others carried banners and they all sang, and tea and cakes were had
in the afternoon.

Jack-in-the-Green featured, described in *Jackson's Oxford Journal* (7th
May 1859):

National and Sunday Schools. The children of these schools had their annual May Day treat on Tuesday 3rd inst. The 'May Queen' elected by the children from the infant school seated in a carriage which was literally both bower and a coach of flowers ... was escorted round the town. First came the boys, as her trusty knights, to clear the way, carrying a number of flags and banners; then came 'Jack in the Green', then followed the state-carriage containing the queen, backed up by a gigantic maypole; the girls also carrying flags and banners, brought up the rear. Wherever the procession stopped, songs and carols suitable to the season, were very prettily sung by the children.

A similar procession was described the following year. By 1932 May Day was far less formal, with children coming round in small groups:

May Day this year was kept on Monday, the second of the month, and many children brought prettily arranged wild and garden flowers to the door. An improvement on the usual 'Today, today is the first of May, Please to remember the garland' was the song of a little boy who came alone. The commencement has quite the olden touch:

My gentlemen and ladies,
I wish you a happy May,
I've come to show my garland
Because it is May Day.

Mary Vane Turner, *The Story of Deddington*, 1932

It is interesting that only one boy seemed to remember the old song – perhaps learned from his mother? Even he only remembered a fragment of the original.

## Drayton St Leonard

From Drayton near Abingdon comes a lovely example of how rhymes changed. Percy Manning (MS Top Oxon d.199) has the song, recorded in 1894:

Good morning ladies and gentlemen,
I wish you a happy day,
I'm come to show my garland,
Because it is the first of May.

May day comes but once a year,
A garland gay I bring you here;
Primroses and violets too!
And besides a bunch of May.
We wish you all a happy day.

Mrs Frank Wilkinson recalled her memories of the 1890s for the W.I. Grandmothers' Tales Competition of 1951, describing how children and their mothers picked flowers on the evening before May Day to make garlands and posies which were carried round from house to house before school – so it sounds as though these children did not get the usual day off. The song she remembered was similar to the one above, but with 'we' instead of 'I' and garlands in the plural, and the second verse ran:

> May day comes but once a year;
> A garland gay we bring you here,
> Roses red and violets blue,
> Primroses and cowslips too.

The last line has been forgotten. When they had finished going from house to house the children often laid their flowers on the graves in the churchyard. The W. I. noted that the custom continued in a modified form. However by 1931 the favoured song was different again:

> Good morning ladies and gentlemen
> I wish you a happy day.
> I come to show my garland
> Upon the first of May.
> Hail all hail, the merry month of May
> The Spring is coming in.
> The cuckoo's voice is heard,
> Come out into the fields
> To hear my favourite bird.
> Cuckoo, Cuckoo he warbles in the tree;
> Cuckoo, Cuckoo, how sweet his voice to me.

Berkshire Federation of W.I.s, The Berkshire Book, 1931

## Fifield

Matthew Arnold wrote of:

> Maidens who from distant Hamlets came
> To dance round the Fyfield elm, in May.

## Fifield Merrymouth

Around 1886 Mrs Harry Cummins joined her first May Day parade:

We had to be up at Fifield at half-past eight and we came to the Rectory. Mr York had big red geraniums outside the front door. We had a Maypole on the lawn. The teacher had taught us the dance. We started at the Rectory with the Garland, then we went to other houses all round. Mrs Casemore always kept it and got it ready each year. There were three hoops with a lot of flowers and always a doll inside, and always what we called 'Crown of Pearls' at the top, but it was really Crown Imperials. She put a veil over it, like a best christening robe. The people paid money and we turned the veil back for them to see. There were two poles to carry it on. It was ever so heavy.

Evelyn Goshawk, Fifield Merrymouth, 1957

## Finstock

The garland, decorated with wild flowers, had a doll in the centre and was made up on a pole, then carried round the village under a cloth by the children who stopped at every house to ask for pennies for showing off the doll, who wore a smocked gown and had a china head. The money collected was spent on Holy Thursday (Ascension Day). The children went around in a large group until the Second World War, and after that May Day was just kept up by individual children who sneaked off from school. Their song was:

May Garland Day,
The First of May.
We've come to show our garland
Because it is May Day.
The cuckoo comes in April,
Sings the song in May,
Whistles a tune and then he flies away.
Cuckoo.

## Fritwell

A May song recorded from here is:

Hurrah for May Day, it has come once again;
With the garland of flowers, so fresh and gay.
With the King and Queen and the Merry-go-round,
With the children who always are ready for play.

We mean you to listen and then we will sing to you,
Songs and carols we learn at our school,
For we want to be off to the Meadow
To join with the king and dancers round the Maypole.

Good morning Ladies and Gentlemen,
I wish you a happy May.
I've come to show my May Garland
Because it is May Day. (This line sung three times)

I've come to show my May Garland,
Because it is May Day,
and now I have sung my little short song,
I have no more to say.
God bless you all, both great and small,
And send you a happy May,
And send you a happy May.
God bless you all etc.

Miss Stanley Smith's Notes, Oxfordshire County Museum

May Day at Great
Rollright in 1937.
Oxfordshire
Photographic
Archive

## Ginge

The children assembled on Ginge bridge with their garlands before taking them round the village, singing:

Good morning young ladies and gentlemen,
I wish you a happy May.
I come to show our garlands,
Because 'tis the first of May.
Happy May! Joyful May!
Winter's gone and passed away.

Nigel Hammond, *The White Horse Country*, 1972

## Great Bourton

Rhoda Baylis of Great Bourton, the daughter of nailmaker William Dale, who was born in 1880, remembered singing on May Day:

Spring has come all bright and gay,
Birds are singing on the spray,
Flowers are blooming everywhere
Gladdening colours bright and fair.
Hail, hail, glorious spring,
Hail, hail, glorious spring.

I love the poor man's garden,
It gives great joy to me,
That little precious plot of ground

Before his door to see.
All day upon some weary task
He toileth with good will
And back he comes at set of sun
His garden plot to till.

## Great Tew

Jack Gibbard, the blacksmith, recalled that around 1910 the children would gather together at school at 9 o'clock, then set off, beginning at the vicarage, spending the morning wandering round the village and in the afternoon venturing further afield to the neighbouring farms. Some of the money collected was used for a tea at the school and some given to the Society for the Propagation of the Gospel.

Mr Legge, the schoolmaster, and his wife organised everything. Their daughter was an actress, and she probably provided the exotic costumes the children used to dress in. The children made a garland from crossed hoops. They elected a King and Queen and sang a song which began: 'See the garland gay we're bringing'.

The exotic costumes ceased to be used during the First World War (1914-18), but May Day customs continued until the 1940s when a new schoolmistress who disapproved of them started at the school.

May Day at Great Tew, 1913, with the children dressed in theatrical costumes.

Photograph: Oxfordshire Photographic Archive

## Grove

May Day was organised by the Vicar's wife, and children and villagers went to dance round the maypole to the music of violins on the vicarage lawn on the second Saturday in May. A May Queen dressed in white was accompanied by a boy carrying her crown and maids of honour who had

new dresses made each year by a lady in the village. After the Second World War the skirts of the dresses were made of dyed parachute silk, with black bodices. The boys wore smocks – sometimes small ones, at other times adult smocks and top hats. The old boys of the Icknield School have a morris dance team which often joins in the Oxford May Day celebrations.

*May Day at Headington Quarry School in 1925. Standing in the centre is May Queen Hilda Washington. Ellen Hare stands on her left and Cathy Cooper on her right, with Liz Coppock and Cicely Kimber seated in front. The queen was chosen by drawing a girl's name out of a hat.*

*Photograph courtesy of the Headington Morris Men*

## Headington and Headington Quarry

Headington is now a suburb of Oxford, but in the 18th century it was a small village situated just off the London Road. L. Jewitt gives a rare description of May Day in the 19th century before it was taken over by the schools:

At Headington ... the children carry garlands from house to house. They are all alert some days beforehand, gathering evergreens and levying contributions of flowers on all who possess gardens, to decorate their sweet May offerings. Each garland is formed of a hoop for a rim, with two half hoops attached to it, and crossed above, much in the shape of a crown; each member is beautifully adorned with flowers, the top surmounted by a fine crown imperial, or other showy bunch of flowers.

Each garland is attended by four children, two girls dresses all in their best, with white frocks, long sashes, and plenty of ribands, and each wearing a cap

Headington Quarry School May Day in 1927, when Dorothy Auger was May Queen. The girls are all dressed in their best white dresses, and the children have made several hoop garlands.

Photograph courtesy of Russell Auger

tastefully ornamented with flowers etc., who carry a garland supported betwixt them by a stick passed through it between the arches.

They are followed by the Lord and Lady, a boy and girl linked together by a white handkerchief which they hold at either end, and who are dressed as gaily as may be in ribands, sashes, rosettes and flowers, the lady wearing a smart tasty cap and carrying a large purse.

They then go from house to house, and sing this simple verse to a very primitive tune:

*Gentlemen and ladies*
*We wish you a happy May;*
*We come to show you a garland*
*Because it is May-day.*

One of the bearers then asks 'Please to handsel the Lord and Lady's purse' and on some money being given, the Lord doffs his cap and taking one of the Lady's hands in his right, and passing his left arm round her waist, kisses her; the money is then put in the purse, and they depart to repeat the same ceremony at the next house.

In the village are upwards of a dozen of these garlands, with their Lords and Ladies, which give to the place a most gay and animated appearance.

*Literary Gazette*, May 1847

### Percy Manning recorded the traditional:

Good morning, mistress and masters,
I wish you a happy May,
I am come to shew my garland,
Because it is May Day.
A bunch of May I have brought you,
And at your door I stand;

It is but a bit and I can't spare it,
'Tis the work of my lord's hand.
And now I have sung my short little song,
No longer can I stay.
May God bless you all, both great and small,
And give you a very happy May.

Headington Quarry was much poorer than Headington with most of the men there working as stone-quarriers and bricklayers, very seasonal work, while their wives augmented the family incomes by taking in washing, so the children had much more need to collect any spare pennies that they could in the 19th century. Raphael Samuel commented on the social status of customs in 'Quarry Roughs':

May Day was a children's harvest, from the point of view of earnings, but the number who went out with their begging tins was limited by notions of family prestige; it was definitely the children of the poorer sort of people ... who went out. The more respectable would keep away.

ed. R. Samuel, *Village Life and Labour*, 1975

In the early 20th century the children started going round with their garlands at 5.45 in the morning, and sang the 'Good morning, master and mistress' rhyme.

The Headington Quarry School Log Book is a good source of information about May Day. For example in 1893 it contains the wry comment:

May 1st... Very bad attendance so many children round with garlands instead of coming to school. A holiday given this afternoon.

Almost the attitude that if you can't beat them, join them! By 1901 a school holiday was given for the whole day. In 1928 the May Queen was Dorothy Auger, and the procession round the village started by placing a wreath on the war memorial. The 1929 entry for 1st May reads:

Holiday for May Day celebration. The children paraded the village with May Queen and Garland. A display of dancing was given in the afternoon in Mr Bushnell's field, followed by tea at four o'clock.

This indicates that May Day was organised by the school, and that the children all went round together rather than in small groups. The Lord and Lady have been replaced by a May Queen.

By 1942 country dancing and old English games have been added to the afternoon festivities.

In 1935, King George V's jubilee year, it was rather different:

May 8th. Jubilee Treat. Children taken to Kidlington Zoo in the morning. Lunch taken at the Zoo, returning to school in time for tea. May Queen paraded playground after tea.

## Hook Norton

William Kirby (1907-1968) told Mr Humphris of Banbury that it was only the boys of Hook Norton who took the garland round. The event was organised by the schoolmaster who took all the money collected and gave it to the Horton Hospital, Banbury, and treated the children to a tea later in the summer. Their song was:

A bunch of May I have brought you
And at your door I stand.
It's a very nice branch and it smells very sweet
And it comes from the Lord's right hand.

Good morning, good ladies and gentlemen,
I wish you a happy May.
I've come to show you my garland
Because it's the first of May.

(Information from Sarah Gosling)

## Idbury

Miss Jones, schoolmistress in Idbury in 1933 wrote:

Idbury children have a veiled Queen on May Day (formerly a doll) who, followed by the rest of the school, some as Jack-in-the-Green or Jesters, visits every house, singing the traditional songs, and wishing the occupants a 'Happy May'.

A fatiguing business, but it is lovely to visit every house, once a year at least, with so cheery a greeting, and to know that this is no artificial revival, but an unbroken custom.

It was organised by the school and the schoolmistress here accompanied the children. It is interesting to note the inclusion of Jack in the Green and Jesters.

Evelyn Goshawk recorded a May song, sung to the tune of 'Nuts in May', in *Idbury History* (1961):

Here we come with the Queen of May,
Queen of May, Queen of May,
Here we come with the Queen of May,
All on a bright May Day.

Come please all your money pay,
Money pay, money pay,
Come please all your money pay,
If you see the Queen of May.

Smiling May, come today,
Come today, come today,
Smiling May, come today,
Sing we merrily.

## Islip

May Day was a popular occasion in the village, and a May Queen was elected. A strange rhyme was used in 1846:

1st May 1846
Good morning master tillipus,
I wish you a happy day
Please to smell my garland
Because it is the first of May.

Velda Henman, Islip, Oxfordshire, 1987

John Brand, in *Observation on Popular Antiquities* (1849) gave a version of the Islip May song:

Good morning, Missus and Master,
I wish you a happy day.
Please to smell my garland,
Because it is the first of May.

By 1904 the *Oxford Times* was reporting that a prominent part in organising the event was taken by Dr South's School in the village. A May Queen was chosen, Jack-in-the-Green made, two boys carried the garland, and the procession comprised about 60 children, who visited each house.

Some time after that, perhaps during the First World War, the custom died out, and Edith Miller in *The History of the Village of Islip* (1930) reported that the custom had been revived, with a May Queen, taking place a little time after May Day:

In the morning the Queen and her attendants parade the village accompanied by the other children in what quaint costume they can procure. The ceremony of crowning is performed amid song and dancing in the afternoon.

By this time the Jack-in-the-Green seems to have disappeared from the proceedings.

Monica Jameson (née Brooks), daughter of the ex-headmaster, remembered her mother's best Nottingham lace curtain being used for the May Queen's train, probably in the 1930s, and how her mother used to get up at dawn to make crowns and circlets for the girls from cowslips and grape hyacinths. By 1950 the procession, maypole dancing and tea were confined to the afternoon.

## Long Wittenham

By 1972 May celebrations in the Vale of White Horse had greatly declined, and the *Berkshire Village Book*, published by the Berkshire Federation of Women's Institutes, commented that Long Wittenham was one of the few villages still celebrating May Day, electing a May Queen who was crowned on 1st May. The children carried traditional three-legged garlands, and gave posies of flowers to the older residents.

The May King
and May Queen
at Lower
Heyford, mid-
20th century.

Photograph:
Oxfordshire
Photographic
Archive

## Lower Heyford

The diaries of George James Dew (edited by Pamela Horn and published as *Oxfordshire Country Life in the 1860s* and *Oxfordshire Village Life* in 1983 and 1986) give useful information about Victorian May Day. Dew started as a carpenter, but later worked as poor law relieving officer and registrar of births and deaths. His first reference to May Day is in 1867, two weeks before the village school was opened:

> May 1. Wednesday ... The children went round as usual with their garland of flowers.

The following year he mentioned many May garlands being brought round and in 1869:

> May 1, Saturday... No less than nine May garlands (as they are called, i.e. a procession of children decorated with flowers and ribands and carrying a garland of flowers) called at Rousham House today. One of them had flags, and some sang very nicely indeed.

Rousham House would have been the nearest 'great house' for the children to visit.

In 1870 the school began to play a role. The entry is ambiguous but it seems to read that children from other villages came round on 2nd May (or perhaps it was the Heyford children doing their own thing), while the Heyford celebration was organised a day later by the schoolmistress Miss Banfield (who later married George Dew):

117

May 2: Many May garlands with children singing came round today. Our
Heyford May garland is coming round tomorrow. I made a flag for Miss Banfield
with 'Lower Heyford School' on it.

May 3: The children came round with their May garland this morning. They had
a good number of flags and two Union Jacks among them. They had a tea at the
School and played in the Paddock at the Rectory afterwards.

In 1872 celebrations were more elaborate, with 'the National School children dressed in every gay colour possible', parading round the village with the
garland and then having tea at school as before and playing in Mr King's [a
local farmer's] yard and barns. They went home at a quarter past eight.'
In 1873:

May 1: It being May Day the children, as has been their custom from time
beyond memory, or record, dressed themselves in their best clothes, with all the
fine pieces of coloured ribbands for adornment they could obtain, and marched
around the village with their flower garlands and flags to gather as much money
as possible in order to have a tea in the afternoon. The total of their gatherings
amounted to thirty six shillings or thereabouts, and they had a good tea in the
School-room of cake, bread and butter, and tea, and afterwards a play in the
Rectory Paddock. The festivities lasted until about eight o'clock.

The following year they collected about forty shillings and in 1877 £2
8s 7d. There is an interesting comment in 1878 about preparing the children's clothes for the occasion:

... the girls in white and everyone with a good assortment of bright coloured
ribbons. Quite a gay sight. Some of the poor women were up nearly all night I am
told in washing and getting up their white frocks in the best style; and the clean,
nay some of the most spotlessly pure, appearance they had spoke well for the
general character of the Heyford poor.

Mrs Dew was succeeded as schoolmistress by her daughter, Miss
Dorothy Dew, who wrote in 1951:

The usual May-day procession was held in Lower Heyford on May 1st 1951.
This has been carried on without interruption for the last sixty years. All the
schoolchildren, boys as well as girls, take part, wearing their best, and usually new
clothes, for it is a custom in the village to have new dresses and suits for May-day.
A Lord and Lady are elected by the children, and at 9am on May 1st a procession
starts round the village, carrying two hoop garlands and four decorated staves
known as Maypoles. Every house is visited and songs are sung outside each.
Formerly traditional songs were given, but these have unfortunately been
forgotten, and others are now chosen. When money is received from any
householder, the four 'Maypoles' are crossed over the heads of the Lord and Lady
who kiss each other under them. The money collected is used to pay for a tea for
the whole school.

*Oxford and District Folklore Society Annual Record, 1951*

## Mollington

The *Oxford Times* of 10th May 1913 reported that two Mollington children carried a large garland on a pole containing a doll about twelve inches high, accompanied by a May Queen dressed in white, and they sang a song which was supposed to date back to the 17th century (unfortunately the words of this were not given).

## North Hinksey

The children collected flowers from the fields which their mothers made into May garlands. The children went round in groups of four wearing May garlands and singing:

Good morning ladies and gentlemen,
We wish you a happy morn,
We've come to show you our May garlands,
Because it is May morn.
Our shoes are very dusty
They're also very thin,
We've got a little pocket
To put a penny in.

Alice M. Harvey, *Memories of a Country Childhood in North Hinksey Village*, 1975

Some of these words from 'our shoes are very dusty...' onwards resemble souling songs sung in the north-east at Halloween.

## North Leigh

May Day celebrations ceased here around 1890. Until then, as Violet Mason wrote in 'Scraps of English Folklore' (*Folklore*, vol 40, 1929), the children had gone round collecting cowslips, primroses, wallflowers and other spring flowers such as polyanthus which they took to school to make three garlands, each made from two crossed hoops, with a bunch of flowers underneath, which was carried on a stick by two children. Banners were also decorated with bunches of flowers. Mrs Guy remembered flags with bunches of flowers on top being carried.

The children processed to church, accompanied by their parents and the brass band. After a service they went to the vicarage for pea soup or tea, then set off in three groups marching two by two round the farms and villages. The big girls went towards New Yatt, the boys to East End and the small girls to North Leigh.

The children sang songs learnt in school and were given cakes and milk, but no money. When they came back they had tea and games on the vicarage lawn, and at the end scrambled for sweets. This ended towards the end of the 19th century, but it has been revived by the school. The lady who traditionally made the Bampton garland taught the technique of making a dome-shaped one to top the maypole. Mrs Elwood took over the responsibility for making it, helped by girls from the school. The basis of the dome was green willow bent over to make eight strakes, decorated with wild flowers –

buttercups, cow parsley, cowslips, honesty, bluebells and May blossom, bunched up and tied onto the frame with green garden twine with a large bunch of May in the centre of the frame. A line of cow parsley was fixed down both sides of each strake of willow, then cowslips and bluebells were added to make the same pattern – yellow, blue and white – on each strake.

## Somerton

In 1903 the *Oxfordshire Archaeological Society Reports* recorded that an elected Lord and Lady headed the procession, and that the Lord would kiss his Lady when they were offered money – the money was used for a tea.

The garland, carried on a pole, was described as a bower containing a doll who, it was thought locally, may have represented the Virgin Mary because of local Catholic connections.

Sometime after that the Lord and Lady, according to Mary Hutchinson in the Oxford and District Folklore Society in 1957, became King and Queen – no child was allowed to perform the role twice.

Somerton May garland c. 1970s. The Victorian doll featured in it has a wax head with moulded blonde hair and a stuffed cloth body. The dark red silk plush cloak hides the fact that her arms are missing. She wears a white spotted muslin dress with a frilled hem. Her ribbon sash is modern. The pyramid shaped garland is made up over a wooden frame decked with flowers tied on in bunches. The wild flowers used in the past have been replaced with garden flowers. Crown imperials are always used on the top if they are out in time.

Photograph:: Rosemary Arnold and Sheila Stephens

The Queen wore a white or light-coloured dress and veil, held in place by a wreath of flowers and her two attendants wore garlands and carried posies. The King wore a tin foil crown, and had a scarf draped over his shoulder and diagonally across his chest. His two attendants each carried a stick surmounted by a bunch of flowers.

The procession included two boys bearing a staff and a banner and two boys carrying the May garland (which had the May doll suspended from the

**Left:** Somerton May Day c.1964-5 showing Stephen Kill with matrons of honour Lynn Stevens, Margaret Kill and Susan Macdonald, carrying the posies of flowers they represent.

Photograph: Rosemary Arnold and Sheila Stephens

**Below:** Somerton May Day c. 1967 when Susan Stephens was May Queen, wearing a white dress and veil. Her sister Lynne stands to the left in blue.

Photograph: Rosemary Arnold and Sheila Stephens

**Below:** May Queen Elizabeth Arnold earnestly reciting her verse c. 1979. The children from left to right are: Jackie Stillgoe, Sherry Golder, Jeanette Beesley, Emma Davidson, Peggoty Hutton, Elizabeth Arnold (Queen), Michael Hirons (king), Charlotte Gornall and Charlie ?

Photograph: Rosemary Arnold and Sheila Stephens

base) on a carrying pole. The doll was over 100 years old, with a round composition face and blonde painted hair. Her long dress of white silk with a blue sash and her red velvet cloak were made in 1953, the year of Queen Elizabeth II's coronation – before that she had a white embroidered dress and a pink sash. The doll was not veiled when carried in the garland. For the rest of the year the doll was stored in the vestry.

The procession set out at 9.15 and carried on round the parish for most of the day, with breaks for lunch and maypole dancing in the school playground. The money collected was used for a tea and Christmas treats. At the end of the procession the female attendants laid posies at the Queen's feet after reciting a short verse. The celebrations were held on May Day except when it fell on a Sunday, in which case they were held on May Eve.

Several May songs were recorded at Somerton in 1976 (14 had been mentioned in 1956, but not quoted):

May Day, May Day, brightly breaking
Through the midst of April showers.
Let us from our slumbers waking
Welcome in our happy hours.
The Queen of May is here today
And gives us all a holiday.

Round the maypole gaily singing
Come and scatter wild spring flowers.
Hark the bells are gaily ringing

Hannah Poulton and Della Grant carrying the Somerton May garland on a pole c. 1980, with Queen Lucy Arnold and King Daryl Grant. Standing from left to right are: Fiona Gattley, Ethel Smith (who with Valerie Newey revived the celebration of May Day – which had died out when Somerton School closed c. 1964 – in the mid 1970s), Peggoty Hutton and Rosalind, Melanie and Lizzie Govier. On the right are Sheila Grant, Rosemary Arnold and Neil Clare.

Photograph: Rosemary Arnold and Sheila Stephens

Somerton May Queen Lucy Arnold and her King Daryl Grant shown with their May garland decked with a mass of bunches of flowers, topped with the traditional crown imperials, c. 1980s.

Photograph: Rosemary Arnold and Sheila Stephens

Peals of joy from village towers.
The Queen of May is here today
And gives us all a holiday.

Another song was:

Come lasses and lads
Get leave of your dads and away to the maypole hie,
For every he has got a she
And the minstrel standing by.
For William has got his Jill
And Johnny has got his Joan
To trip it, trip it, trip it, trip it, trip it up and down.
To trip it, trip it, trip it, trip it, trip it up and down.

Another traditional song was:

There came to my window
One morning in spring,
A sweet little Robin he came there to sing.
The tune he was singing
Was pretty afar [prettier far?]
Than ever I heard on the flute or guitar.
He raised his wide wings

Somerton May Queen Justeene Hirons and King Johnny Beesley, c. 1980s, standing by the garland, shown with its carrying pole, with their matrons of honour behind them. Ethel Smith, the organiser, stands on the right in a pink coat, with Ellie May Steele. Matrons of honour are Peggoty Hutton, Lucy Arnold, Rosalind Govier and Elizabeth Arnold.

Photograph: Rosemary Arnold and Sheila Stephens

124

To fly away and rested
One moment so sweetly to say
How happy, how happy this
World seems to be.
Await little child and be
Happy with me.

The other song is a traditional folk song:

Early one morning, just as the sun was rising,
I heard a maiden singing in the valley below:
'Oh don't deceive me, oh never leave me,
How could you use a poor maiden so?
Remember the vows that you gave to your Mary.
Remember the bowers where you said you'd be true.
Oh don't deceive me, oh never leave me.
How could you use a poor maiden so?

## Souldern

May Day was not automatically given as a holiday. A new teacher commented on the thin attendance in 1872, and bowed to the inevitable the following year, giving the children a day off. The teacher who took over in 1876 reinstated it as a school day although he commented that several children were absent taking their garlands round. Those who came to school were rewarded with refreshments sent in by villagers.

Mr and Mrs Gough wrote in *Historical and Descriptive Notes of the Parish of Souldern* (1887) that children dressed in their Sunday best and walked from door to door carrying garlands decorated with spring flowers such as kingcups and daisies chanting:

Gentlemen and ladies,
We wish you a happy May.
We come to show our May garland
Because it is May Day.
*Chorus*: Because it is May Day etc.

A branch of May we bring to you,
And at your door it stands,
It is but a sprig, but it prospers a bough,
The work of our Lord's hands.
*Chorus: repeat first verse.*

## South Stoke

Mary Hutchinson recorded ceremonies here, probably from Miss Nind, a relative of a former rector, in the 1950s:

Every year a May Queen was chosen. She and the Queen of the last year, dressed in their prettiest clothes and decked with garlands of 'barges', as the village golden kingcups are called in the village, were seated in a low cart drawn by a donkey.

Maids of honour, and a guard of boys carrying drawn swords, with gilt blades, escorted them through the village. After the new Queen had been crowned by the old Queen, proceedings finished up with a dance round the Maypole in the school yard. 'That was the worst part', remarked a former participant, 'for it you had no partner to help you out, you just had to trust to your own brains'. At one time a large, gaily-dressed doll was a prominent feature of the procession. It was presented to the child who had the best school record for the year.

Christina Hole Collection

## Spelsbury

In 1894 the children processed round the village with a garland carried on a stick. The Lord and Lady dressed in white, with coloured ribbons, the other children carried maces: sticks decorated with ribbons and flowers. After they sang the Lord kissed the Lady and then onlookers were asked for contributions. Their song went:

> Hail, all hail! the merry month of May.
> I'm come to show my garland
> Because it is the first of May.
> Hail, all hail! away to the woods, away,
> And to the fields and lanes so gay.
> Hail! all hail!

P. Manning, Folklore, vol. 14, 1903

Elsie Corbett wrote that from at least 1884-1927 the afternoon of April 30th was given as a holiday for the children to gather wild flowers for May Day. From 1928 children over eleven went to school in Charlbury which changed the procession. Before the transfer a King and Queen were elected and the whole school paraded round the village with the garland. By 1962 practice had changed again, with no King chosen, although the May songs were the same:

They assembled at 9 a.m. when the Queen, previously elected, was robed and crowned and the 'garland' with its crossed hoops was decked with flowers and ribbons. Preceded by their banner and carrying the garland the children visited the church where they were met by the choir and hymns were sung, including 'Brightly gleams our Banner'. They then went in procession round the farms and hamlets singing:

> Spring is coming, Spring is coming
> Flowers are coming too,
> Pansies, lilies, daffodillies
> All are coming through.

and

> Come lasses and lads get leave of your Dads
> And away to the Maypole hie.

They collected a few pence at each house and returned to the school in the middle of the afternoon. Tea in the schoolroom was followed by prizes given by Lady Dillon for the most regular attendance. The school was closed the next day for cleaning and tidying. In later days I am told, the children assembled at 6 a.m. on May Day to make the garland, and Miss Conduct had tea and bread and butter ready for them.

E. Corbett, *A History of Spelsbury*, 1962

## Standlake

The *Oxford Times* of 8th May 1897 reported:

On May morning the schoolchildren to the number of eighty or ninety, assembled at the Rectory at eight o'clock, dressed in garlands of cowslips and daisies, and sang a May morning song, after which they were presented with a large bun and a bag of sweets each, by the Rector and Miss Tuckwell. They then paraded the streets accompanied by their teachers, and afterwards assembled at the school where they were photographed, and after singing the National Anthem dispersed. The proceedings were quite a novelty in this village, and aroused considerable curiosity. Their singing was very nice, and reflects great credit on the schoolmaster, Mr Phillips.

It is interesting that May Day had obviously not been regularly celebrated in the village, and may perhaps have been done that year partly as a celebration of Queen Victoria's Diamond Jubilee.

## Stanton Harcourt

Percy Manning (MS Top Oxon d.192) wrote that children went round the village until 1908 decked with ribbons and singing:

I bring you May roses
And lovely posies
And the Lord shall kiss the Lady.

## Stoke Lyne

Around 1885 when Annie Elizabeth Aishfield was May Queen her mother made her a dress and she had a floral crown. The school organised it, and in the morning the older children paraded round the village and further afield to Tusmore House singing May songs. The younger children joined the procession in the afternoon and they all had tea at school. One of their May songs began:

Here we come a-maying
Through the meadow straying.

## Swalcliffe

The garland, made of two crossed hoops, decorated with wallflowers, daffodils, cowslips and forget-me-nots, with crown imperials at the top and a doll in the centre, was carried on a pole. The May Queen wore a long white veil and the King had a broad blue ribbon sash over one shoulder and carried a money-box. They had several attendants, and the other children followed this group.

The main May song in Swalcliffe was:

Awake! Awake! Lift up your eyes,
And pray to God for grace.
Repent, repent of your former sins
While you have time and space.

I have been wandering all this night
And part of the last day,
So now I'm come for to sing you a song
And to show you a branch of May.

A branch of May I have brought you,
And at your door it stands
It does spread out and it spreads all about
By the work of our Lord's hand.

Man is but man, his life's but a span,
He is much like a flower.
He's here today and gone tomorrow,
So he's all gone down in an hour.

So now I've sung you my little short song,
I can no longer stay,
God bless you all, both great and small
And I wish me a happy May.

Dorothy G. M. Davison, *The Story of Swalcliffe*, 1943

Afterwards the school feast was held in the park with played games such as 'Thread the needle', 'I wrote a letter to my love', 'Nuts in May', 'Here we go round the mulberry bush', 'Open the gate and let me through', and the boys brought along their tops and played cricket and football.

## Swerford

The *Oxford Journal* of 8th May 1897 said that as usual the children processed through the village calling at the principal houses. Here the May Queen and her two boy attendants dressed as sailors and all three rode suitably decorated donkeys. Afterwards the children enjoyed tea and sports in school, but the school managers had decided not to have dancing although it had been popular.

## Tetsworth

Six couples dressed in white, decorated with ribbons and flowers, went round Tetsworth. The first couple carried the garland, the second were the Lord and Lady, the latter carrying a bunch of flowers, followed by the waiting man and maid who held the Lord's hat and the Lady's flowers while they kissed. Two or more couples holding white handkerchiefs between them followed. They sang:

Good morning, ladies and gentlemen,
I wish you a happy day;
I'm come to show my garland,
Because 'tis the first of May.

The first of May is Garland Day,
So please remember my garland.

Percy Manning, *Seasonal Customs*, Ms Top Oxon d.199

## Thame

The children wandered round in groups of four in the late 19th century. Two girls walked in front carrying the flower and ribbon decked garland, followed by the Lord carrying the money-box and his Lady dressed in white or a light colour, trimmed with coloured ribbons. They sang:

Good morning, ladies and gentlemen,
I wish you a happy May,
I'm come to show my garland,
Because it is May Day.

The first of May comes once a year,
Garland Day now brings me here;
Please to see my garland, sir,
Because it is the First of May;
Please give me a penny, sir,
And then I'll run away.

After the Lord had kissed the Lady he handed round the money-box. (Percy Manning, *Seasonal Customs*, MS Top Oxon d.199.)

## Waterstock

The Ashurst family gave each girl a red cloak and each boy a pair of boots to wear in the May procession, which they were allowed to keep afterwards.

## West Hendred

The children began singing round the village at about seven o'clock in the morning, collecting pennies. They sang:

Good morning, young ladies and gentlemen;
I wish you a happy May.
I am come to show our garland,
Because 'tis the first of May.
Happy May! Joyful May!
Winter's gone and passed away.
Hail, all hail, the merry month of May!
We'll all hasten to the woods away,
Among the flowers so sweet and gay,
Away to hail! Away to hail!
To hail the merry month of May.

Eleanor Hayden, Travels Round Our Village, 1901

## Weston-on-the-Green

The children sang as they carried their May garlands and dolls:

Gentlemen and ladies, I wish you a happy May.
So please to smell my garland, because it is May Day.
I've brought you flowers, I've brought you May,
So at your door I stand and clap. Clap away.

It is the happiest time we have
Throughout the month of May,
When soft winds blow and kiss away the snow,
When the blackbirds sing for the dear, warm, Spring,
Then we'll go a maying,
In the meadows straying,
Maying, Maying, you and I.

C. E. Prior, Oxfordshire Archaeological Society Reports, 1903

## Wheatley

Children made garlands and brought them round on May Day until about 1914. Two May songs were recorded in W. O. Hassall (ed), *Wheatley Records*, 1956:

Come and see the Queen so gay,
The Queen so gay,
Come and see the Queen so gay,
All in the merry month of May.
You may look at our garland and see the sweet flowers,
And see the sweet flowers, and see the sweet flowers,
All in the merry, merry month of May.

The other is:

Spring is coming, spring is coming,
Birdies build your nest,

May Song from
Wheatley recorded
with its music in
W. O. Hassall,
*Wheatley Records*,
Oxfordshire
Record Society,
1956

Weave together straw and feather,
Doing each his best, doing each his best.

Spring is coming, spring is coming,
Flowers are coming too,
Rosies, lilies, daffodillies,
Now are peeping through, now are peeping through.

Spring is coming, spring is coming,
All around is fair.
Shimmer and shimmer on the river,
Joy is everywhere, joy is everywhere.

There must have been a revival, because in 1953 a Wheatley teacher wrote to Iona and Peter Opie, and was quoted in *The Lore and Language of Schoolchildren* (1959):

I have made enquiries among my children in school and I find that... little groups are formed and a May Queen is chosen. A small maypole is made and

131

decorated with a garland a-top, and the Queen carries a stool upon which she sits for the ceremony, which is performed at intervals along the streets. She, by the way, wears a lace curtain and a ring on her finger, if possible. The rest of the company dance round her singing:

> Round and round the maypole,
> Merrily we go, tripping, tripping lightly
> Singing as we go.
>
> O, the happy pastime
> On the village green,
> Dancing in the sunshine –
> Hurrah for the Queen!

Here they all kneel on one knee and the Queen stands up and sings:

> I'm the Queen, don't you see,
> Just come from the meadow green;
> If you wait a little while
> I will dance the maypole style.
>
> My hair is long, my dress is short,
> My shoes are laced with silver,
> A red rosette upon my breast
> And a guinea gold ring on my finger.

Then all the company rises and, oddly enough, begins to hop round the maypole singing:

> Hop, hop, hop to the butcher's shop,
> I dare not stay any longer,
> For if I do my ma will say
> You naughty girl to disobey.

## Witney

The sweeps held a procession in the latter part of the 19th century, recorded in *Jackson's Oxford Journal* in 1875, and the custom was still carried on, although the reporter sounds a little surprised to find it, in 1896:

> At Witney they still have a Jack-in-the-Green, a man enclosed in a bower made in the shape of a pyramid about ten feet high. He is accompanied by various attendants, one bearing a drum or triangle and another a large silver ladle for the reception of the monies of the speaker.
>
> P. H. Ditchfield, *Old English Customs Extant at the Present Time*, 1896

## Wootton-by-Woodstock

In the early 20th century the boys made a rough bower for the May Queen from poles and carried her round in it. The children collected

May Day at Wroxton c. 1910. The celebrations were organised by Wroxton School, as proclaimed by the banner displayed above the children. A garland has been made from crossed hoops, shown between the May Queen and King.

Photograph: Oxfordshire Photographic Archive

bunches of any flowers they could get, and paraded round the village, sang songs and danced round the queen. Songs included:

Gentlemen and ladies
We wish you a happy May,
Come kiss my face and smell my mace,
And give the Lord and Lady something.

*Notes and Queries*, 3rd series, vol. 7

Another song in the Percy Manning collection, recorded in 1897, is:

Good morning, mistress and master,
We wish you a happy May,
We're come to show my garland,
Because 'tis the first of May.

A bunch of May I have brought you
And at your door I stand,
It is but a bit, but it will sprout out.
'Tis the work of our Lord's hand.

Then we will go a-Maying
Through the meadows straying
Maying, maying, maying,
You and I.

## Wroxton

Oliver Grant, a past headmaster of Wroxton School, recalled the celebrations in Wroxton in about 1910 for Banbury Museum: garlands were made by the teachers, using flowers gathered down by the brook and garden flowers. The garland had two crossed hoops with a carrying pole through the centre and was carried by the older boys aged about twelve. They also had a large heavy banner with 'SUCCESS TO WROXTON SCHOOL' on it. Another boy carried a collection box. Girls acted as maids in waiting to the Queen, who, like the King, was elected in a proper ballot using paper slips. Usually she was one of the most popular girls in the school, or the prettiest, and the boy was the most popular.

The children gathered at the school, then the first stops were made at the homes of the King and Queen. Although the children had the day off school their master was there to keep order. The vicar said a prayer and they all sang a hymn, then the children marched to Wroxton Abbey to visit Lord and Lady North and show them the garland and sing to them – often a hunting song like 'Ken John Peel'. After the Norths had given money the children went under the arch into the courtyard to visit the servants who all gave something. Then it was time to go to church for a service before parading round the village, ending up at the school around one o'clock. They had a rest in the afternoon then went to the vicarage paddock to play cricket and games and the vicar provided lemonade and buns.

# 29th May: Oak Apple Day

May 29th was both the birthday of King Charles II, and the day on which he was proclaimed king after his triumphal entry into London in 1660. It was ordained that commemorative peals of bells should be rung in the churches. The day rapidly became associated with the use of oak apples, commemorating the fact that Charles had escaped after defeat at the battle of Worcester in September 1651 by hiding in an oak tree at Boscobel. The day was given a variety of names – Oak Apple Day, Royal Oak Day, Shick-Shack Day and Nettle Day – and was widely celebrated, if in a low-key manner, until the early 20th century, even though the prayers commemorating the date of Charles I's execution and Charles II's Restoration were removed from the Prayer Book in 1859.

Anthony Wood described a decline in the enthusiasm for celebratory bonfires lit in the King's honour in Oxford in 1682, twenty-two years after the Restoration:

> May 29... but one bonfire to be seen in the four great streets, made by any townsmen, whereas there hath been thirty.
>
> ed. Andrew Clark, *The Life and Times of Anthony Wood*, vol. III

James Newton of Nuneham Courtenay wrote in his diary on 29th May 1761 of 'Oaken boughs set at many People's Doors' (quoted in R. W. Malcolmson, *Popular Recreations in English Society*, 1973), which sounds similar to the May custom of decking the houses with hawthorn boughs.

In the 19th century Oxfordshire boys would shout 'Show your oak!' to each other, and those who had neglected to wear oak would suffer pinching as punishment for being disloyal. The oak was only worn until twelve noon, and anyone found wearing it after that time was liable to be stung with stinging nettles, which boys took to school for that purpose, according to J. R. Wodhams in *The Midland Garner*, Vol. II., 1884.

George James Dew of Lower Heyford mentioned the day in his diary in 1874:

May 30th... Yesterday being the day on which Charles II was restored in 1660, the children had oak leaves stuck on their hats and bonnetts (sic), in commemoration thereof. They call it 'Shick Shack Day'...

ed. Pamela Horn, *Oxfordshire Village Life*, Beacon, 1983

His daughter Dorothy Dew recalled the same practice in the early 20th century. It was found throughout Oxfordshire, with slight variants on the practice. Angelina Parker ('Collectanea', *Folklore*, 1913, vol. 24) commented that in Oxford after noon the shick shack or oak apple, was discarded and replaced by ash leaves or monkey-powder, and these disappeared in the evening, or wearers would be stung with stinging nettles. In Charlbury the oak apples worn were gilded, according to John Kibble in *Historical and Other Notes on Charlbury* (1927).

Mary Bright Rix of Boars Hill hated the day:

That day every boy and girl must wear an oak-apple. If anyone appeared at school without the royal emblem they were stung unmercifully with nettles, and the bare legs and face revealed painful red patches. Being the daughter of a dissenter and a liberal I was neither supposed to wear primroses to commemorate Lord Beaconsfield, nor oak apple to honour the Stuarts, but went along Jarn hedge on my way to school and surreptitiously broke off an oak-apple to save myself from torture.

Mary Bright Rix, *Boars Hill, Oxford*, 1941

At Over Norton children divided themselves into Roundheads and Cavaliers, the latter wearing oak apples. They recited the rhyme:

Oak apple day, 29th of May,
If you don't give us a holiday,
We'll all run away.

Mollie Harris recalled a similar rhyme used in Ducklington in *A Kind of Magic* (1969):

Shick Shack day,
Twenty-ninth of May,
If we don't have a holiday
We'll all run away.

Another rhyme was used in Oxford, according to Mrs Thicke:

Oak tree, oak tree,
On a summer's day,
When leaves were green in May.
Hidden by your leafy spray
The bonny Charlie lay.
Though unfurled by years you stand,
Still your name true to fame does our love command.
With a ribbon blue
We will bind your spray
On the 29th of May.

At Leafield a bath was filled with water and apples were dropped in and the children had to catch them – presumably with their teeth. At Ramsden, according to D. H. Allport in *Ramsden* (1965), the children went round collecting 'largesse' in return for providing painted oak apples to hang on people's doors. In Eynsham in the 1970s Hugh Cooper went up the church tower each 29th May to place an oak spray including an oak apple up there.

At Souldern the 29th May celebrations coincided with the annual meeting of the Souldern Friendly Society in 1887:

On the 29th of May, the anniversary of the restoration of King Charles II, a large branch of oak is displayed in the principal street, and oak apples are extensively worn.

Mr and Mrs Gough, *Historical and Descriptive Notices of the Parish of Souldern*, 1887

In Charlbury the Forester's Club met on 29th May, and the members, according to Mrs Pumphrey in *The Charlbury of Our Childhood*, prided themselves on wearing the 'biggest and rosiest oak-apples'. Stalls, target shooting and a merry-go-round were set up in Church Street.

# Whit Hunts and Whitsun Ales

**Whit Sunday, or Pentecost, the seventh Sunday after Easter, is an** important date in the religious calendar, commemorating the time the Holy Spirit came down to the Apostles. Whit Monday and Tuesday were holidays and time for more revelries, some connected with spring or hunting rights. There were also customs seemingly unrelated to the time of year such as that of distributing smoked farthings at Eynsham (which attracted Oxford students who picked fights with the local people), while at Minster

Lovell the village children sat at trestle tables and were regaled with cakes and ale, sometimes imbibing so much that they fell off their stools in a drunken state. At Ducklington, according to Mollie Harris, at Whitsun everyone who could afford it wore new clothes, with the better off girls dressing entirely in white: dresses, socks, shoes and hats.

Whitsun and May Day came close together in some years, and there are many similarities in the way they were celebrated with flowers and dancing. The Queen of the May perhaps became the Lady at Whitsun.

## Robin Hood Games

A feature of May and Whitsun in the 15th and 16th centuries was the election of a summer king and queen, sometimes called Robin Hood (or King of the May or Whitsun King or Summer Lord) and Maid Marian (who was at first played by a woman, later becoming a man-woman

Robin Hood Games: painted window from Betley in Staffordshire, now in the Victoria & Albert Museum, which illustrates characters from the Robin Hood games including Friar Tuck and Maid Marian. Several of the characters wear the bells associated with the morris men.

Illustration from John Brand and Henry Ellis, *Observations on Popular Antiquities*, 1841.

character). Henry VIII himself played the part of Robin in one such play and his nobles dressed in costume. Other characters included Friar Tuck and Little John. The ales were a way of raising money for the church: records of them are found in churchwardens' accounts including those of Henley-on-Thames, Thame and St Helen's Church, Abingdon.

At Thame there was a tradition of Whitsun celebrations from the mid-15th century up to the Elizabethan period (also Hoketide celebrations and in 1482 a play about St George). The character of Robin Hood gathered the money three times before 1501. In the early 1550s a Summer Lord was chosen, who in 1553 was accompanied by 'vices' who played the fool, a taborer (from London) and piper. Money was paid in 1554 for buying thirteen yards of green fabric and two-and-a-half of yellow to make coats for the morris men, and to buy them bells. J. Howard Brown and William Guest quoted the costs paid by the churchwardens for the ales in 1555 in *A History of Thame*:

| | |
|---|---|
| 5 bushels of wheat | 5s 11d |
| 2 qr 2 bushels malt | 15s 9d |
| 7 gallons of ale | 18d |
| 2 calves | 19s 2d |
| Fish | 5s 2d |
| Butter and eggs | 3s 4d |
| 3 loads of wood | 10d |
| Cook | 18d |
| Helper | 10d |
| Dressing the barn | 4d |
| Piper | 6s |

In 1557 the Lord of the May was paid a fee of five shillings.

In Henley-on-Thames the Corporation Accounts in the reign of Henry VIII record money collected at the Robin Hood play, which was saved up over several years and used to buy a silver censer. The festivities were sometimes termed 'The king game' here. In 1520 it was known as 'Robin Hood's money'.

J. S. Burns quotes from the Corporation Accounts in *A History of Henley-on-Thames* (1861):

18 He VII 'the seid John hathe rec' of the King Playe mony gadred when Ric Andrew his son was semer [Summer] King vviis'

12 HVIII '...Also of Robyn Hood ys money ... iiijli xiijs iiijd'

'Also received of the King's money by the seyd warden the xxvith day of June – the xiijth yere of King Henry VIII xxxs ixd

20 H VIII 'And for the King's Ale in the Easter week...'

22HVIII '... and for the kynge... by young men, called the may game xxxis xsijd'

'24.H.8 Received of Artur for suche money as he gatheryd at Whittsentide when he was King Play kyng for that tjme of Whittsuntide xxxs ijd and of ill money xvjd

26 Hen 8 The Kyng's gam att Whittesontyd. Received of John Gravett for the

kynge's game this yere xxxiiis viiid. Payde for a minstrel that went to the chosing of kyng and quene.

John Gravett was recorded in the same accounts as making payments:

'for the gartering of the morrys bells iid'
'for the morrys bells and for the cotes iiijd'
'Item threde to sow the same coots iid'
'Payd to John Granger for playing the fole at Whitsontyd iiis iiijd'
'payd to Vell for playing wt his tabor at Whitsontyd iijs iiijd.'

Abingdon has a tantalisingly brief reference in 1566 when eighteen pence was paid for setting up Robin Hood's bower. The play was performed in Enstone at the surprisingly late date of 1652.

There are references to a Robin Hood play, perhaps a version of the mummers' play, being performed at Bloxham until the 19th century, but the text has completely disappeared.

The Robin Hood games involved a procession with dancing, at which bystanders were sold paper livery badges, accompanied by feasting and drinking in green bowers. In many places it was accompanied by an element of combat, such as jousting, symbolising ritual combat between winter and spring. The games are another strand in the common motif found in customs of role reversal: working class people aping aristocracy and royalty, here with Robin Hood the outlaw and rebel taking authority. Robin Hood symbolised youth and the coming of spring. Although the May Games died out in the 16th century, one can see elements of them in the Whitsun Ale.

Another early example of Whitsun festivities comes from Oxford in 1598:

The inhabitants assembled on the two Sundays before Ascension Day, and on that day, with drum and shot and other weapons, and men attired in women's apparel, brought into the town a woman bedecked with garlands and flowers named by them the Queen of the May. They also had Morrishe dances and other disordered and unseemly sports, and intended the next Sunday to continue the same abuses.

*Calendar of the Cecil Papers*, 1899, viii, 201

# Bringing in the Fly

The Whitsun custom of Oxford college cooks 'Bringing in the Fly' began with a sermon preached in Oxford after which they processed to St Bartholomew's Chapel off the Cowley Road to capture a cranefly and bring it back in a cage, amidst drinking and hilarity. The earliest reference is in the Register of the University for 1463, of which Percy Manning wrote that:

Thomas Dalton and Tibot Coke, proctors of the Guild (artis) of the Cooks of the University, lodged a complaint against John Coke, of S. John's Hospital (later Magdalen) because he had neglected to provide certain wax candles called the 'Coke-lyght', in the church of the Blessed Virgin Mary in Oxford, and had neglected or broken the custom of contributing to a certain feast which was wont to be held yearly in the month of May, 'on the day of the riding of cooks.' Robert Coke, of Hamton Hall, and others, proved that this custom was ancient, and that the College cooks and cooks of the Halls chose each one proctor to collect subscriptions.

*Address to the Folklore Society, 19th March 1913*

The custom was described in detail by John Aubrey in 1686-7:

Before the Civill warres the custome was that some day of ye Whitsun-holydayes, ...the Master-cooke (for that yeare) with the rest of his brethren were marched in silke doublets on horseback, and rode (I thinke) to Bartholomews or Bullingdon-green, fetch in the Flye: the sd master-cooke treated his brethren before they rode out (at Exeter Coll. 1642). I saw them drinke their mornings draughts, and on Michaelmas Day they rode thither again to convey the Fly away.

*Remains of Gentilisme and Judaisme*

The custom became a by-word for rowdy behaviour, as Anthony Wood remarked ironically in *The History and Antiquities of the University of Oxford*, vol. II that when the Earl of Pembroke was installed as Chancellor of the University in 1648 the ceremony was so disorderly that 'the rout or rabble of the City' declared 'that they had often seen Sir Cranion or the Fly at Whitsuntide fetched in by the Cooks of Oxford from St Barthlomew's Hospital with much more grace and solemnity'. 'Sir Cranion' was referred to by Ben Johnson in *Bartholomew Fair*: 'He looks... like one that were made to catch flies, with his Sir Cranion legs'.

A comical 'explanation' for the custom was given in the burlesque speech written for a college porter in an appendix to a *Narcissus, a Twelfth Night Merriment*, performed at St John's College in 1602:

... few of them (the cooks) will take rest this night and suffer as few to take rest in the morning. They have sett a little porch before so great an house, and have called their show the fly.

Some say because a maid comming to towne with butter was mett by a cooke and by him deceaved in a wood adjoyning, whose laments the dryades and hamadryades of the place, pittieng, turned her into a butterfly; and ever since the cooks are bound to this anniversary celebration of her metamorphosis; but soft, if the cooks hear that the porridge pott of my mouth runnes over soe, they will keele it with the ladle of reprehension; therefore, I will make haste away, onely asking this boone ... that your ladyshipps servant Monsieur Piers may ride tomorrow with the fierye fraternity of his fellow cookes and make upp the worthy company of the round table, which they are resolved not to leave till the whole house goe rounde with them.

The playwright Gayton referred to Sancho Panza having made a cassock into a wallet in *Festivious Notes upon Don Quixote*:

It were serviceable after this greasie use for nothing but to preach at a Carnivale or Shrove Tuesday, and to tosse Pancakes in after the exercise; or else (if it could hve been conveyed thither) nothing more proper for the man that preaches the Cook's Sermon in Oxford, when that plump society rides upon their governours horses to fetch in the Enemie, the Flie.

Quoted in John Brand and Henry Ellis, Observations on Popular Antiquities, volume 1, 1841

The 'fly' of the ceremony was the focus of confused beliefs: at some times it seems to have been thought of as a malign influence, sometimes as a cranefly, sometimes a butterfly. Percy Manning commented:

It might be conciliated by gifts of food, be honoured for being carried in procession, or receive that supreme token of esteem – to be solemnly and ritually eaten by its devotees. But, on the other hand, the attitude of compulsion was equally present; it was 'fetched in', as Wood says, and might be over-awed and hunted to its death.

'Bringing in the Fly', Folklore Vol 26, 1914

Percy Manning pointed out similarities between this and other May Day and Whitsun ceremonies, such as the Whit Hunt which, like the 'Fly', included the use of horses. They rode out very early in the morning, as was done on May morning. St Bartholomew's well seems to have been decorated in a similar way to Derbyshire well dressing while the bower of green boughs built against the college gateway resembled those constructed for Whit and Lamb Ales. He suggested that it was originally connected with a medieval festival of the Cooks Guild, about which very little is known.

The capture of the cranefly has parallels with carrying and killing a live victim, part of which is eaten by each person (like the division of the deer's skin at the Whit Hunt and the eating of the Bampton morris men's cake). There was a Danish festival in which a mayfly was carried in procession with green boughs. Strowell at St Bartholomew's must have been considered a holy well in the middle ages and the cranefly may have been thought of as its guardian spirit.

Some references connect the custom with May Day, so it may have been changed from this date, as was the New College singing. It continued into the early 18th century, referred to by J. Burman in 1705 as a custom which had not been described by Dr. Plot.

# Wychwood Forest Whit Hunt

On Whit Monday Morning, as beauty shone clear,
We hadn't been hunting for the space of a year;
Our deer being fresh, our hounds being strong,
We spurred up our horses and chased him along.

Percy Manning, MS Top Oxon d.200

Wychwood was a large royal forest, which at one time stretched between Woodstock, Witney, Chipping Norton and Burford. That does not mean that the entire area was thickly forested, but it was an area within which forest laws were strictly enforced. Normally only the King and a few favoured local nobles had permission to hunt deer and other animals within

141

the forest, and no-one was allowed to hunt for forty days before the king was expected. Among other things medieval forest law laid down that all inhabitants over the age of twelve had 'to be of good behaviour towards his majesties' wild beasts' – hart, hind, boar, hare and wolf – and all dogs must have their fore-claws removed. The main purpose of the forest was to provide deer for the king's table (about a thousand a year were killed in the thirteenth century, and salted venison sent off to wherever the king was staying), and timber (which was used for buildings and ships). The timber was so coveted that Philip of Spain is said to have issued instructions to bring back oaks after England had been conquered by the Spanish Armada, but as he lost, he never got his timber.

On one occasion each year villagers were permitted to hunt in the forest, under the strict supervision of the keeper. This usually took place on Whit Monday, but was looked forward to for weeks beforehand in Witney, where processions of about fifty people paraded round playing horns, while:

> On Whit Monday morning, the horn band, followed by almost everyone in the town (on foot or mounted on horses or donkeys), marched in front of a rough pack of harriers to Chase Green, where they solemnly broke their horns on the stile at Codling Corner, leading to Hailey.
>
> W. J. Monk, *History of Witney*, 1894

The horns were made and used by local villagers too, being blown loudly at midnight on Whit Sunday, and some survive in the collection of the Pitt Rivers Museum:

> These 'peeling horns' were made of green willow-bark, peeled in a long spiral strip from a bough previously well soaked and beaten, in order to loosen the bark. This strip was then rolled up in a long funnel shape, about eleven inches long and two and a half inches in diameter at the larger end. To the smaller end was fitted a reed, about two inches long, made of willow bark stripped from a twig without any incision being made in it. This reed was called the trumpet. The edges of the reed, which entered the mouth of the player, were pinched closely together to produce the sound. The whole horn was pinned together with the long thorns of the blackthorn.
>
> Percy Manning in *Folklore*, vol. 8, 1897

At daybreak the men of Brize Norton, Charlbury, Crawley, Ducklington, Finstock and Leafield and from the towns of

A 'peeling horn' made of twisted willow bark, with a reed in one end, held together with thorns, made to summon men to the Whit Hunt on the outskirts of Witney in the early 19th century.
Photograph: PR100H Pitt Rivers Museum, University of Oxford

Bampton and Witney who could lay their hands on a horse rode off to meet at Hailey. Accompanied by dogs, usually including a pack of harriers, greyhounds, sheep dogs, lurchers, and others, they hunted twelve Chase Woods: Bretch Wood, Cowley Wood, Henley Wood, Dean Wood, Barley Hall, Water Vine, Little Water Vine Wood, Pigstie Wood, Spoonley Wood, Blaindell Wood, St Johns and Smalley Wood. They were permitted to kill only three deer, one for Hailey, one for Crawley and the other for Witney.

It was a source of great pride to be the one first in at the death, and this person was permitted to keep the head and antlers which were often preserved as a treasured trophy and considered very good luck.

The deer carcases were taken to the nearest inn to be skinned, so that small pieces of skin could be scrambled for; it was considered very lucky to acquire a piece of skin to wear in the cap, which was supposed to indicate marriage within the year. The deer killed for Witney is said to have been cooked in an enormous frying pan.

The Whit Hunt was still going strong in 1837 when *Jackson's Oxford Journal* of 20th May reported:

> Our annual chartered hunt had a numerous attendance on Monday last. At an early hour in the morning the whole of the athletic population of Witney appeared to be in motion, and were seen pouring in crowds to the Forest Copses, the scene of the action. The noble stag hounds of Lord Churchill threw off at five and by eight o'clock a brace of deer were killed. The sport was suspended for a time to refresh the hounds and another deer was shortly afterwards killed.

Another aspect of the Whit Hunt was the settling of long-standing grudges and quarrels by fights, sometimes between the actual people concerned, sometimes represented by village champions. It was not uncommon to find half a dozen fights going on at once. There was also fighting over the distribution of the venison.

While the hunt was in progress those not participating set up a maypole on the green of one of the villages, and were entertained by:

> a party of Morris dancers, accompanied by a fool and a pie-and-tabour player ... With the dancers went a sword-bearer, as at Bampton, carrying a cake impaled on a sword, which brought good luck to all who partook of it. The dancers afterwards marched off to Witney, where they gave a similar exhibition, and collected money for the feast.
>
> Others of the villagers got ready the Bowery, a barn dressed up and decorated with flowers and green boughs. On the return of the hunters and the Morris-dancers, the whole company repaired to the Bowery to take part in a feast known as the Youth Ale.
>
> Percy Manning, *Folklore*, Vol. 8, 1897

The ale lasted a week, then on the Saturday following the Hunt the venison was dressed and cooked. The hunters were allowed as much as they could eat, but outsiders paid a shilling for a portion. The Morris dancers travelled from village to village each day to dance and compete with fellow groups, and each evening returned to the Bower. The Youth Ale was last held around 1847. After that a big procession to church took place on Whit Sunday, while on Monday and Tuesday races were held on Curbridge Downs outside Witney, culminating in a donkey race from Church Down to Staple Hill and back.

The people of Burford had a similar right to hunt in Wychwood Forest on Whit Monday, but the town suffered an outbreak of plague in 1593 so the right was withdrawn because of the danger of infection, and instead the Privy Council proposed:

Order shalt be given to the keepers of the said forest to deliver unto you two buckes to be spent amongst you at your own disposicions; besydes this your forbearinge for this tyme shall not be any prejudice to your said ancyent custom hereafter.

Quoted in Wilson Macarthur, *The River Windrush*, 1946

After that the Rev. A. C. Dallas, on taking up his post in Burford was shocked at the small size of his congregation on Whit Sunday which consisted of the parish clerk, two old women and three small boys. He was horrified to discover that the remainder of his congregation was out hunting and determined to remedy the matter, and after a discussion with the Ranger, Lord Churchill, the hunt was abolished.

Instead a Whitsun ale was set up: a boy and girl elected as Lord and Lady processed to Capps Lodge where they formally demanded their 'brace of best bucks and a faun, with their horns and hoofs, without fee or reward'. These were delivered to Burford the following August when a Venison Feast was held in the Town Hall for all residents, who ate off pewter plates owned by the churchwardens.

The procession into the forest continued until 1827, and the feast longer, but after disafforestation in 1857 deer were no longer available, and instead a donation of £150 to the Burford Apprentice Fund was negotiated by the commissioners for the disafforestation:

And whereas it appeared to us ... that the Aldermen and Bailiffs of the Township of Burford did satisfactorily establish their right to two bucks to be delivered annually to them from the said Forest ... we determine that the sum of one hundred and fifty pounds is the proper amount of compensation to be paid to the said Alderman and Bailiffs of the Township of Burford in respect of this claim.

Quoted in Percy Manning MS Top Oxon d.200

There are various references to the Venison Feast in *Jackson's Oxford Journal*: in 1765 it recorded that the venison for the feast had been stolen, and on 16th July 1776 that year's feast was held at two p.m. In 1807 three bucks were cooked. The proceedings in 1898 were also described:

... an excellent custom is still maintained every year at the Lamb Hotel, when Mr John Wyatt provides for his numerous patrons an excellent repast of that which was in days gone by, such a very esteemed dish to English people [ie venison]. On Saturday night last a good company sat down and enjoyed the annual dinner, as so many have in years gone past, and the function proved in every respect a happy and successful one.

By this time Wychwood Forest had been disafforested for over forty years, and the deer would no longer have come free, but the custom of having the dinner persisted.

## Whitsun at Eynsham

There are few references to medieval customs, but the Whit celebration at Eynsham in 1230 is documented as it led to problems:

> Upon a grant of the Bishop of Lincoln, for observing of processions and other solemnities to Ensham [sic] Church, in obedience to the Mother Church of Lincoln during Whitsun Week, many of the Oxford Scholars, repairing thither to see jovial doings, were assaulted by the country people who killed some and wounded others, and made the rest fly home in fear and danger of their lives.
>
> The bishop, hearing about the riot, excommunicated the authors and abetters of this sedition, in all the churches of Oxfordshire, excluding them from the society of all Christians, and depriving them of the benefit of confession till the Feast of St Bartholomew; the scholars also resented this injury so highly that they interrupted all lectures and would not resume them till the offenders had undergone the severest punishments; and when they did, the bishop procured of the Pope a permission for the doctors and masters of Oxford to become lecturers and regents in any other University without an examination.
>
> Cox, *Magna Britannia*, vol 4.

The Eynsham clergy processed at Whitsun, carrying the holy water vat. Mrs Bryan Stapleton suggested that place names 'Vocat Alleluiah' and 'Paternoster Farm' in Yarnton indicated that they could have formed part of the route.

Whit Monday was the only day Eynsham residents were permitted to fell timber from the Forest. According to Dr Robert Plot in *Natural History of Oxfordshire* (1676), the churchwardens went into the woods first, and marked each tree that the Eynsham people were permitted to cut down. The timber was taken to the yard of Eynsham Abbey, and the Abbey servants, before the Dissolution of the Monasteries, grabbed some for abbey use, and the Eynsham men took the rest away, some to repair the church. The custom continued until the mid-eighteenth century.

## Whitsun Ales

Churchwardens used to raise money for the church by brewing ale to sell at Whitsun festivites, which the Puritans disapproved of because it engendered drunkenness and over-enthusiastic revelry:

> Against Whit Sunday, or some other time, the Church Wardens of every parish ... provide half a score or twenty quarters of malt ... which malt being made into very strong ale or beer, it is set to sale, either in the Church or some other place

assigned. Then when the Nippitatum, this Huf-Cap (a they call it, this Nectar of Life) is set abroad ... he that sitteth the closest to it, and spends the most at it, he is counted the godliest man of all the rest.

Philip Stubbes, *The Anatomy of Abuses*, 1583

This disapproval was felt in other quarters too, as shown by the questions in visitation articles in the Oxford diocese in 1619:

Whether the Minister & Churchwardens have suffered any Feastes, Banquests, Churchales, or Drinkings in the Church, or any Lords of Misrule, or Sommer Lord or Lady, or any disguised persons; and players of May games or any Moris dancers at any time to come unreverently into the Church or Church-yard, and thence to dance or play, or shew themselves disguised, and what they be that commit such disorder, or that accompanied or maintained them: or any Paies to be plaied in the Church.

V. A. Diocese of Oxford (1619) quoted in John Forrest and Michael Heaney, *Annals of Early Morris*, CECTAL, 1991

Despite Puritan disapproval, many Whitsun ales were held in Oxfordshire into the 18th or even 19th centuries. Sometimes, as at Wantage, they became entwined with Robin Hood games, as in 1867 when Robin Hood and Little John appeared in costume in the festivities.

## Woodstock Whitsun Ale

An elaborate Whitsun Ale was held at Woodstock, graphically described by Thomas Little in *Confessions of an Oxonian*, Volume 1, 1826:

I was suddenly aroused from my reflections by the sound of tabors, flutes, pipes, tambourines and fiddles, mingled with shouts of merriment and rustic songs, all indicative of glee and rural festivity; and having now passed the gates of the park I was able to discern the quarter from whence the sounds of this merrymaking proceeded. On inquiry, I learned from an honest, chubby-looking 'clod-pole', that the present occasion was one of no small importance in the vicinity of Woodstock, since it recurred once only in the space of seven long years, and that the period of its celebration was always at Whitsuntide, and that it was denominated by the ancient appellation of an ale.

Off I walked to be a spectator of the festivities of the Whitsun ale. On elbowing through the throng, the first fellow I met who was engaged as a party in the revels was an old man dressed up in the motley garb of a Tom Fool or clown, and I must say he looked his character to perfection.

'How do, master?' cried he. 'May I ask your honour what you call that yonder?' pointing to a painted wooden horse, placed in the middle of a ring.

'A wooden horse, to be sure.' said I. 'What should you think it was?'

'A shilling, Sir, if you please,' answered the clown, 'a forfeit if you please, Sir.'

'A forfeit! a forfeit! what for?' I inquired. 'I'll give you no shilling, I assure you!'

'Bring out his lordship's gelding. Here's a gentleman who wishes for a ride! Bring out the gelding! His lordship's groom hey! Tell her ladyship to be mounted!'

Here I was seized by four or five clumsy clodpoles dressed up in coloured rags and ribbons. They were forthwith proceeding to place me on the wooden hobby just mentioned, behind an ugly red-haired freckled trull, who personated the lady

An illustration of the Woodstock Whitsun Ale held in Blenheim Park in 1826. Churchwardens used to raise money for the upkeep of their churches by brewing and selling ale, and often sold it in a tent or Bowery at a Whit Ale. At the larger ales a Lord and Lady were selected and, as at Woodstock, unwary passers-by were requested to name the parrot in a cage and flail hung above the entrance to the Bowery. If they did not call the owl 'My Lady's Canary Bird' or similar and the flail 'My Lord's Nutcrackers', they were liable to pay a forfeit or be threatened with marriage to the ugliest girl in the town.

Illustration from Percy Manning, 'Stray Notes on Oxfordshire Folklore', *Folk-lore*, vol.XIV, June 1903

of the revels. I bellowed out that I would pay the forfeit without more to do, and thus I was sconced of a shilling for not calling the cursed wooden hobby his lordship's gelding. Shortly after one of her ladyships maids of honour came up to me, and begged me to look at the pretty bird in the cage, hanging over her Ladyship's saloon, or dirty oblong tent made of tarpaulin. This was a great ugly white owl, stuffed; and I thought I should be safe by answering that it was the very handsomest owl I had ever seen! No sooner had I uttered this, than the fair maid of honour screamed out in treble, shriller than the squeak of a Christmas porker, or a pig driver's horn, 'A Forfeit, Sir, if you please. A shilling forfeit!'

'Pooh!' said I, 'I've paid forfeits enough.'

On which, continuing in the same strain, 'Bring out her ladyship's cook! Here's a gentleman wishes to marry her!'

On this all the dirty baggages, which formed the group of her ladyship's maids of honour, brought out a fat ugly wench with a nose and cheeks reddened with brick dust, and bearing a toasting fork in one hand and a dishclout in the other; and were on the point of commencing a mock ceremony of marriage between myself and the fair siren of the kitchen, in the course of which I was to have received three pricks with the toasting fork on each buttock, and to have had my nose wiped with the dishclout, had I not saved myself by producing a shilling as the penalty of my mistake, which consisted, as I was afterwards given to understand, in not denominating the stuffed owl her ladyship's canary bird...

At short intervals tents were erected for the purpose of dancing; and and the maidens and swains of the whole country around were hoofing and clumping up and down the middle and up again, beneath their welcome canopy.

147

The Ale was held every seven years, beginning on Holy Thursday and lasting for a week. It raised significant money for the church – in 1609 £7 1s 6d was raised, which paid for several years' repairs. A Lord and Lady were chosen – Ellinor Collins, the Lady in 1614, was presented with an apron by the Mayor. A dancing bower was constructed, originally from green boughs, (later, it seems from the description above, a tarpaulin was used), situated on the green on the main Oxford-Stratford road through the town, near the entrance to what is now Blenheim Palace. A refreshment booth was erected nearby. Obviously details varied over the years, and in John Aubrey's time there were a pair of owls in a cage, known as 'my lady's parrots' (sometimes an owl and a hawk), and a pair of flails, known as 'my lord's nutcrackers', while the wooden horse was 'my lady's palfrey'. If these were mis-named by visitors (many students came out from Oxford for the occasion, and villagers from miles around came too), they had to pay a forfeit of a shilling or ride shoulder high behind the lady on the wooden horse, round the maypole. If they still refused to pay the forfeit, their hats were taken.

A maypole was erected – after the building of Blenheim, begun in 1705, it was provided by the Duke of Marlborough – and decorated with ribbons and flowers. Sometimes the lower half of the pole was greased, and a leg of mutton was tied on, together with a silk hat, won by whoever could climb up and get them. Evergreens and young oaks were taken from the park, with the permission of the Duke, to make a large bower about six yards wide and thirty yards long. The Lord and Lady each carried a mace, made from small squares of board with semi-circular hoops crossed diagonally attached to the four corners, each with a small stick to hold it, the whole covered with ribbons. In the centre of each mace was a small rich cake like a Banbury Cake, known as the Whit Cake – small pieces were offered to passers-by in return for a payment. Additional cakes were carried in a basket by a man. The Lord and Lady were attended by a waiting man and a waiting woman, two men to carry the painted horse on its two carrying poles, and morris dancers. This group progressed round the town.

The last maypole was left standing for about a year and bought by Mr Holloway who wanted to keep it as a relic of the last ale, but the Yeomanry in the town pulled it down one night and destroyed it.

It was said locally that if the Whit Ale was not kept up, a turnpike would be put across the road from Woodstock to Bladon and Percy Manning was told that this in fact happened after the feast was discontinued.

There are various references to the Whitsun Ale in *Jackson's Oxford Journal*, as on 6th June 1837:

On Monday last one of the finest May Poles ever seen was set up in Woodstock, as the signal for the rural sports of Whitsun ale; and on Thursday, being Holy Thursday, My Lord and My Lady, with their usual attendants - the tabor, pipe, and the fiddle, with an excellent set of Morris dancers, paid their respects to their neighbours, to invite them to My Lord's Hall and Bower during the Whitsun-week.

The *Oxford Chronicle* of 7th June 1851 said that there would be a pageant at the Whit Ale, which was probably the last one held.

## *Adderbury*

A poem entitled 'At Whitsuntide' was written about the Adderbury ales:

'In olden days' (and the greybeard shakes
His head, as he says), "Twas gay, Sir!
There was Whitsun Fairs and Ales, and Cakes.
And the fun was all the day, Sir!
There was wrastling bouts on the village green
Play-acting in the booth, Sir;
And the lasses so gay as never was seen, –
They were merry, merry times in sooth, Sir!

The Morris-Dancers shook the ground
Wi' stamps and hops in time, O!
They flicked the handkerchers around,
Wore silver bells to chime, O!
In white array wi' ribbons gay
Tall-hats and limbs to lace O!
They rattle their sticks, and fiddlers plat
The Morris tunes a-pace O!

They danced 'fore housen all around;
We followed at the tail, O!
The gentris gave 'un pence or pound
Or broached the home-brewed ale O!
The Hobby-horse did prancing go
'Sakes! But those times were gay, Sir!
But that were sixty years ago; –
Now all the fun's away, Sir.

Our village lads they go to town,
To factories and shops, Sir
The lasses far too fine have grown,
To wield the brooms and mops, Sir!
The farmers scarce can find the hands
To tend the beasts, or hose, Sir;
To fell the trees, or plough the lands; -
Schollards no muscle grow, Sir!

But still at Whitsun-tide they come
By 'scursion trains so new, Sir,
To see t'old folks – the village home, -
And bring the children too, Sir,
For English lads love country air
In sunshine or in rain, Sir.
I'm thinking that they soon will fare
Back to the land again, Sir.'

J. H. S., *The Pancake Bell, and other Jingles*, 1908

This poem was written after a conversation with an old Morris dancer and farmer, so describes the late 19th century. The reference to the hobby horse is interesting, if puzzling, as there is no tradition of using a hobby horse with the morris teams in this area.

Bampton Club feast was held on Whit Monday in the late 19th and early 20th centuries. Here the procession is seen outside the church, with the band ready to play, c. 1905.

Oxfordshire Photographic Archive

## Bampton-in-the-Bush

Bampton Whit Monday celebrations still attract many visitors – children display their garlands, and the morris men dance around the town, and the place takes on a carefree atmosphere.

Whitsun is more important here than May Day, and has taken on many May characteristics including the garlands, which are usually made of two crossed hoops (often egg-shaped) decorated with greenery and flowers, with a doll in the centre (she is not veiled). Some local people used to say that the doll represented Minerva or Our Lady. Probably the custom originated with May Dolls, and was transferred to Whitsun when this became more important. Prizes were sometimes offered for the best doll until the 1940s and the custom was revived in the late 1950s. The garlands up to the 1940s were made with wild flowers only. More recent garlands often have a stick through them with flowers at the end, for ease of carrying.

In the 19th century the Bampton Club Feast was held on Whit Monday, and a procession round the town was held, consisting of:

- A drummer and a piper with a whittle and dub (later replaced by a fiddler)
- Eight morris dancers in finely pleated white shirts, white moleskin trousers and top hats decorated with red, white and blue ribbons
- Squire or Clown with a calf's tail and bladder, carrying the money box

150

The Cakebearer with the Bampton cake impaled on a pole, in 1992. Any woman wanting a baby was supposed to be guaranteed fertility if she ate a piece of the Bampton cake. Several Wychwood area morris teams used to have similar cakes.

- A sword-bearer whose sword impaled a cake decorated with ribbons

When the dancing began anyone could ask the sword-bearer for a taste of the cake, said to bring good luck and fertility (anyone who wanted a baby in the coming year ensured they had some cake!). Some people stored their piece of cake carefully in a box and kept it to ensure good luck for the next twelve months. Any cake remaining was shared among the morris men and their friends.

At the beginning of the 20th century the men danced on the lawns of houses when asked to do so. Sometimes one man would do a solo dance over two crossed sticks placed on the grass.

The Club Day was described in *Jackson's Oxford Journal* on 18th June 1859:

Club Day had arrived, and the various necessary preparations had to be made. Soon after ten o'clock the members of the two benefit societies donned their holiday suits – the best toga was not left at home on that day, and were soon at their respective hostelries, where the bands played a tune or two on their arrival. Visitors, more than usually numerous, presented themselves, and the dresses of many of them vied with the colours of the brightest rainbow, and which were only outshone by the dazzling brightness of their eyes. The clubs met – one at the Fleur-de-lis, the other at the Horse Shoe, from which houses they walked to church, preceded by their bands, the clergymen and some of the honorary

members. The services of a drill sergeant were required here, for to our mind the procession appeared to want the order and precision of former years; however they all reached the church, where the Rev. F. E. Lott, the Vicar of Lew preached...

The banner made for the Bampton Friendly Society in 1843 was gilded, and had the motto 'Love the Brotherhood, fear God, honour the King'.

The Bampton morris men performing a handkerchief dance on Whit Monday 1992.

Whit Monday dancing, 1992, with the clown who played the Fool.

Photographs: Christine Bloxham

## Bicester

Dunkin described the festivities, which have much in common with Woodstock, in his *History of Bicester* (1816):

The object of this entertainment appears to have been a burlesque on greatness; hence a barn, the scene of their festivity, is called a hall, two of the principal male and female characters are dubbed Lord and Lady and others bear the names of My Lord's Waiting Man and My Lady's Waiting Maid. A treasurer who carries a tin box before him, a set of morris dancers, a merry-andrew to clear the ring for dancing, etc., form the remainder of the group; and these fantastically dressed and decorated with ribbons, dance or parade among the spectators. The barn doors are ornamented with an owl and monkey, who bear the appropriate names of my lord's parrot and my lady's lap dog, and to miscall any of these, or accept of my lord's cake or ale, which are carried about in profusion and offered to everyone, subjects the offending party to a forfeiture of sixpence, for which however he is treated to a ride on my lord's gelding [a monstrous wooden horse carried on men's shoulders to a certain distance amidst the shouts of a large company of followers] (if a man behind my lady, or if a female before my lord) who of course considers himself entitled to a salute: but if this honour is declined, for an additional sixpence the forfeiting party is privileged to enter my lord's hall, and is entertained with cake and ale.

By the sums collected in this manner, together with those arising from the voluntary visits of parties to the hall, the expenses of the entertainment, which are very considerable, are defrayed, and oftentimes the surplus is applied to charitable purposes. At Bicester ... a few years ago a funeral pall for the use of the poor was purchased in this way...

A towering May pole erected some time before Whitsuntide serves to announce the amusement to neighbouring villages, and the crowds which usually attend attract great numbers of those itinerant traders who frequent markets and fairs, so that the festival may be considered one of the most entertaining in the country.

At the neighbouring village of Kirklington [sic] is a similar amusement held annually on Lammas-day, and from thence denominated a Lamb-ale. The common people say, if the latter were discontinued in that village, the inhabitants of Bicester King's End would be privileged to establish it in that township.

Dunkin's comment about the 'burlesque on greatness' applies well, not only to this festivity, but to the sweeps' processions, and mock mayors. The commercial nature of the custom is interesting – it must have been as important as a fair, attracting trade into the town, as people came from miles around.

## Blewbury

In the late 18th century Thomas Martin allegedly stole a maypole from a nearby village, and set it up in Playclose, where it formed the centrepiece for Whitsun sports.

## Bucknell

According to the *Oxfordshire Archaeological Society Reports* (1903) ales were held here until towards the end of the 19th century. The Rectory Barn was requisitioned for the purpose, and in latter years a rick-cloth tent was erected in the parish pound instead. Morris dancers attended, and in addition about fifty couples danced country dances in front of the barn.

## Chalgrove

The last ales were held here in 1805 or 1806, according to Laura M. P. Gannon in 'Chalgrove, A Sketch', in *Pelican*, vol. V, no. 25, Feb. 1883. A maypole was erected, and the festivities lasted for several days, with a court of misrule, headed by a Lord and Lady, who were carried round the village on a wooden horse to the tithe barn, which was renamed for the occasion 'Lord's Hall'. There was feasting, maypole dancing and morris dancing. The maypole, engraved with the initial 'M', was built into the rafters of a barn. The Whitsun Ale was replaced by the village Club Day.

## Charlbury

As in Woodstock, the Whitsun Ale was only held every seven years. The Bowery was set up in front of the Bell Inn, a maypole was brought in from Wychwood Forest, and throughout Whit week people enjoyed festivities and dancing.

## Eynsham

The Whitsun Ales died out here in 1754 because of an outbreak of smallpox.

## Finstock

A Lord and Lady led the festivities which were held in Webbs' barn. They called the owl 'my lord's parrot' and the flail 'my lord's bagpipes'. A tree from Wychwood Forest was put up on the green for a year, then cut up and sold to raise money for the Youth Ale at Finstock.

## Forest Hill

The churchwardens bought or were given vast amounts of malt to make beer, which they sold at the church house. Anyone who did not attend and buy some was fined. As an added inducement to get people to attend games and entertainments were organised including archery, shooting, bowling and dancing in Squire's Close (now Spire's Close). Later it degenerated into drunkenness and was suppressed. Interestingly Ella Miller says in the *Forest Hill Village Book* (1933) that part of the churchyard here was known as 'Robin Hood's bower', perhaps suggesting that at one time Robin Hood plays were performed.

The stone font in the church, dated 1710, is thought to have been bought with the proceeds of a Whitsun ale, and the seventeen sets of initials carved on it are said to be those of the young men who went round collecting the money.

In the 19th century Whit Monday instead became Club Day, and the club members marched round the village to church with a band. The children scrambled for nuts and oranges at the vicarage.

## Hailey

Whitsun ales or sports were held in 1763.

## Headington

The Marsh and Bush Revel was held on Whit Sunday until towards the end of the 18th century, and was attended by gypsy fiddlers and groups of country dancers – who may perhaps have been morris dancers. Rural sports and games were held in the afternoon.

## Hampton Poyle

The Whit revels survived until 1841, but by that stage were no more than drunken revels, and the 'Lord', who was carried on a wooden horse, was hired from Oxford.

## Mitlon-under-Wychwood

The Ale was eloquently advertised in *Jackson's Oxford Journal* on 14th May 1808 to encourage more visitors and raise more money:

MILTON WHITSUN ALE, NEAR BURFORD, OXFORDSHIRE CELEBRATED BUT ONCE IN TWENTY YEARS

Come then, ye votaries of pleasure, and pay your adorations to the shrine of Venus, Bacchus, and Comus: lose not this charming opportunity of hiding from care, in the bowers of love, festivity and harmony. You may not live twenty years more: hilarity, jocularity, and rural simplicity will move hand in hand conducted with the greatest discretion, modest demeanour, and appropriate etiquette, by his Lordship, attired suitably to the occasion, assisted by his Lady, specially elected for the pleasing task from the youth and beauty of the neighbourhood. - Be not afraid, nor encourage unfounded prejudices (if any exist), for the utmost attention will be paid to due decorum. So strong has been the resolutions of the Honourable Committee in that respect, that a retired Castle has been provided in the neighbourhood, where nothing can be heard more divine than the croaking of a Crow, or the braying of an Ass, to which all the enemies of innocent mirth will have the liberty of retiring during the merry week. Barrels of home-brewed Ale (9 months old) and Cakes, as numerous as gnat flies in the summer, with various other elegant repasts, tastefully set out in his Lordship's Hall and Her Ladyship's Boweries and Tea Gardens, Will be at the service of the Company. A May Pole, as lofty and well decorated as ever was seen, will nod its assent on Holy Thursday; and the superb fete will commence on Whitsun Monday and continue during the week, in a Hall and Bowers, rurally decorated for the Occasion, and attended by a Band of eminent Musicians.

Club Day in Banbury in 1907, featuring the town's 'mascot' – the lady on her white horse from the nursery rhyme, who is said to have ridden to Banbury Cross.

Photo: Oxfordshire Photographic Archive

Despite the claim that the next ale would not be for twenty years another was organised just one year later in 1809.

### North Leigh

According to Violet Mason in 'Scraps of English Folklore', *Folklore*, Vol. 40, 1929, through the ale the parishioners raised money for the upkeep of the church, with the exception of the chancel – the lay rectors, who owned Bridewell Farm, took responsibility for the chancel. All occupiers of parish land gave a bushel of malt each year, which was brewed into ale and sold on Whit Monday.

## Club Feasts and Wakes

During the 19th century the climate of opinion changed, and rustic pleasures which involved days of drinking became frowned on, particularly by the Church, which was taking on an increasingly important role in the village. Non-conformity also grew greatly in importance in the 19th century. Various movements started which condemned drink, and the idea of raising money through brewing ale was no longer considered proper. After enclosure more labourers were employed on a wage basis, and worked strict hours, all of which militated against the Whitsun ales.

Various Friendly Societies, promoted by the clergy and the gentry, were formed to provide insurance and help for the labouring classes, and reduce the amount that had to be collected on the poor rates, in the days before a National Health Service and Social Security. These Clubs had an annual feast day which in many places replaced the old Whitsun ales by the Victorian period, although club days took place throughout the summer and autumn period. An article in *Jackson's Oxford Journal* about the Valencia Club Feast in Bletchingdon in June 1862 reflects the new view on the world:

> It was a pleasing sight to see nearly a hundred young, fine, clean, and well-dressed labourers follow their banner ... to the quiet old church – it was a convincing proof of what unanimity and good feeling can effect ... This was a meeting bearing strong contrast to those of years gone by, when riot and drunkenness was the result...

Club day was important for the whole village, and was looked forward to and saved for. Many servant girls and others who had moved away from the village tried to get back for that day. Often bands were hired in for the day, onlookers enjoyed watching the members of the club parading with their banner to church, to the music of the band.

As almost every village had a club it is not feasible to write about them all, so here are a few representative examples of their activities.

## Charlbury Clubs

Charlbury Club Day was 29th May, with a clearing-up supper held the following day. J. Clifford recalled that two bands were employed, and that after the church service the men belonging to the clubs based on The Bell and The Crown processed round the village, then ate at their respective clubs, and morris dancers from Finstock and Leafield danced. Some flavour of the Whit Ale remained, as the men tended to get drunk in the afternoon and often adjourned to Walcot Meadow, which was outside the jurisdiction of the village constable, for fights. It sounds as though the clubs were organised on an irregular basis and spent money on their club feasts which should have been used for members' benefits, so Lord Churchill regularised matters by sponsoring an Act of Parliament which insisted on yearly accounts, which proved the death knell for the two Charlbury clubs.

## Filkins Club

The Filkins Benefit Club, which existed from 1879 until 1912, when the National Health Scheme came into force, was nicknamed the Red, White and Blue Club. Its Club Day was Whit Tuesday. George Swinford remembered the band marching through the village to the club room, playing at about 9.30 a.m., where members were regaled with bread and cheese in baskets, and ale served from watering cans. At 10 o'clock there was a roll call of members, who each placed sixpence in one box to pay the secretary and threepence in another for those who cooked and washed up for the feast.

Next they lined up in pairs to march behind the band to church, and while they were there the cooks prepared dinner consisting of roast beef, mutton and ham, vegetables, plum pudding and jellies, with beer and ginger pop to drink. The meal was held in a big tent. After dinner there were short speeches from prominent local men including the Vicar and Club Doctor, who all gave a donation to club funds. At the end the band played 'For he's a jolly good fellow'.

After dinner the stewards (drawn from the committee members), who carried long staves topped with bunches of flowers, usually red or white peonies, accompanied the band round the village, playing as they went, and visiting the larger houses collecting money, working their way back to the clubhouse by about 6 p.m. No tea was provided, but from seven until nine the band played for dancing – usually waltzes and polkas. Then toasts were made to The King and three cheers given for the band, which was conveyed home on a horse-drawn wagonette, while the club members carried on drinking and singing in the pub.

The following evening a clearing-up supper was held to eat up the left-overs. Anything still left by nine o'clock was auctioned off.

## Headington Quarry

The village, where most of the men were brickmakers and stone-quarriers rather than farm labourers, had two clubs, the Old Club and the Foresters, both of whom celebrated Club Day on Whit Tuesday. They kept everything strictly fair, so one club would lead the way to church and the other the way back, and each entertained the Vicar in alternate years. The banner carried by the Old Club had one pole while the Foresters' banner had two. After the service the members went to their club headquarters for dinner, and on one occasion the unfortunate baker burned the dinner and was punished by being bundled into a barrel and rolled down a stone-quarry in the village.

In the afternoon traditional rural sports and games were organised such as climbing the greasy pole to win a leg of mutton, men with their hands tied behind them chasing after cocks to catch them with their teeth, and grinning (i.e. making hideous faces) through horse-collars. Another game sounds more like a medieval torture: a man would lie on his back and hold a huge stone over his chest, then the quarrymen would try to break the stone.

The Quarry morris dancers came out and danced that day, then festivities closed with a supper.

## Iffley

The Foresters' Club at Iffley celebrated Club Day in early July. The men met outside The Tree at ten o'clock in the morning, dressed in their best, wearing large buttonholes and sashes in red and green, decorated with silver beads and sequins. They carried their banner and set off in procession for Iffley Turn, where they met the band, which came from a country village. They walked back up to Iffley Church for a service, then paraded round the village, visiting most of the large houses. They had dinner at The Tree, then booths were set up in a field nearby. After tea there was dancing at a cost of threepence per head, with music provided by the band. The proceedings ended at about 10 p.m.

Chasing the pig at the last Scouring in 1857.

## Scouring the White Horse

The owled White Harse wants zettin to rights,
And the Squire hev promised good cheer,
Zo we'll gee un a scrape to kip un in zhape,
And a'll last for many a year...

There'll be backsword play, and climmin the powl,
And a race for a peg, and a cheese,
Aud us thenks as hisn's a dummell zowl
As dwont care for zich spwoorts as theze.

Thomas Hughes, *The Scouring of the White Horse*, Minet, 1972

A very different custom took place at the Uffington White Horse, the prehistoric hill-cut figure. It was the treasured privilege of the villagers of the Vale to 'scour' the White Horse or keep it clean about every five years. This was often done at Whitsun. The antiquary Francis Wise wrote in 1736 that the scouring was already an old-established custom:

The ceremony of scouring the Horse, from time immemorial, has been solemnized by a numerous concourse of people from all the villages round about. I am informed, though the horse stands in the parish of Uffington, yet other towns claim, by ancient custom, a share of the duty upon this occasion.

In the 18th century there was horse-racing for a silver cup, and prizes were in kind, such as gold-laced hats and buckskin breeches. A handbill dated 1776 detailed the activities:

WHITE HORSE HILL, BERKS, 1776
The Scowering and cleansing of the White Horse is fixed for Monday the 27th day of May; on which day a Silver Cup will be run for near White Horse Hill, by any horse, etc, that never run for anything, carrying eleven stone, the best of three two-mile heats, to start at ten o'clock.

159

Scrambling down the hill below the White Horse chasing after a wheel.

Between the heats will be run for by Poneys, a Saddle, Bridle and Whip; the best of three two-mile heats, the winner two heats will be entitled to the Saddle, the second best the Bridle, and the third the Whip.

The same time a Thill harness will be run for by Cart-horses, etc. in their harness and bells, the carters to ride in smock frocks without saddles, crossing and jostling, but no whipping allowed.

A flitch of Bacon to be run for by asses.

A good Hat to be run for by men in sack, every man to bring his own sack.

A Waistcoat, 10s 6d value, to be given to the person who shall take a bullet out of a tub of flour with his mouth in the shortest time.

A Cheese to be run for down the White Horse Manger.

Smocks to be run for by ladies, the second best of each prize to be entitled to a Silk Hat.

Cudgel-playing for a gold-laced Hat and a pair of buckskin Breeches, and Wrestling for a pair of silver Buckles and a pair of pumps.

The horses to be on the White Horse Hill by nine o'clock.

No less than four horses, etc. or asses to start for any of the above prizes.

The only traditional sports mentioned were wrestling and fighting with cudgels. Another potentially dangerous activity was racing down the Manger to catch a cheese – a sport still practised at Cooper's Hill in Gloucestershire, where bones are often broken!

Another Scouring took place in 1780, on Whit Monday, 15th May, which was described in the *Reading Mercury* of May 22nd:

The ceremony of scouring and cleansing that noble monument of Saxon antiquity, the White Horse, was celebrated on Whit-Monday, with great joyous festivity. Besides the customary diversions of horse-racing, foot races etc., many

Back-swording
at the Scouring.

uncommon rural diversions and feats of activity were exhibited to a greater number of spectators than ever assembled on any former occasion. Upwards of thirty thousand persons were present, and amongst them most of the nobility and gentry of this and the neighbouring counties; and the whole was concluded without any material accident.

Additional games that year included 'a jingling match by eleven blind-folded men, and one unmasked and hung with bells, for a pair of buckskin breeches'.

In 1803 one competition was for grinning through a horse collar, and in 1808 a gallon of gin or half a guinea was presented to the woman who could smoke the most tobacco in an hour, a competition which only attracted two gypsy women as entrants. At the Scouring of 1813 one prize was a loaf made from a bushel of flour for the winner of the race running up the Manger.

The 1825 Scouring attracted even more people, and the games were held two miles away at the Seven Barrows of Lambourn. The Scouring in 1838, revived by the patronage of Lord Craven, took place in September. The next Scouring in 1843 was augmented by a visit from Wombwell's Menagerie – hauling the elephant's caravan up the hill was far from easy!

The last Scouring took place on 17th and 18th September, 1857. Uffington Castle, the hillfort above the White Horse, was filled with a double line of booths and stalls selling apples, nuts, gingerbread, other food and drink, ribbons, knives, braces, toys etc. Various shows were set up, together with drinking booths with skittle games, a stage, and a greasy pole for climbing. Nearby stood the County Police stand to keep people in order. Sports mentioned on the handbill that year were:

Backsword Play Old gamesters £8
Young gamesters £4
Wrestling Old gamesters £5

The men of the Vale of White Horse valued their privilege of Scouring the White Horse to keep it clean.

Illustrations from Thomas Hughes, *The Scouring of the White Horse*, facsimile of the first edition of 1859, published by Paul P.B.Minet, Chicheley, 1972

Young gamesters £4
A jingling match
Foot races
Hurdle races
Race of cart-horses in Thill harness (for a new set of harness)
Donkey race (for a flitch of bacon)
Climbing pole (for a leg of mutton)
Races down 'the Manger' (for cheeses)

A pig will be turned out on the down, to be the prize of the man who catches him (under certain regulations); and further prizes will be awarded for other games and sports as the funds will allow.

Thomas Hughes, *The Scouring of the White Horse*, 1859

In the 19th century the Scouring gradually lost all connection with Whitsun, and took place at irregular intervals with long gaps, which the locals put down to political problems and changing conditions in the countryside. It was less easy to get time off to attend such events, and it suffered from the growing disapproval of 'rough' events that led to drunkenness.

163

# Whitsun Sports

Some places held sports rather than ales. Cock-fighting was traditional on Whit Monday at Wantage and Wheatley, and bull-baiting was popular in Wheatley (despite being officially banned in 1835) – the vicar, Rev. E. Elton wrote of the 1840s:

> Rude sports lingered here as in their last resort... Before this the custom was at the feast or at Whitsuntide to parade a bull through the streets covered with ribbons and during the next day to bait him tied to a stake., i.e. everyone who had a savage dog was allowed to let him loose at the bull. This was done in an old quarry and a brutal scene it was.
>
> Quoted in W. O. Hassall, *Wheatley Records*, 1956

Bull baiting was also found in Garsington and Leafield, and both badger baiting and dog fighting were common over the Whitsun period.

# Trinity Sunday and Lamb Ales

Trinity Sunday is the Sunday after Whitsun. It was the day usually chosen for beginning to strew grass in the church in Shenington (sometimes it began on Whit Sunday), which was also done on the two following Sundays. A piece of ground was left to provide rushes for the purpose, but by 1905 this was let as allotments, according to the *Oxfordshire Archaeological Society Reports* of 1905.

It was also the date of the Kirtlington Lamb Ale, which has much in common with Whitsun Ales. There is controversy as to whether there was also a Lamb Ale at nearby Kidlington, to which there is only one reference, which may be a misprint for Kirtlington:

> At Kidlington ... Monday after Whitson week, there is a fat live Lamb provided, and the Maids of the Town having their thumbs ty'd behind them, run after it, and she that with her mouth takes and holds the Lamb is declared Lady of the Lamb, which being dress'd with the skin hanging on, is carried on a long Pole before the Lady and her Companions to the Green, attended with Music and a Morisco Dance of Men, and another of women, where the rest of the day is spent in dancing, mirth and merry glee.
>
> The next day the Lamb is part bak'd, boyl'd, and roast, for the Ladies feast, where she sits majestically at the upper end of the Table, and her Companions with her with music and other attendants, which ends the solemnity.
>
> T. Blount, *Ancient Tenures*, 1679

Thomas Hearne was convinced that Blount was wrong in ascribing the custom to Kidlington unless it was once held in both places. He said that at Kirtlington it originally took place at Whitsun (and Henry Taunt suggested that it was sometimes held at Easter). He commented that a similar custom used to take place at Wightham in Berkshire.

At one time the Kirtlington ale was brewed from barley grown on land belonging to the parish (long since appropriated for other purposes) and wheat was specially grown to make the crown cakes sold at the feast. When

parish lands were no longer available for barley, the lord of the manor provided the ale, which was brought from Oxford; villagers and morris men escorted the dray from Bletchingdon and the beer was taken to the evergreen-decked barn that was then used as the Bowery. After 1858 when the Ale was discontinued the Dashwoods instead gave £2 12s for the use of the poor.

At early ales a Bowery of evergreens was erected on the village green where the ale was sold. A Lord was chosen, who selected his Lady (the race mentioned by Blount was obviously discontinued). The Lady, a girl of good character, was paid a fee of twenty five shillings, and great deference was paid to her – in fact forfeits were paid if she was jostled. At

**Above and right:**
Grass strewing in Shenington church on Whit Sunday 1967. The shorter man on the left (above) is Mr Cook, the Parish Clerk, whose family carried out the custom over several generations.

Photographs by Kenneth Cardus from the Christine Hole collection

eleven o'clock on the Monday morning the Lord set out from his Bowery to collect his Lady from her home; then they processed round the village:

First came a man carrying a live lamb on his shoulders, which was, if possible, the first-born of the season, and the finest of the flock. Its legs were tied together with blue and pink ribbons, and blue ribbons were hung round its neck.

Next came the 'Lord' and 'Lady' gaily dressed and decked with pink and blue ribbons. (On alternate days the 'Lady' wore pink

# KIDLINGTON "LAMB-ALE" LECTURE.

These drawings featured in the *Oxford Journal* of 21st February 1912 in an article about a lecture given on the Kidlington Lamb Ale by T. Tindall Wildridge.

and white and blue and white.) The 'Lord' carried slung over his shoulder a tin money-box called the 'treasury'. Both he and his consort held in their hands badges of office known as 'maces'. These 'maces' are short staves, on the top of which is fastened a square horizontal board. To each corner of this square is attached the end of a semi-circular hoop which intersects in the middle. The whole 'mace' is covered with pink and blue silk, with rosettes at intervals, and from the four corners hang silk streamers. The colours of the two 'maces' are counter-changed.

Following the 'Lord' and 'Lady' came the Fool, known as the 'Squire', who wore a dress of motley, and carried a long staff with a bladder and a cow's tail at either end. His duties were to belabour the bystanders and to clear a ring for the dancers. Next came six morris-dancers, who were dressed in beaver hats, finely pleated white shirts, crossed with blue and pink ribbons and rosettes, and white moleskin trousers with bells at the knees. Their music was supplied by a fiddler,

The Kirtlingon Lamb Ale declined in the late 19th century and was superseded by the Lamb Ale Club Feast. This photograph of the Feast was taken in 1880 outside the Dashwood Arms. Participants include, in the front row: Mr Spittle, Tom Shillingford (the bandmaster), boy – Charles King, Mr Busby and Mr Plant.

Photograph: David Watts

and a 'whittle and dub man', as the musician was called who played the pipe and tabor. At the end of the procession were two men carrying the 'forest feathers', which were wooden clubs about three feet long, covered with leaves, flowers, rushes and blue and pink ribbons.

Percy Manning, 'Some Oxfordshire Seasonal Festivals', in *Folklore*, Vol 8, 1897

The use of pink and blue was a tribute to the Dashwood family of Kirtlington Park, the first place visited by the procession, which by the end of the week had visited every important house in the parish. Morris dancers performed at intervals throughout the day, after parading round among the spectators with the Lord, showing off the crown cakes they wore on their hats. The cakes were about nine inches in diameter, with minced meat and batter inside a coating of rich currant and plum dough. The spectators paid to look at them, and could purchase an entire cake for half a crown. The cakes were considered luck-bringers, and often carefully kept throughout the year. Unsold cakes were divided among the 'Lamb Ale boys'. Refreshments were free, but donations solicited. At nine o'clock in the evening the Lady was escorted back home.

The procession took place on Monday, Tuesday and Wednesday, then a lamb (often less valuable than the one carried around) was killed and several pies made, including the 'head pie' which contained the entire head, including wool – the latter was sold for a shilling, and pieces of the others distributed around. Taunt, who visited Kirtlington in 1905, said that the Lamb Ale cake was carried by two sword-bearers on flower-decorated staves. After about 1820 the lamb was not killed, and often became quite tame. The rest of the week was spent in feasting and drinking, with the morris dancers returning from their tours of the local villages each evening.

**Above:** The Kirtlington Morris at the Lamb Ale accompanied by 'Elmo', a replica of the gryphon on the Dashwood coat of arms. He was made by Paul Davenport of the Green Oak Morris who revived the Kirtlington Morris. Elmo happily swallows coins fed to him and says 'Thank you!'

**Below:** The Lady of the Lamb sits in her Court – a toy lamb has replaced the real lamb used in the past.

Photographs: David Watts

William Wilson Saunders wrote in *A Short Account of my Life* (unpublished, quoted by Keith Chandler in *Ribbons, Bells and Squeaking Fiddles*, 1993) that twelve young men were chosen as Lamb-Ale boys, the prettiest girl became the Queen, and that the Lamb-Ale boys danced in front of her as they processed round the village.

The Lamb Ale was replaced after about 1858 by a Club Feast on Trinity Monday for the Oddfellows and Box Club Friendly Societies (later replaced by the Provident and the Oxford Arms Friendly Societies), accompanied by stalls and entertainments. In 1876 George James Dew commented that the drunkenness was 'most disgraceful' (ed Pamela Horn, *Oxfordshire Village Life*, 1983). Rev Gutch wrote in 1951 that a church service was held, followed by a dinner of roast lamb, after which the Kirtlington men played the Merton Mayflies at cricket, while in the evening there were sports and dancing, organised for fifty years by the Edgington family.

The Kirtlington morris men were revived in 1979, first dancing at the Feast in 1980. They organise a weekend of dancing with about twenty teams invited to join them from all over the country, including a parade to church for a service where some of the morris men sing, and the foreman does a solo jig. Then they parade to the school and dance round a Lady of the Lamb, and tour the local pubs.

Eynsham also held a Lamb Ale on Trinity Monday, where Mrs Bryan Stapleton wrote in *Three Oxfordshire Parishes* that the prettiest girl was chosen as the Lady, and after catching the lamb she rode, gaily dressed, on the front horse of the team which brought the Lamb home. Sarah Stayt, who died in 1840, was the last 'Lady'.

Morris dancing
illustrated in John
Brand and Henry
Ellis, *Observations
on Popular
Antiquities*, 1841

# Morris Dancing

...they bedeck themselves with scarfs, ribbons and laces hanged all over with
gold rings, precious stones and other jewels. This done they tie about either leg
two or forty bells with rich handkerchiefs in their hands, and sometimes laid
across over their shoulders and necks, borrowed for the most part of their pretty
Mopsies and loving Bessies, for bussying them in the dark. These things set in
order, they have their hobby horses, dragons and other antiques, together with
bawdy pipers and thundering drummers, to strike up the Devil's Dance withal,
then march these heathen company towards the church and churchyard, their
pipers piping, drummers thundering, their stumps dancing, their bells jingling,
their handkerchiefs swinging about their heads like madmen, their hobby horses
and other monsters skirmishing amongst the throng and in this sort they go to
the church (though the minister be at prayer or preaching) dancing and swinging
their handkerchieves over their heads, in the church, like devils incarnate.

Philip Stubbes, *Anatomy of Abuses*, 1879

**Philip Stubbes, as a 16th-century Puritan, was not enamoured of**
morris dancing, which was first recorded around 1500 as a court entertainment. It gradually filtered down to the towns and then in the 17th century

diffused into villages. Oxfordshire boasted more morris teams than any other area, with at least sixty-six different teams recorded. It remained popular in this area until the late 19th century, carrying on into the 20th century in some places, and enjoyed a revival in the latter part of the 20th century. Unfortunately there is little written information before the 19th century, although there was certainly dancing earlier to accompany Whit ales. Three dance sides in particular, Abingdon, Bampton and Headington Quarry, which still perform today, claim an extensive history.

Early historians of the morris dance such as Cecil Sharp suggested pagan origins and postulated that the name morris came from 'morisco' or Moorish, but more recent scholarship has not substantiated these claims. Michael Heaney and Keith Chandler, who have done extensive research on local morris dancing, have focused on its social context, and concentrated on what is revealed by the available sources. Keith Chandler has published two books on dancing in this area, *Ribbons, Bells and Squeaking Fiddles* (Hisarlik Press, 1993) and *Morris Dancing in the English South Midlands, 1660-1900* (Hisarlik Press, 1993), which contain a wealth of information.

Traditional morris dancing, as a rural pursuit, was performed largely by working-class men, especially agricultural labourers or tradesmen, but there is little information about their background before the 19th century. The times they could dance depended on how busy the agricultural season was, so the early summer lull at Whitsun became the most popular time, although many dancers came out earlier for May Day, and they sometimes danced at other times of year. As Whitsun ales declined, many morris dancers attended the club feasts which replaced them.

There were two different types of morris dancing described by Michael Heaney. One he called the 'Whitsun ale' form, because it was often danced at these functions, in which dancers used handkerchiefs and bells, and the 'bedlam' form where sticks were used, with no bells. These appear to have combined in the 18th century.

There are few early descriptions of the dances, but G. A. Rowell, who probably saw dancing in the City of Oxford or nearby around 1800-10, wrote:

The dances were in various forms, but in all the six [dancers] had to move in unison; sometimes with a white handkerchief in one or both hands, waved about in various manners; in other dances there was a clapping of hands, either by each bringing the palms together or by each meeting those of his partner; and, in others, each had a staff, of about two feet in length, and these were flourished and clashed together in various ways. There was no display of 'footing' in the dancing, but the great aim seemed to be to keep the time and figure, so that every sound and movement should be strictly in unison.

'Notes on some old-fashioned English customs: the Mummers, the Morris Dancers, Whitsun Ales, Lamb Ales', *Folk-lore Journal*, vol. IV, (1886)

An early reference to morris dancing in Oxfordshire (although the town was in fact in Berkshire until boundary changes in 1974) is in Abingdon in 1560, where the purchase of bells for the morris men was recorded in the Churchwardens' Accounts, probably indicating that they danced at church ales. The 16th century Thame Churchwardens' Accounts also referred to purchases for the morris men.

In the late 16th century morris dancing was condemned by Puritans who disliked most amusements, and particularly the morris because it was performed on May Day and at Whitsun Ales, which they thought encouraged drunkenness and immorality. However the dancing was favoured by the Cavaliers, who were entertained by morris men in Witney in May 1646, as Anthony Wood wrote of:

some six or seven Country fellowes with Napkins and Scarfes, and Ribons tyed about them, and bells at their knees, according to the manner of that sport, and with them a Mayd Marian, and two fooles, who fell a dansing and capering.

ed. Andrew Clark, *The Life and Times of Anthony Wood*, Oxford, 1891

The Puritans did their utmost to ban dancing, but it revived at the Restoration in 1660, when sides were recorded at Kirtlington, Somerton, Bicester and Burford, and oral traditions exist of teams at Abingdon and Bampton, and almost certainly many others.

The gap between the social classes widened during the 17th century, as the upper and middle classes became more literate and looked down on the illiterate 'common folk' and their activities. Morris dancing became more important to the agricultural labourers who danced as the growth of the enclosure movement lessened their independence and led to a decline in agricultural earnings, as dancing was a useful additional source of income – the morris men who danced at Churchill Whit ale in 1721 received six shillings (probably divided between them), their fiddler John Phillips half a guinea, and the Fool a pound. Some teams, including Abingdon Morris, went from Oxfordshire to London and the south to work on the early hay harvests, gradually working their way back to Oxfordshire, dancing on their travels to earn extra money. Even this potential declined as the growing trend away from drunkenness towards temperance, imposed on the lower classes by the higher ones, influenced a decline in recreations such as Whit Ales.

Morris dancing was to a certain extent dependent on patronage. It is a very physical dance, requiring stamina, which in return required a good diet. Often labourers found it hard to make ends meet, and consequently had poor diets, so in some villages, such as Kirtlington, the lord of the manor would supplement the diet of the dancers with regular joints of beef. The dancers prided themselves on their athleticism – the Abingdon dancers used to say that the higher they could dance in the air, the higher the corn would grow. Often several teams danced in the same location, so there was an element of the dancers representing the honour of their villages.

Dancing was seasonal, so the men began practising about six weeks before their first performance, often for an hour each day. Sometimes the art of dancing was passed down from generation to generation in the same family. The team at Bampton over much of the 19th century (and many others) showed much intermarriage, and the dance steps were often quite a closely guarded secret.

The morris dancers were accompanied by several other characters. Perhaps the most important was the Fool, who belaboured the passers-by with his weapon – a stick with a calf's tail attached to one end and a pig's bladder blown up like a balloon on the other – to create room for the men to dance, and acted as a comic master of ceremonies. His role was described in 1753:

Every Body that knows what a Whitsun-Ale is, knows that the Fool, or more properly the 'Squire', claims the Privilege of cracking Jokes upon the Women, and exercising the Calves Tail, the immemorial and tremendous Ensign of his Office upon the Men, – We never pretended to a right of flogging the Ladies, – Never fear me Lady, you need not put on your Breeches; the most I shall have do with you will be a brush at your Petticoats: But as to the Men, especially those that crowd where they have no Business, and break in upon the antient and undoubted Rights and Privileges of the morris Dancers, I shall have no mercy on. My brave Boys of Oxfordshire are going to begin a Dance and I shall endeavour to keep a clear Stage for them. All unfair Play I shall guard against as well as I am able, – I shall be very busy with my Calves Tail, and give you Raps where I can reach.

'Thomas Motley' in *Jackson's Oxford Journal*, 5th May 1753

The Fool acted the Clown, and sometimes, as in the case of Jingy or Jinky Wells of Bampton in the 20th century, dressed as one. It was his job to persuade the onlookers to part with their money, and he generally took charge of the cash. For this reason he often had to remain more sober than his colleagues. John Kibble wrote of a Wychwood Fool:

The man in charge of the Morris, who carried the collecting box and conducted matters generally, was called the 'Fool', he kept the crowd back, flourished a stick with a bladder tied on one end, and a calf's tail on the other, cracking jokes and generally adding to the fun.

He was the only man who had a wage. He had to keep his head, not drink too freely, so the others paid him to keep things straight, whilst they danced.

On one occasion Charlbury Morris agreed to pay the 'Fool' thirty shillings for the week. When the pay day came and he received the money, knowing the dancers, now their week's capering was over, had only empty pockets, tired limbs, and owing to the quantity of drink consumed, aching heads, said to them, 'Who is the fool now?'

John Kibble's Manuscript Notes, Oxfordshire Museum

A Ragman, who looked after the men's clothes, was another member of the team. A treasurer carried a money box. Around the Wychwood area particular, there was often a sword-bearer, who had a cake impaled on his sword, which was cut into pieces and sold to onlookers, with the implication that it brought good luck and fertility to the purchaser.

The dancers' costumes have since the 18th century usually consisted of white shirts and white or black breeches (latterly trousers), with ribbon baldricks and decorated beaver or silk hats or caps. The boots were the lightest available.

173

Music was provided by the bells worn round their calves, the style varying from team to team. Some sides, like Headington, carry sticks, others handkerchiefs.

Apart from the jingling of the bells, music was traditionally provided by a pipe (wooden, about twelve inches long with a mouthpiece like a whistle) and tabor (a small shallow drum), sometimes known as a whittle and dub. These were sometimes replaced by a fiddle or a concertina in the nineteenth century.

As well as those mentioned below, there were teams at Bletchingdon, Broadwell, Buckland, Chadlington, Charlton-on-Otmoor, Chesterton, Clanfield, Cropredy, Deddington, Duns Tew, Faringdon, Fewcott, Fifield, Glympton, Great Milton, Hethe, Kingham, Launton, Long Hanborough, Lyneham, Noke, North Aston, Ramsden, Shipton-under-Wychwood, Sibford, Somerton, Souldern, South Leigh, Standlake, Steeple Aston, Stoke Lyne, Stratton Audley, Swalcliffe, Swerford, Tadmarton, Weston-on-the-Green, Witney and Wootton.

## Abingdon

Abingdon has the distinction of very early records of the morris men in the churchwardens' accounts of St Helen's Church from 1554 to 1592, which record expenses such as buying bells for the morris men and setting up Robin Hood's Bower. However after this enticing information, no references to the morris have survived until the 18th century.

An unusual feature of the Abingdon team regalia is ox horns mounted on a wooden bull's head carried as a standard. According to the team's publicity leaflet:

It is said that in 1700 a farmer named Morris (perhaps the Abingdon benefactor John Morris) presented a black ox to roast in the Bury for some celebration. The people who assembled took up some form of dancing, and an argument arose as to who should have the ox horns. This developed into a fight and the residents of Ock Street challenged those of the Vineyard for possession. This being the west end of the town versus the east, a chalk line was drawn at the foot of the vineyard and another outside the 'Cock and Tree' in Ock Street. The fight began on the Bury (or Market Place) and those who drove or beat the other over the chalk line were to be the winners of the horns. Sticks, stones, fiery torches and bare fists were put into this grim tussle for ownership. The Ock Street men were victorious and through one of them, a Hemmings, the Horns have come down to the Morris.

At the end of the dance 'Maid of the Mill' the dancers face the musician and the standard bearer and bow slightly, which is known as 'honouring the horns'.

According to a speech given at a concert in Abingdon in 1975, the team is entitled to the name 'Royal Morris' as it is said to have performed for Henry VIII when he visited Abingdon, leading to a tradition that it should be performed for every monarch visiting the town, and Queen Victoria is said to have enjoyed watching the team on several occasions. One of the Abingdon

William and James Hemmings, stalwarts of the Abingdon morris team, who met Cecil Sharp in 1910 and 1922. The concertina is inscribed 'Presented to William Hemmings'.

Scrapbook of the Abingdon Traditional Morris Dancers

dances is called 'Princess Royal', but several other teams have a dance of this name. The tradition was maintained when the Abingdon Morris danced for Queen Elizabeth II when she visited the town in 1956. When the team dances before royalty red, white and blue ribbons are added to the decorations on the hats.

The 'Berkshire' style of dancing varies from the Cotswold Morris found in Oxfordshire in that it is set to a distinctive regular beat and the dancers use high leg movements with heavy stamping and energetic arm movements.

The annual dancing takes place later than in most places, around midsummer, for the election of the mock mayor of Ock Street (of which more later). The team was based in Ock Street, a poor and rather insalubrious area outside the original town boundary. Dancing was not just confined to the one day in June, as in 1783 the men were seen dancing miles away:

In the summer of 1783, the editor saw at Richmond in Surrey, a company of Morris dancers from Abingdon, accompanied by a fool in a motley jacket, etc., who carried in his hand a staff or truncheon, about two feet long, with which he either buffeted the crowd to keep them at a proper distance from the dancers, or played tricks for the spectator's diversion. The dancers and the fool were Berkshire husbandmen, taking an annual circuit; and collecting money from whoever would give them any.

ed. F. G. Waldron, *Ben Jonson's The Sad Shepherd*, 1783 edition

Cecil Sharp recorded that the costume of the men around 1900 was:

a high hat with a silk ribbon or handkerchief for band, streamers at the back and flowers in front and feathers 'if you like'; white shirt and white duck trousers; waist ribbon, attached to which were two bunches of ribbons eighteen inches long hanging down from the hips nearly to the knees (as at Brackley); sixteen inch ribbons 'doubled over' fixed to each shoulder, shoulder blade, and breast, and the usual wrist and upper arm ribbons.

C. J. Sharp and H. C. Macilwaine, *The Morris Book*, 1924

The Abingdon morris dancers c. 1938, wearing chequered sashes and carrying the ox horns. The men on the right are from the Eynsham morris team.

Photograph: scrapbook of the Abingdon Traditional Morris Dancers

The ribbons and baldrics are bright green and yellow, and a member of the morris recently said that the colours represented the growing and the ripened corn, and that there was a traditional belief that the higher they danced in the air, the higher the corn would grow.

The costume worn in 1977, according to the Abingdon Morris Regulations, consisted of:

White shirt, trousers and socks.
Shiny black shoes.
Top hat, decorated with ribbons and flowers.
Neckerchief, red with white spot markings.
Baldricks, green with central gold line.
ATMD badge at front cross, Abingdon town badge at back cross.
Armbands with ribbons: red, green, yellow and blue.
Belt with horizontal ribbons: red, green, yellow and blue, with a rosette and ribbons at the fastening, which must be on the left hip.
Bellpads on each leg, decorated with ribbons.
Badges and emblems, other than as stated, may be worn at the discretion of the Mayor and his Deputy.

The morris team avoided the general decline towards the end of the 19th century because of the Hemmings family and their relatives, who claim a connection several centuries old with the team. They feature prominently over the years in lists of dancers – who in 1879 had jobs such as labourer, fellmonger (who prepared skins for a tanner), fellmonger's labourer, railway porter, wool draper, horse dealer and scholars. Other occupations in different years included mason's labourer, flax dresser, weaver, baker, currier (a tanner) and basket maker.

There was a brief lull from 1902-1910, then dancing revived. It nearly died out in the 1950s, when the older dancers were in their sixties, but they persevered until they found younger men to carry on. The team that doggedly kept going in the 1950s consisted of:

Jack Hyde, who became temporary bagman in 1939 and stayed with the team for 37 years. He promised the dying Tom Hemmings that he would keep the tradition going, and was true to his word. At the age of 79 he played his harmonica all afternoon and evening because there was no other musician, despite being in pain.

Johnny Grimsdale, the hornbearer, who took on the role in 1937, was famous for singing 'Buttercup Joe'. He last danced in 1977.

Charlie Brett first became Mayor of Ock Street in 1964, and was well known for his charity work.

Fred Stimpson, the President and Returning Officer, served three times as the real town mayor of Abingdon. He was unable to dance because of wounds sustained during the First World War.

The music was similar to country dance music. The whittle and dub were used over many years, to be replaced in the late 19th century by a melodeon, and after the Second World War by a concertina. More recently a melodeon has been used again.

The steps of the Abingdon dances form a jealously guarded tradition. A favourite is 'Princess Royal', which includes a song:

Old Mother Harvey, Old George Hunt,
Went to Nuneham in a punt,
Lost the pole and down they wunt,
And they never got to Nuneham!

The Ock Street horns are said to have been won in a fight between the men of the Vineyard and those of Ock Street in 1700, when a farmer by the name of Morris had presented a black ox to be roasted in the Bury in Abingdon. The Ock Street men won the horns, and through the Hemmings family the horns have become part of he regalia of the Traditional morris team.

Photographed at the mock-mayormaking in 1990 by Christine Bloxham

This was sung to the tune of 'Old Molly Oxford'. After the singing, the dancing begins, to a totally different tune.

A dance unique to Abingdon is 'The Duke of Marlborough', danced to the tune of a traditional Danish cobbler's song. The team thought that it might have been taught to Abingdon soldiers by continental soldiers in the first Duke of Marlborough's army, and became a morris song in celebration of his victories.

'The Maid of the Mill' is thought to depict the wheel of Ock Mill, a watermill first mentioned in the Domesday Book and acquired by Abingdon Abbey in 1115. In this dance the Mayor of Ock Street becomes the hub of a wheel formed by the dancers, who form 'spokes', 'posts', 'iron bands' and 'rim' as they dance.

'Constant Billy' may perhaps refer to William of Orange, who may have seen the dancers when he visited Milton Manor in the late 17th century, but this link is tenuous as it is a common morris tune.

'Sally Luker' is danced to the medieval tune 'The Tempest', with a little song in the middle of the dance:

Sally Luker, Sally Luker, Sally Luker,
Pretty little girl, don't you tease her, try to please her,
For she is a pretty little girl.

Luker is a common Abingdon surname.

'The Squire's Dance', exclusive to Abingdon, has sequences which the dancers suggest could have magical undertones, as they equal three times three. It is performed each year in honour of the newly elected Mayor of Ock Street.

Abingdon men dancing at the mock-mayormaking on 23rd June 1990, wearing the now traditional green and yellow baldricks which are said to represent the unripened and ripe corn.
Photograph: Christine Bloxham

'The Girl I Left Behind Me' is a sedate dance, selected by the older dancers, and is also used as the team's signature tune to introduce their dancing. It was used as a marching song by the Berkshire Regiment.

'The Curly-Headed Ploughboy' is part of the Abingdon 'Royal Morris', and has the same number sequence found in 'The Squire's Dance', but ends in a circle.

'Jockey to the Fair' builds up to a fast climax using different step and arm movements from the other dances, and is said to have a hypnotic effect on the audience.

'Shepherd's Hey' is a jig for two men including a demanding singing and clapping sequence.

'The Berkshire Broom Dance', more of a step dance, is sung to the tune of 'The Noble Duke of York' and was traditionally danced at fairs.

'The Nutting Girl' is the final dance at each performance, and begins with a song:

A-nutting we will go, me boys,
A-nutting we will go
We'll catch a little fox
And put him in a box
And never let him go!

The dancers use a rocking motion, following the example of the lead dancer who ad libs until all the dancers form a circle, which then splits into single file.

The Hemmings family were not very forthcoming with Cecil Sharp, being reluctant to show him the detailed steps of their dances, so he only published 'Princess Royal' from their repertoire, and that is said to be incorrect.

The Abingdon men frequently dance at ceremonies and festivals elsewhere, including sheep fairs at East Ilsley; they travelled to Belgium in 1973 to promote British Trade Week and joined the Morris Ring in 1937. They danced in London in 1941 to promote war bonds, at Windsor in 1951 to celebrate the Festival of Britain, at the Albert Hall, London at the English Folk Dance and Song Society Festival in 1952 and at the International Rose Conference in Oxford in 1976 which celebrated the centenary of the Royal National Rose Society. As part of the fee for the latter, Mattocks presented roses to be planted in the Charter Complex landscape in Abingdon. The team have appeared on television several times. They are immensely proud of their heritage, aiming to preserve their own traditional tunes rather than incorporating new dances from other teams.

## Adderbury

There were three distinct morris teams when dancing was at its peak before 1860, which danced on Adderbury Green and then round a different circuit of villages each day during Whit week, when the Adderbury Club feast was held. All the local teams attended the Banbury fair held on the Thursday of Whit week. They often danced at local wedding celebrations.

After the 1860s interest gradually declined and the last public performance took place around 1879.

The dancers carried sticks, and wore bells round their knees and ankles. Their double baldricks were red and blue, with rosettes in the same colours. One of their tunes was 'Lads o'Bunchum', alternatively known as 'Lads o'Beecham'. Others were 'Constant Billy', 'Sweet Jenny Jones', 'The Buffoon' and 'The Black Joke'. The dancers sometimes sang between dances to give themselves a chance to catch their breath – 'The Happy Man' and 'Postman's Knock' were favourites. One dancer, William Walton (born in 1837), a mason, was also a noted singer. Walton led the morris men for twenty years before the dancing ended. One team was made up just from his family members.

The team members had jobs such as mason, servant, carpenter, thatcher, innkeeper, carrier, maltster, stonemason, coachman, slater, hawker and shepherd.

Their dances included 'How d'ye do Sir', 'Laudanum Bunches' and 'Jockey to the Fair'. One unusual move performed by the dancers here involves tweaking one's partner's nose.

For several years the Adderbury Fool was William Castle, otherwise known as 'Old Mettle', who came from Banbury. Sarah Beesley described him in *My Life*:

I have seen him with the eight Morris dancers in Banbury, all of them in their shirt sleeves, with bells tied by ribbons of all colours on their arms and legs, and wearing white trousers, 'Mettle' acting as merryman to the lot, dressed in similar style, and with his face painted. They all danced, and each had two white pocket handkerchiefs to whirl about in time with the music.

William Castle, nick-named 'Old Mettle' or 'Old Metal', a match-seller, acted as fool for the Adderbury morris men. He died on 2nd June 1841 while mending his patchwork Fool's outfit. He was regarded as a figure of fun in Banbury and is seen here in an academic dress he was given.

Photograph: Banbury Museum

180

He was born around 1789 and died on 2nd June 1841, in the process of mending his patchwork fool's outfit ready for his next performance. Castle was a matchseller, a local figure of fun, occasionally dressed in an old mortar board and gown he had been given.

Janet Blount did much research into the Adderbury morris dancing in the early 20th century, and she encouraged Cecil Sharp to come and record the local dances. The dances were revived in 1948, and again in 1974.

## Ascott-under-Wychwood

There was a probably a team here from at least the 1820s if not before, which toured during Whit week. The team wore red and blue ribbons, top hats, pleated shirts, white trousers, bells and blue ribbons, and performed both stick and handkerchief dances.

In 1864 the team consisted of six labourers: Daniel Smith (foreman), Will Smith, John, Will, Benj and Joseph Moss, Squire Will Cook from Lyneham, and sword-bearer Will Moss senior. Thomas Langford of Finstock played the pipe and tabor. Most were agricultural labourers, but Stephen Dore who played the pipe and tabor in the mid-to-late 19th century was a carpenter, and William Moss became a railway servant in 1871.

That year they danced at Pudlicot House on Whit Monday morning and then boxed for money. The first to draw blood from his opponent received two shillings and sixpence, the second two shillings. The men were paid fourteen shillings for the entertainment and given as much free beer as they could drink.

## Asthal Leigh

Dancing probably began here about 1820. The sword-bearer was responsible for carrying the cake tin, knife and treasury. The Squire or Fool was known as the Rodney. Music was provided by a pipe and tabor. Percy Manning wrote (MS Top Oxon) that the team consisted of: Thos Dix, James Dix, Will Syford, Will Smith, Chas Spruce and Jas Smith, the Squire was George Eeles, sword-bearer Charles Syford and musician Shepherd Cripps. They were wood labourers, agricultural labourers, a retired farmer, a blacksmith and a journeyman blacksmith.

## Bampton-in-the-Bush

J. A. Giles in his *History of Bampton* (1848) wrote about the morris:

Another season of festivity is Whitsuntide, when the Morris-dancers exhibit their saltatory powers for the amusement of the people, and to gather a few shillings for their own private emolument. As these functionaries do nothing but dance, and thoroughly fatigue themselves before nightfall, they may be considered to have earned the hot suppers and mulled ale which probably terminates the festival.

The team must have danced outside many of the houses, as in 1859 one inhabitant complained that his home had not been visited so he had not

The Bampton
morris men
dancing at Thame
in 1951, with the
fiddle being played
by 'Jinky' Wells.

Scrapbook of the
Abingdon
Traditional Morris
Dancers

been 'favoured with any evidence of their saltatory powers' (nothing super-natural – merely their dancing and jumping skill!).

There is oral tradition that the dancing goes back at least 600 years, but although this may well be true, there is no written evidence to support it.

As with all the teams, there were changes in practice over the years, and in 1858 *Jackson's Oxford Journal* commented adversely on the substitution of a 'squeaking fiddle' for the traditional pipe and tabor.

The Wells family had a long association with the Bampton Morris. In the mid 19th century it was led by George 'Jinky the Green Pea' Wells, who, as his nickname suggests, was brilliant at growing peas. The family had a tradition of similar nicknames, as George's father was known as 'Jingle' and William Wells (1868-1953) the famous Fool was known as 'Jinky' or 'Jingy'. As at Abingdon, there were close family relationships within the team which gave it stability.

The team came out on Whit Monday, and as Whit celebrations declined, linked up with the Whit Monday Club Feast. As the Club processed round the town, it stopped at intervals for dancing. However the dancing outlived the club feast, and spread outside the town, as the dancers toured Clanfield, Aston and other local clubs. The morris lapsed temporarily during the First World War as the men went off to fight, but is still going strong today.

Cecil Sharp visited Bampton around 1910 to gather information about the morris and team members William Wells and Arthur Dixey were invited to go to London by Mary Neal to teach girls at the Esperance Guild morris dancing.

William Wells was the Fool for many years. He wrote of his role:

The Bampton
morris men c.
1950.

Oxfordshire
Photograqphic
Archive.

The Fool a merry man is he, with ever ready wit,
With his elastic limbs as nimble every bit,
A rare head-dress, sashes broad, with ribbons bright.
The village people they all shout. Oh. my what a fright!
His cadging hat he passes through; in and out the crowd.
And every penny he doth get, I'm sure he's mighty proud.
If he tires them with his chatter patter
The money helps the box to fill, so what matter!
With fat calf's tail and horse's bladder strung,
To a short stout staff, tied on with a leather throng;
Bells on his shoulders and around his knees,
They said he was the perfect Fool, one and all agrees.
On galley-baldie gosson dresses,
If but a knave they give him best,
But if that part he now has dropped out
The people still turn to shout.
All the children laugh and clap
At his silly acrobat.

But if they don't precaution take
They taste his bladder, not the cake.
The dogs they bark, they show their teeth and yap,
But they don't come back for his bladder's second rap...

Quoted in 'William Wells', in *Journal of the English Folk Dance and Song Society*, Vol. VIII, No 1, 1956

Wells described his Fool's outfit:

The Dress is simply a Blouse made loose like a lady's loose jumper, with elastick (sic) round the bottom to fit tight to the waist, a frill round the neck and frill round the two wrists say with a little round elastick, a full Back as any ordinary pair only loose roomy, its just a simple periot's Dress and Clown's hat but as you will see the old Fool's Dress of the Olden Days were very different as my Old Grandmother made mine when I started with the Morris here in '86 was handworked and they put a lot of work into things in those days ...

*Folk Music Journal*, 1970

The dancers wear white shirts with rosettes and wrist ribbons, dark trousers, a dark crimson ribbon sash, billycock hats decorated with either real or artificial flowers, with red white and blue ribbon streamers and bell pads with scraps of coloured fabric or ribbons.

The team is larger than most, consisting of eight dancers so that two could step in when required, a Treasurer carrying the money box, a ragman to carry the clothes, and a sword bearer with a cake in a crown-shaped tin decorated with ribbons impaled on a sword so that it rested on the hilt. A posy of flowers, known as the mace, decorates the point. The cake used to be presented by the Lady of the Manor on Whit Monday.

The occupations of the team between 1841-91 included: carrier, labourers, road labourer, chimney sweep, dealer, carter, basket maker, thatcher, stable boy, footman, bricklayer's labourer and carpenter's assistant.

The dancers practised from Easter onwards for several nights a week, the younger men paying the older ones fourpence a week for instruction. They had a wide repertoire. 'Constant Billy', a jumping half through dance was a favourite, here described by William Wells:

'Constant Billy' is the longest dance in the Morris – six-handed dance. They used to do it three different ways – Jumping Through – that's the proper old dance – then, they used to dance him Half Through – change hands and come back next time, you see – that was too much trouble for 'em. They got from that to Sho 'Im In where you just step in, you see, and wave your handkerchief cross corners. Then comes the jump, you see – 'When fishes flies over the water' – then turn – 'When shall I see Billy again', that's four jumps – that's a long jump and a long jump, and turn (it's like a twizzle – you know, you turn round quick), then jumping through again.

*When the fishes flies over the water,*
*Then shall I see Billy again.*
*Constant Billy, my Billy, my Billy boy,*
*When shall I see Billy again?*

When I first started in the Morris, they hadn't got no more than half the dances as they had when I finished, because I found a lot of dances.

'William Wells', in *Journal of the English Folk Dance and Song Society*, Volume VIII, No 1, 1956

A similar style dance was 'Bobbing Around' or 'Bobbing Joe'.

The Bampton team danced eight six-handed side-step dances: 'The Forester's Jig', 'The Bride in Camp (The girl I left behind me)', 'The Nutting Girl' and 'Old Tom of Oxford' were said to be named after a forester from Wychwood Forest, who lived in a caravan and married Molly and travelled round hawking. The song went: 'Old Tom of Oxford and young Jim Kent [his nephew], they married old Moll and off they went'. 'The Quaker' is almost a nonsense rhyme: 'vivetty vob' means tug of war, or too many agitators or dictators:

Verily heigh; Verily ho; vivetty vob like the Shaker;
All this world seems awfully wrong and it terribly puzzles the Quaker.

'Plum pudding' included the words:

Lumps of plum pudding and pieces of pie,
My mother she gave me for telling a lie.

'Highland Mary' was another side-step dance:

Around sweet Highland Mary's grave,
We'll plant the fairest of lilies,
The primrose sweet and violet blue,
Likewise the daffodillies.
But since the world's been grown too wide,
In some lonesome place we'll tarry,
Welcome then come gather me to sleep
With my Highland Mary.

'Johnny's So Long at the Fair' is also a side-step dance:

Oh dear, what can the matter be?
Three old women tied to the apple tree.
One ran away, the other stopped till Saturday,
Oh dear, what can the matter be?

Oh dear, what can the matter be?
Johnny's so long at the fair.
He promised to buy me a basket of linen,
A little straw hat and a bunch of blue ribbon,
Before he spent his very last shilling.
Oh dear, what can the matter be?

The clap dances were 'Glorishears' and 'The Maid of the Mill':

There's fifty fair maidens that sports on the green,
I gazed on them well as you can se,
But the Maid of the Mill, the Maid of the Mill,
The Maid of the Mill for me.
She is straight and tall as a poplar tree,
Her cheeks are red as a rose,
She is one of the fairest young girls I see,
When she's dressed in her Sunday clothes.
The Maid of the Mill, the Maid of the Mill,
The Maid of the Mill for me.

The corner dances were 'The Shepherd's Hey', 'The Rose Tree' and 'Banbury Bill'. 'The Flowers of Edinburgh' was a knee dance, while the jigs danced were 'The Webley', 'Princess Royal', 'The Fool's Jig', 'Jogging to the Fair' and 'The Pipe Dance' (also known as 'Greensleeves'):
Dances based on country dances were 'The Green Bushes', 'Trunkles', 'Tommy Make Room for Your Uncle' and 'The Old Myrtle Tree'.
Other dances mentioned by Wells as being performed annually were 'The Soldier's Cloak', 'The Cuckoo's Nest' and 'Bob and Joan':

I won't be my father's Jack,
And I won't be my mother's Jill,
But I will be some fiddler's wife,
Then we can muse it at our will.
T'other little tune, t'other little tune,
Bob at night and Bob at noon.

And finally, 'The Willow Tree':

Once they said my lips were red,
Now they're scarlet pale;
When I, like a silly girl
Believed his flattering tale.
But he vowed he'd never deceive me,
And I so fondly believed he,
While the stars and the moon
So sweetly shone
Over the willow tree.

'Bonny Green Garters', a processional dance, also had local connections:

My sister's going to Abingdon Fair,
Bonny green garters I'm buying you each a pair,
A pair here for Mary and a pair for Sue,
A pair for Molly and a pair for Lou,
And a pair for the girl that I'm after.

Alfred Williams, in *Folk Songs of the Upper Thames*, mentioned that another song was sung and used for a step dance:

There was an old woman tossed up in a blanket,
Ninety times as high as the moon.
Where she was going I then did ask her,
For in her arms she carried a broom.

'Old woman, old woman, old woman', said I,
'Where are you going with your broom so high?'
'Sweeping the cobwebs out of the sky,
And I shall be jogging with you by and by'.

He also quoted a song entitled 'Then my love and I'll be married', obtained from Charles Tanner of Bampton and probably used by the morris men:

When roses grow on thistle tops,
And brimstone's took for sugar candy,
And women can't eat sugar sops,
Oh, then my love and I'll be married.

When gold is thrown about the street,
And lies from June to January,
And dogs will not spare bones for meat,
Oh, then my love and I'll be married.

When a cobbler works without an awl,
And London into York is carried,
When smoke won't rise, nor water fall,
Oh, then my love and I'll be married.

Another Bampton song recorded by Percy Manningwas 'Handsome John':

John is a handsome youth complete,
A smarter lad never walked the street;
And still the Lady's tongue runs on –
Oh what a handsome man was John.
Sing fal, the ral, a li do.

## Bicester

A morris team from King's End, Bicester which danced at the town's Whitsun Ale in 1790 may have had to learn dances specifically for the Ale, as one had not been held for thirty years. The team consisted of Edward Prior, William Handland, a pauper (butcher), Richard Humphrey, William Boffin (shoemaker – perhaps the son of the brewer who supplied the ale), Humphrey Elston and Matthew Neal.

## Bloxham

One Fool before 1841 was 'Old Mettle', William Castle, who also acted as Fool for the Adderbury men (see p180). The team danced for a week at Whitsun, at the statute fair in October until c. 1846, and travelled round the local villages. They sometimes competed with the Souldern team.

## Brize Norton

The team participated in a competition at Minster Lovell in about 1854 and last danced here on Whit Tuesday in 1870. The dancers wore top hats, white shirts, white trousers and bells, and carried handkerchiefs. The last team consisted of William Bellinger, Henry and Charles Bellinger (quarrymen), Jonathan Hurst, Rich. Knock and Maspin Hart (labourers). The Squire was local sweep Robert Beatle, and the pipe and tabor were played by John Hedon of Shilton.

## Bucknell

The village was a 'closed' one, under the tight control of the squire and clergyman, and the morris benefited from local patronage: on one occasion Colonel Hibbert of Bucknell Manor offered the team a guinea if they returned from their week's tour as clean as they had left, so to get the money they washed their clothes the evening before they came home! The men danced on the rectory lawn, and later in the parish pound. Dancing lasted for a week at Whitsun, and despite a decline, with no dancing for several years after 1863, they revived to dance to celebrate Queen Victoria's gold and diamond jubilees in 1887 and 1897 and the coronation of Edward VII in 1902. They travelled round neighbouring parishes as far as Middleton Cheney, and attended the Kirtlington Lamb Ale in Trinity Week. It could be financially rewarding for them, as they are said to have earned up to nine shillings a day dancing (when they only earned ten shillings a week as farm labourers) in the 1870s.

The men wore the usual white outfits decked with ribbons (in fact it may have been one of the morris men, William Rolphe, whose family was prominent in the morris team, who was convicted in 1826 for trying to steal twelve yards of ribbon in Oxford just before Whitsun). The Squire dressed in motley and carried the obligatory bladder and calf's tail. He invented doggerel suitable to the occasion, and to honour prominent members of the audience. The music was played on a pipe and tabor – the last musician was Joseph Powell.

## Burford

There are records of a Burford team dancing in the town and at Sherborne in the late 18th century, and dancing probably continued until the 1850s.

## Churchill

A team was paid six shillings for dancing at the the Churchill Whitsun Ale in 1721, while John Thornett received one shilling and sixpence for 'dancing and belles' and John Hyatt and Robert Brooks were given money for bells. The fiddler was paid half a guinea and the Fool a pound. A team was dancing in the mid-19th century.

## Ducklington

There was a team here from around the 1830s. In the 1840s men had to be at least twenty before they could join. The team, which included a sword-bearer, danced around the maypole on Whit Monday, paraded round the village, and went to Witney to dance, returning to Ducklington to dance for the Youth Ale run in conjunction with the celebration of the Whit Hunt. After this ceased in 1854 they carried on dancing in the village on Whit Monday and for the Club Feast on Whit Tuesday. They danced for about a week in surrounding villages and Witney. There may have been two or even three village teams dancing simultaneously around the 1850s.

One team was made up entirely from the Fisher family. John Fisher commented that around the 1840s it had 'cost Three Pounds for a Set of Six Dancers to turn out. Each had to Purchase a Light Pair of Boots three weeks before the time so as to get them well to their feet by the Day.' (Manning MS Top Oxon, d. 199 fol.176). They recouped some of their expenses by ensuring that they visited the lawyer and the vicar first, as they could afford to give them decent money.

The men were proud of their clean appearance and danced very neatly. They did not perform stick dances. Percy Manning recorded that in the 1870s at the time the morris in Ducklington finished, the foreman was John Hall, the team consisted of Moses Midwinter (bootmaker and publican), Robert Jordan (shoe maker), Wm Ayres or Ayers (in the Union – i.e. the workhouse), James Boston or Bason (farm labourer), Charles Munk or Monk (sawyer), Thomas Larner, the Squire, Thomas Boston or Bason, sword-bearer, with music played on the whittle and dub by John Lanksbury or Lanchbury (a labourer).

## Eynsham

Percy Manning recorded (MS Top Oxon d.200) that the morris was still performed in Eynsham in 1902 on the Wednesday of Whit Week and at Christmas (when the morris men apparently performed with the mummers). The dancers wore caps instead of hats and their ribbons were red, white and blue. Their Squire (also known as Feathers) carried a money box and bladder stick – when Ed Russell was a young Squire the team visited Blenheim Palace, and he hit the Duchess of Marlborough over the head, to the horror of the others, but fortunately she took the incident in good part. Music was provided at different times by a pipe and tabor, fiddle, banjo and mouth organ. The team consisted of Edward Russell, foreman, William Russell, Horace Belcher, Ernest May, Charles Masters, Henry Hedges, George Masters, Fred Harwood and Ben Hares. Around 1900 William Nicholson painted a picture of a man in a morris outfit with feathers in his hat – this shows Ed Russell who was then foreman of the morris men.

In 1900 a boy team performed with the adults at Christmas. It was said that a team of Eynsham men danced in South Africa while fighting there during the Boer War.

## Field Assarts

The team was said to be active in the 1830s and to have competed against the Bampton side. Dancing continued until around the 1870s. The team wore white pleated shirts and knee breeches, stockings, bells and blue and red ribbons. Their sticks were painted in alternate bands of blue and white, and handkerchiefs were carried.

The team recorded by Percy Manning was foreman: Robert Lock (stonemason), John Lock, Will Lock, Joseph Shaler, Mick Pratley and George Busby, all labourers. The Squire, known as Rodney, was played by Richard Eeles (father of the Leafield fool, Richard and the Asthal Fool, George). The sword-bearer was Charles Scyphas, and John Dix played the pipe and tabor. The men apparently ensured they did not get drunk until they had finished their dancing.

## Filkins

The Filkins team danced for the festivities at Broughton Poggs to celebrate Queen Victoria's coronation in June 1838. The side was noted for its quality and practised all year round, dancing in public for about six weeks, and travelling in a thirty-mile radius. One fiddler was lame and had to be pushed around in a carriage. George Swinford recalled that the team danced the whole of Whitsun week, visiting different Club feasts each day.

## Finstock

The key day for dancing here was Holy Thursday, when a bowery was built on Well Hill, but the men also danced at Whitsun. Six dancers formed the team, together with a Squire with bladder and tail and sword-bearer who carried sword, cake, knife and treasury box. The cake was not in a tin, it just rested on the hand-guard. Percy Manning wrote that Thomas Langford and Stephen Dore played the whittle and dub for them, the sword-bearer was James Turner, the Squire George Stratford and the dancers Charles, John, William and Stephen Dore (the latter the foreman), and John and Edward Oliver.

## Headington Quarry

Headington Quarry is the third team still dancing which has a long and important almost unbroken record of morris dancing. Oral tradition takes it back several hundred years, but written records only go back to the 1820s, when William Kimber's great-grandfather Anthony Kimber, who was born in 1791, would have begun dancing.

The village was established because of the stone quarries, and most male inhabitants were involved in seasonal work such as quarrying, brickmaking and hauling, dependant on the weather, so it was not unusual for men to be laid off for several weeks in bad weather, so dancing formed a useful addi-

Opposite:
This is thought to be the earliest photograph of the Headington morris men, taken around 1876 outside the Chequers Inn, Headington Quarry. The team are, from left to right: Francis Cummings (musician), William Kimber senior (foreman until 1887), James Hedges. John Horwood, Robert Cooper, John Haynes (the fool), an unidentified man carrying the collecting box and Joseph and Robert Trafford seated in front.

Oxfordshire Photographic Archive

**Below**: The Headington Quarry Morris Men photographed outside the Chequers on 26 June 1899. The men are: back row, 3rd and 4th from left, John Horwood and 'Gran Hedges'. Middle row, 3rd, 5th and 6th from left, William 'Sip' Washington, fiddler Mark Cox and Charles 'Mac' Massey. Front row: Mrs John Cooper, George 'Spuggle' Coppock, William 'Mac' Massey, George 'Cobby' Coppock and Thomas 'Russian' Jones.

Oxfordshire Phptographic Archive

William Kimber, who taught Cecil Sharp a great deal about morris dancing, is shown playing the fiddle while the Headington Quarry team perform a stick dance., c 1899. The Fool is 'Sip' Washington.

Oxfordshire Photographic Archive

Elsie Caistor taught some of boys at Margaret Road School morris dancing, and here boys from the school are seen dancing on Shotover Mound in 1955. Left row, front to back: Geoff Hill, Jack Morris and Terry Phipps, right row: Mervyn Cox, Peter Craft and John Graham.

Headington Quarry Morris Dancers' Scrapbook

'The White Rose', the anthem of the Headington Quarry Morris Men, from their Scrapbook.

tion to their income. The women often supplemented the family income by taking in college laundry. It was a fairly poor and often lawless community, with poaching rife.

They danced at Whitsun in the Quarry and in Oxford, but from around the 1870s the team came out on the Monday before Whitsun, beginning in Headington, then touring round for a week, sleeping rough, visiting Wheatley, the Miltons and Long Crendon. They danced on Whit Monday afternoons at the Feast of the Havelock Lodge of Oddfellows, at the Britannia Inn, Headington and sometimes at Easter and at Christmas to earn extra money. The team occasionally danced on request, as when they were invited to entertain guests at Old Headington Hill House in 1847. They often won the morris competition at the Kirtlington Lamb Ale.

The team disbanded around 1887, perhaps dispirited by the death of their Fool, John 'Black Jack' Haynes in 1884 and fiddler of forty years, Frank Cummings in 1885. He was lame, so when younger he was carried round on the men's shoulders, and later taken round in a donkey cart. The side performed at Queen Victoria's jubilee celebrations given by Hall's Brewery at Oxpens in 1887, when William Kimber senior led them, both in the Quarry and in Oxford, and once after that, then only among themselves. Then Percy Manning, a lecturer at Oxford University, in the course of his study of Oxfordshire folklore, persuaded them to dance for him then paid

John Horwood and James Hedges to teach younger men the local morris dances. This side performed at Manning's lecture at Oxford Corn Exchange in March 1899, then in Oxford at Whitsun and in the Quarry in June. Mark Cox, the new fiddler, picked up the old tunes by hearing them whistled by Mr 'Gran' Hedges, who led the new team. William 'Sip' Washington was the Squire, dressed as a clown. That Christmas the weather was particularly bad and it snowed, and some men had earned no money for three

Headington Quarry morris dancers forming a triumphal arch with their sticks at the wedding of Sylvia Gilland (nee Spokes) and John Graham on 20th November 1970. Francis Parsons, Bob Turrell and Terry Phillips are on the left and Bob Grant, Peter Scudder and Eddie Whitehouse on the right.

Headington Quarry Morris Dancers' Scrapbook

weeks, so they danced around Headington on Boxing Day, and it was on this occasion that they were seen by Cecil Sharp, who was staying with his mother-in-law Mrs Burch at Sandfield Cottage in the London Road, Headington. William Kimber, who worked for Knowles the builders, saw her about alterations to the house; they talked about morris dancing, and he promised that they would call at her cottage next time they danced. This was the first time that Sharp had seen morris dancing performed, he noted down the tunes and made a point of talking to Kimber the next day. He was so fascinated that he subsequently spent many years studying the subject and collecting information about the morris.

HERE ON BOXING DAY 1899
CECIL SHARP FIRST HEARD
WILLIAM KIMBER PLAY THE
HEADINGTON QUARRY MORRIS
DANCE TUNES.

William Kimber was a leading light in the resurrection of the Headington Quarry morris team in the late 19th century, and a stalwart member for much of his long life. He also became a close friend of Cecil Sharp, who saw morris dancing for the first time outside Sandfield Cottage, London Road, Headington. This plaque commemorates the occasion.

Photograph: H. A. Shatford

William 'Merry' Kimber is a noted name in dancing fraternities. He had a great influence on the revival of interest in the morris in the early 20th century, thanks to his friendship with Cecil Sharp. His family had danced in and led the morris team over at least four generations, including himself, and he later played the fiddle for the side. He claimed that: 'You were never a morris dancer unless you had plenty of beer, there was not time for food.' He taught Mary Neal's girls the Headington dances at the Esperance Club, where he met Sharp again, and their friendship grew from there.

William Kimber was presented with the English Folk Dance and Song Society's Gold Badge at a folk-dance performance in Oxford in 1922. On Boxing Day in 1959 the side danced once again outside Sandfield Cottage and a plaque was unveiled commemorating that first meeting, and two years later to the day Kimber died at almost ninety. The side dance each Spring Bank Holiday Monday in William Kimber Crescent, New Headington, named in his honour.

Some dancers, such as Joseph Trafford and William Kimber, started dressing in morris costume and dancing as young boys – Trafford claims to have danced as a stand-in in the set at the age of seven or eight, and Kimber at twelve, although he did not dance regularly until he was eighteen, and claimed to have led the set aged twenty-two. Trafford claimed that he once ruined a pair of shoes after three days through dancing.

The Headington dances published in 1901 by Mary Neal in the *Esperance Morris Book* were 'Bean Setting' (a stick dance imitating the process of dibbling beans into the earth), 'Rodney Drawback', 'Blue-eyed Stranger', 'Double Set-back', 'Laudanum Bunches' and 'Old Mother Oxford', which included the words:

Old Mother Oxford's just come home,
Had to light a fire in the big back room,
Step and fetch her,
Down the middle, down the middle,
Step and fetch her, my pretty little dear.
Don't you tease her, try to please her,
'Cause she is my pretty little dear.

'Constant Billy' and 'Rigs o'Marlow' were performed for Cecil Sharp. Manning recorded that they also danced to 'Jacks the Lad', '29th of May', 'Haste to the Wedding', 'Trunk Oles', 'How do-e do Sir?' 'Banks of the Dee', 'Queen's Delight', 'Country Garden', 'Lillie Dale', 'The Old Woman Tossed up in a Blanket', 'Balance the Straw', 'Brighton Camp' and 'Jockey to the Fair'.

Percy Manning (MS Top Oxon d.200) recorded another song:

Take an Old Woman and Roast her
And Baste Her Well with Cheese,
Taker out on a Cold Winter night
I am sure the Lady Would Freeze.

Take her out the Next Morning
Put her in a bundle of Straw,
Then set Fire to the Bottom
I am sure the old Lady Would Thaw.

## Idbury

The team probably danced from at least the 1840s until the 1860s. Their musician, Charles Benfield, also played for the Bledington men, and the two teams shared the same dances. One dance was called 'Idbury Hill'. Evelyn Goshawk wrote (*Idbury History*, 1961) that the last team of dancers was made up of John and William Lainchbury (labourers), Benjamin Paxford and William and Charles Toms, both of Westcote, the latter a fiddler.

## Kencot and Langford

There was dancing at Kencot from at least the 1820s, from Holy Thursday until Whitsun, and the team sometimes competed with the Langford side for a cake presented by the landlord of Langford's 'Five Bells' inn. The winner was the team that made the least false steps in three different dances. The team included a sword-bearer.

## Kirtlington

The team was closely connected with the Lamb Ale (see pp164–169) held at Trinity. Thomas Blount wrote in *Tenures of Land and Customs of Manors* (1874) that during the 17th century there was a 'Morisco of men and another of women' at Kidlington, but it is thought that this is more likely to be a reference to Kirtlington. The women are said to have danced until 1679. Women's teams were unusual and often frowned upon by the men.

The Lamb Ale ceased about 1860, but the dancing continued until about 1863. The Dashwood family of Kirtlington Park were patrons of the morris from 1732 until about 1858 when they decided to support the poor of the parish instead. In the 1840s the team was entertained at Kirtlington Park on the Tuesday of Trinity Week. The team wore ribbons in the Dashwood colours of light blue and pink.

## Leafield

There was dancing here from at least the 1830s. The team wore billy-cock hats with blue ribbons, pleated white shirts decked with red and blue ribbons, white waistcoats and knee breeches, bells, white stockings, sticks and handkerchiefs. They had a sword-bearer, and people paid for slices of his cake, which were cut with a penknife.

The team travelled round the villages throughout Whitsun week, and often came out again for the autumn Forest Fair. They once fought with the Longborough side because they found them poaching on 'their' dance territory, but they later went on joint excursions with them and with teams from

Bledington, Finstock, Shipton and Ascott-under-Wychwood. Some of their tunes were taught to the Bampton men through sharing musicians. They had a reputation for dancing very energetically and leaping as high as they could.

Their dances included 'The Country Garden', 'Highland Mary', jigs over tobacco pipes – and 'Greensleeves', which included the song:

> Green sleeves and yellow laces,
> Get up, you bitch and work apace
> Your father lies in an awful place
> All for want of money.

Percy Manning (MS Top Oxon, d.200)

During one dance the men circled round clutching each other's ears.

## Milton-under-Wychwood

Whitsun Ales were held here in the 18th century, with morris dancing as the chief attraction. *Jackson's Oxford Journal* wrote on 24th May 1828 that cakes specially baked for the ale would be 'carried away with triumphant joy by the sprightly MORRIS-DANCERS'.

The team danced to celebrate the marriage of the Prince of Wales in 1863, but dancing is not recorded after this date.

## Minster Lovell

There was a team here in the 1840s and perhaps earlier, dancing at Whitsun and for Club feasts. A competition was held around 1850 between sides from Brize Norton, Ducklington, Minster Lovell, Standlake and Leafield, which the latter won easily.

## North Leigh

The team here danced from around the 1850s to the 1860s, travelling the Woodstock Whitsun Ale. One of their dances involved tying coconut halves to the men's hands and clapping.

## Spelsbury

Spelsbury is unusual in having a women's team as well as a men's one. In the early 19th century unmarried farmers' and labourers' daughters aged about eighteen to twenty danced at Whitsun. When both teams danced at the same time the women had to use fiddler William Ivings, though both teams preferred to use Thomas Hedon, who played the pipe and tabor.

The women danced on top of Spelsbury church tower to celebrate a victory, possibly in 1815 after the battle of Waterloo, and the team probably continued into the 1830s. They wore head-dresses with ribbons and flowers, short-skirted dresses, bells on their legs and white handkerchiefs. Manning records the team as Elizabeth Fowler, Jane Hern, Charlotte Cross, Sarah Fowler, Mary Knight and Mary Couling.

Both teams danced at the Ascension Day Club Feast and in November at Taston Wake. One of their songs went:

My father's a hedger and ditcher,
My mother she cards and she spins,
And I am a pretty young lassie,
And the money comes tumbling in.

Elsie Corbett, *A History of Spelsbury*, 1962

## Stanton Harcourt

Music was provided in the 1850s by John Potter, who was noted for his skill with the pipe and tabor. Their dances included 'Black Joke', 'Princess Royal', 'Nightingale', 'Bean Planting', 'Greensleeves', 'Clock', 'Brighton Camp', 'Constant Billy', 'A Nutting We Will Go' and 'Jockey to the Fair'. The men danced with white handkerchiefs knotted to their little fingers.

## Wheatley

Dancing flourished here at least from the 1820s until the 1890s and was revived in the late 20th century. The men were proud of their skill which they practised all winter ready for the Whit Week dancing. The costume was a tall hat, pleated white shirt, moleskin trousers, red, orange and blue ribbons (one source says red and blue), bells, sticks (half red, half blue) and handkerchiefs.

They had a unique dance called the 'Wheatley Processional' in their repertoire.

## Woodstock

Dancers here came under the patronage of the Duke of Marlborough from the early 18th century, as they were asked to dance when the foundation stone was laid for Blenheim Palace on 18th June 1705 – three teams performed that day, consisting of young men, young women and old women, who may have been from Woodstock. Morris dancers were paid by the Duke to provide entertainment at the election in 1727 and celebrated the victory over the French in 1794. They would also have danced at the famous Whit Ales.

# Midsummer Madness

Strawberry Man, Strawberry Man,
Bring me good luck,
Today or tomorrow,
To pick something up.

**This rhyme was chanted by Oxfordshire children the first time they** saw a man wearing a straw hat in early summer. As soon as they saw him, they would touch elbows and hands alternately, then pick up a stone or small object and throw it over the left shoulder, hoping to receive a gift shortly, or at least have good luck.

The midsummer solstice on 21st June was a time for magic and divinations. Percy Manning (MS Top Oxon d.199) mentioned a divination practised in Oxford at Midsummer, and elsewhere at Halloween: a girl would go to the church porch at midnight, sprinkling hempseed and saying 'Hempseed I sow, Let the one I love come and mow'. If she looked over her left shoulder, she should see her future husband mowing the hempseed, which had magically grown behind her, with a scythe.

Some places had the custom of paying a rose as rent: Elsie Corbett quoted one, dating from 1295, in *A History of Spelsbury*:

> Margery of Dichelege, widow of John of Dichelege, gave two houses with one yardland in Clevely which she had as her marriage portion from her brother Thomas Colonna to her daughter Isabell, to have and to hold for ever on payment to her mother of one rose every year on St John Baptist's Day, and to William Colonna twelve pence on the feast of St Kenelm.

Another example which still takes place is at Long Wittenham, where on Midsummer Day a red rose is paid by Oxfordshire County Council to the Hedges family to lease land for a car park at Wittenham Clumps.

Midsummer bonfires were lit, well into the 18th century, to purify and bring fertility and protect cattle against witchcraft and murrain.

With Christianity, 24th June, St John the Baptist's Day, became more important. There is a stone pulpit in the quadrangle of Magdalen College which is used for the sermon preached each St John the Baptist's Day, which originated because the college was built on the site of a hospital dedicated to St John the Baptist. Anthony Wood referred to it:

> June 24. Su., Midsomer Day, the bell rang and tol'd at Magd. Coll. for an University sermon ... Which being done, Mr Philip Lewis appeared in the pulpit in the chappell and preached. Grinning and laughing, and had water squirted on

them. The University took no notice of it, but had their sermon at St Marie's where Mr [John] Hudson of Univ. Coll. preached.

*ed Andrew Clark, The Life and Times of Anthony Wood, Oxford, 1894*

John Pointer wrote that it had become highly organised in the 18th century:

Custom of having the University Sermon preach'd in the Stone-Pulpit every Year on St John Baptist's Day; at which Time there are Seats plac'd in the Quadrangle for the Vicechancellor, Proctors, Masters etc., and the walls adorn'd with green Boughs and Flowers, and the Ground cover'd with green Rushes and Grass; And all this of St John Baptist's Preaching in the Wilderness, and in commemoration of the said St John, as being the great Saint to whom an Hospital by K. Henry III was here dedicated.

*Oxoniensis Academia, or the Antiquities and Curiosities of the University of Oxford, 1749*

The practice of filling the courtyard with green boughs died out in the mid-18th century. It has resonances with the green boughs erected on May Day and at Whitsun.

Midsummer and December were the times for paying rents on college properties. T. Berry, a New College scout, told Christina Hole in 1949 that at Midsummer the tenants were given a substantial lunch at eleven a.m., then presented with a pair of white doe-skin gloves with red backs, which the men wore home, and to church next Sunday. If the farmer was not seen wearing the gloves that Sunday it would indicate that he had not paid his rent on time.

# Burford Dragon: St John the Baptist's Day, June 24th

St George: 'Here am I St George, from Britain did I spring, and I will fight the fiery Dragon, my wonders to begin, I'll clip his wings he shall not fly, I'll cut him down, or else I die.'

Dragon: 'Who's he that seeks the Dragon's blood, and speaks so angry and so loud? That English dog, will he before me stand. I'll cut him down with my courageous hand, with my long teeth and scurvy jaws, of such I'd break up half a score, and then stay my stomach, till I had more.'

*Burford Mummers' Play*

Folk memory of Burford's dragon ceremony, which died out in the 18th century and was revived in 1971, is very strong, as typified by the use of the character of the dragon in the mummers' play. The most complete description of it comes from Dr Plot in 1677:

The town of Burford ... [is] most remarkable for a Battle fought near it, about the year 750, perhaps on the places still called Battle-edge, west of the town betwixt it and Upton, between Cuthred or Cuthbert, a tributary king of the West Saxons, and Ethelbald, King of Mercia, whose insupportable exactions the former king not being able to endure, he came into the field against Ethelbald, met and

MIDSUMMER EVE PROCESSION AT BURFORD IN THE DAYS OF KING CHARLES 1st

A postcard depicting a 19th or early 20th century idea of how the original Burford dragon ceremony would have looked.

overthrew him there, winning his banner, whereon was depicted a golden dragon: in remembrance of which victory, the custom of making a dragon yearly and carrying it up and down the town in great jollity on Midsummer Eve, to which they added the picture of a giant, was in all likelihood first instituted.

*Natural History of Oxfordshire*

This may refer to a battle fought in 752, although there is controversy as to whether it actually refers to Burford:

752. In this year, the twenty second of his reign, Cuthred, king of Wessex, fought at Beorhford against AEthelbald, king of Mercia, and put him to flight.

ed. G. N. Garmonsway, *The Anglo-Saxon Chronicle*

The latest research into this area in the Saxon period is by John Blair, who wrote (*Anglo-Saxon Oxfordshire*, 1994) that Aethelbald had some sort of overlordship over the West Saxons, and that the battle fought in 752 might have been over lands in the Thames Valley, but the sources are unclear, so one cannot prove or disprove the theory.

Legends became attached to it over the years: Camden, in *Britannia*, embellished Plot's description saying that Cuthred captured Aethelbald's standard 'which, we read, was the pourtraicture of a golden dragon'. Further legends suggest that Cuthbert's standard bearer, Aethelhun, speared his opposite number with the pole of his banner.

However the connection with the battle may be spurious, as it is likely that the dragon and giant are connected with the Merchant Taylors' Guild. Burford's wealth in the Middle Ages came from being a Cotswold wool

Burford owed its wealth to the wool trade, and it is likely that the dragon ceremony was connected with the Merchant Taylors' Guild. Guild figures of a Giant and Hob Nob – also known as a dragon, used in a similar ceremonial role – are preserved in the Salisbury and South Wiltshire Museum. Photograph: Salisbury and South Wiltshire Museum

The dragon ceremony died out in the early 18th century and was revived by Burford School in 1971. The secondary school children and staff made and carried the dragon. The character of the ceremony has varied over the years. The dragon's head is usually remade each year – the version shown here was used in 1975.

Photograph: Freda Kitcher

The Gloucester City Morris Men dancing after the church service in 1975.

Photograph: Freda Kitcher

Detail of the dragon's head (carried on wheels because of its weight) from the 1992 celebration.
Photograph: Christine Bloxham

**Right**:

The vicar, magnificent in his patchwork cope made by Averil Colby, conducts a service in the courtyard for participants in the dragon ceremony in 1975.

Photograph: Freda Kitcher

town, and St John the Baptist was the patron saint of the Guild. The dragon and giant were probably Guild emblems, paraded through the town at Whitsun and again for the patronal festival. Records of such a procession survive from Salisbury, and the processional figures of a giant (who may represent St Christopher, the patron saint of the Merchant Taylors) and Hob Nob (a hobby horse) are preserved in the museum. Hob Nob is also known in Salisbury as 'Old Snap' and 'Dragon'. The first records there are from 1496 when the two figures, accompanied by a sword-bearer, mace-leader, a yeoman with a staff of office surmounted by a lamb (the badge of the Guild), the mayor and corporation and morris men went to greet Henry VII and his queen. It is suggested in Salisbury that

Hob Nob may have been part of a spring festivity originally, perhaps belonging to the Guild of St George. Dragons featured in Whitsun ceremonies up to the 17th century.

Whatever its origins, the dragon and giant were last paraded in Burford in 1796 and it was not until 1971 that they were seen again in the town. This time

**Right:**

The dragon procession approaching the church in 1975.

Photograph: Freda Kitcher

The giant carried in the 1975 procession.
Photograph: Freda Kitcher

the festivity was organised by Burford School: the procession went from the school to the roundabout and down the hill to the church, where the dragon shed the twenty or so children who formed its tail so that they could all participate in a church service (held outside in good weather). That first year the primary school children did maypole dancing. The Gloucester City Morris men are regular visitors at the ceremony, which is still kept up, with some changes – the dragon is remade each year, and now there are several giants.

Children emerging from the dragon's tail outside the church.

One of the several giants used in Burford in1992.
Photograph: Christine Bloxham

## Port Meadow Round-up

Port Meadow in North Oxford is owned by the Freemen of the City of Oxford, and is cared for by the Sheriff of Oxford. Many people graze their horses and cattle on the meadow, and without warning one day each summer the Sheriff, accompanied by a group of freemen, conducts a round-up of all grazing animals at dawn, sometimes impounding them in Godstow nunnery. They are released on payment of a £3 fine – or more for unauthorised grazers. One sheriff who had served in the R.A.F. conducted the round-up from a helicopter instead of on horseback!

A similar round-up used to take place on Otmoor, organised by Lord Abingdon, to drive all cattle found on Otmoor into Beckley. Any beasts not claimed by their owners became his property.

The Port Meadow round-up: the cattle and horses permitted to graze on Port Meadow, Oxford are rounded up annually by the Sheriff of Oxford, as shown here in 1983.

Oxfordshire Photographic Archive

## Yarnton Lot Meadow Mowing

In comes the jolly scythes-men,
To mow the meadow down,
With the good old leather bottle,
And the ale that was so brown;
There's many a stout young labouring man
Comes there his skill to try,
While he sweats and blows and stoutly mows,
For the grass cuts very dry.

From 'The Haymakers', quoted in Alfred Williams, *Folk Songs of the Upper Thames*

Many villages had common hay meadows shared by the villagers, who drew lots to select their portions. This was done at Fencott and Murcott on Otmoor until about 1920, and at Kingham where a feast was held afterwards. Candle auctions were used to allocate strips at Combe and Bicester.

For many years the rights to mow hay in the Yarnton meadows of Pixey, Oxhay and West Mead were auctioned in the Grapes public house as shown here c. 1921.

Oxfordshire Photographic Archive

A detailed system was developed at Bampton, where the government of the common land was regulated by the Lord of the Manor, sixteen men called 'The Sixteens', and four grass stewards (often the most influential of the Sixteens), who were selected from those who had rights of common; they provided two bulls at their own expense to run on the common, which they sold at the end of the season, and were entitled to claim one shilling and sixpence for every cow grazing on the common.

> When the grass is fit to cut ... the Grass-Stewards and Sixteens summon the tenants to a general meeting, and Four of the tenants come forwards, each bearing his mark out on a piece of wood, as for example the 'frying pan', the 'hern's foot', the 'bow', the 'two strokes to the right and one at the top', etc.
> These four marks are thrown into a hat, and a boy, having shaken up the hat, again draws forth the marks. The first drawn entitles its owner to have his portion of the Common Meadow in Set One, the second-drawn in Set Two, etc., and thus four of the tenants, having obtained their allotment, four others come forwards, and the same process repeated until all the tenants have received their allotments.

Rev. G. A. Giles, *History of Bampton*

At Yarnton the Meadow Mowing was developed to a fine art. Before the building of the Witney by-pass there were three meadows involved: Pixey, West Mead and Oxhay. Rights to the land were held by several villagers and the parishes of Begbroke and Water Eaton, who did not always require the

rights themselves, so on the Monday after St Peter's Day (June 29th), or when the hay was ripe. an auction was held at the Grapes public house at Yarnton to sell the rights. Over the last few years all the rights have been bought by one person so the lot drawing itself has not been required.

When several people bought rights, the lot drawing was organised by the two Head Meadsmen, who decided when it should take place, and arranged for all concerned to meet in the meadow at eight o'clock in the morning. The strips were marked out with wooden pegs, while the tydals (areas belonging to the rectories of Yarnton and Begbroke) were marked with stones to indicate they were not part of the drawing.

The lot drawing was done using small wooden balls marked with the names Boat, Boulton, Dunn, Freeman, Gilbert, Green, Harry, Perry, Rothe, Walter Jeoffrey, Waterey Molly, White and William of Bladon. The origins of the names are long forgotten but may refer to characteristics of the meadow or to long-forgotten owners of rights. Each ball now represents a defined acreage, measured according to how much a man can mow in a single day or 'man's mowth'.

Mrs B. Stapleton described in *A History of Kirtlington, Yarnton and Begbroke* the practice in 1893:

Marking out the
lots drawn before
the mowing.

Mowing the hay
with a scythe.

Photographs on
this and opposite
page taken by
Freda Kitcher in
1967.

The 'Meadsman' has the management of the business and upon a certain appointed day at the end of June he takes a bag, containing thirteen coloured balls, down to the meadows and begins the drawing. 'Oxhay Mead' has 80 acres and is drawn five times; 'Pixey' has six acres and is drawn twice. N.B. The drafts of 'Pixey' are drawn together. Each draft consists of thirteen lots. In 'Oxhay' thirty-nine lots; in 'West Mead' sixty-five lots, in 'Pixey' twenty-six lots. Each lot has a name, marked upon a ball, and belongs to a particular farm, and when such a name is drawn it shows to whom such a lot belongs. An acre is a lot. An acre or lot is sometimes three or four acres. A habaker, two or two and a half. The yard, one or more.

A man's mowth is reckoned at a scratch acre. When each lot is large, the habaker is large too, and so the yard, and when small, they are small too. The custom used to be to cut the grass in the first mead, 'Oxhay' on the first Monday after Old St Peter's; to cut the grass in 'West Mead' on the following Monday; to cut the grass in 'Pixey' the Monday following.

As each lot was drawn a few sweeps of grass were cut with a scythe so that the initials of the owner could be cut into the strip, then the party followed the same procedure at the next strip. The boundaries were delineated by men 'running the treads', shuffling their feet. Now it is done by a tractor.

Originally all the strips were cut on the same day, but this caused problems, as in 1815:

The plan of cutting each meadow upon one day gave rise to an immense amount of disturbance and riot in the village. As a great influx of disorderly people flocked to the place, where a fair was held, with all its attendant drunkenness. No respectable person was able to go near the meadows, and the riots ended in loss of life. Moreover the restriction of time obliged the farmer to employ outside labour, whereby wages were spent outside the parish to the detriment of the home labourers.

Owing to these considerations, Mr Vaughan Thomas, the vicar, urged upon the landlords and tenants the desirability of extending the time of cutting the grass from one day to three. It was shown that if this plan were adopted, two home labourers could do as much as ten upon the old system.

In 1815 the excitement was ran so high that Mr James Walker of Yarnton was sworn in as Justice of the Peace, and special constables were held in readiness for any emergency.

Mrs Stapleton, op. cit.

In the early 19th century each labourer received a special payment of two shillings and sixpence per day. The end of the mowing was celebrated until 1840 with morris dancing, shows and races – the main prize was a garland, which the winner placed in Yarnton church, where it was displayed for the year. The farmers decorated their wagons with ribbons, the carters wore ribbons and flowers in their hats and a dinner was enjoyed by all on Camp Acre.

However the Rector, Dr Vaughan Thomas, disapproved of the festivity, perhaps because it encouraged drunkenness, and wrote to the landlord, Sir Henry Dashwood requesting that he forbid his tenant Slatter from making the garland, because he thought it encouraged riotous behaviour.

After the hay was cut, cattle were put to graze there: each ball gave the right to graze fourteen cattle or seven horses in West Mead.

A similar festivity was held at the end of the mowing at Revel-mede at Bicester, with stalls erected, and competitions in various rural sports. It ceased when Chesterton Field was enclosed.

## Swan Upping

The swan has been designated a royal bird, regarded as one of the greatest delicacies at aristocratic tables. From the early middle ages the sovereign was the Seigneur of Swans, with the right to grant ownership of them to favoured subjects: in 1482 no-one with freehold and tenements valued at less than five marks could own a Game of Swans, and in Henry VII's reign fines and a year's imprisonment were imposed for stealing a swan's egg. Even in the 19th century the punishment for killing a swan was seven years transportation.

To this day all unmarked swans on open water are deemed to belong to the Crown, although anyone may own captive ones if they are kept on private lakes. However some swans on the River Thames belong to two of the oldest City Livery Companies, the Dyers and the Vintners, a privilege granted around 1493.

Swan Upping is the process of checking and marking the swans and cygnets on the stretch of the Thames between Henley and London belonging to the Dyers and Vintners. (The sovereign's swans have been unmarked since it was so requested by Queen Alexandra). It is done over six days in July. In the 16th and 17th centuries Swan Herdsmen were paid ten shillings for the Swan Voyage, with another ten shillings for lodgings. From the 18th century a ceremonial aspect was added: the Companies used their magnificent state barges, and invited guests, who were feasted and entertained by musicians and gunfire. Today the barges are gone, but guests from other Liveries and the City Livery Club sometimes participate on two days.

Three Swan Herdsmen, wearing magnificent gold-braided uniforms, conduct the proceedings: one is the Queen's Swankeeper, one from the Dyers and the other from the Vintners, who often also served as their Bargemasters. The role was often hereditary, as in the case of the Turk family, several generations of whom held the post in the 20th century. The procedure is probably named Swan Upping because the birds are taken from the water so that the cygnets can be marked to show ownership: one nick on the beak for the Dyers and two for the Vintners. (This has led to the common pub name of 'The Swan with Two Necks', 'neck' being a corruption of 'nick'.)

The herdsmen are skilled in handling swans. About six hundred are examined each year for markings, and to identify the parent swans of each group of cygnets, so that the latter can be appropriately marked. If they are of mixed parentage, half receive the cob's mark, half the pen's. Any odd cygnets are allocated to the cob. The swans and cygnets have their legs tied when they are captured, then the cygnets are marked and have their wings pinioned before being released back into the water. It is all done swiftly and skilfully so that they suffer no pain.

The Swan Upping boats set out from Southwark Bridge and slowly proceed up river to Henley, led by the Royal Swanherd's boat, flying a flag with the Queen's initials and another portraying a swan with raised wings. Another royal boat follows, with two for each of the Companies, the latter four each with one flag portraying their Livery Arms and swans. As the boats pass Windsor Castle the Swan Uppers fall to attention with oars raised and salute 'Her Majesty the Queen, Seigneur of the Swans'. Each man participating in his first Swan Upping, who is known as a 'colt', is ducked in the water. The Swan Herdsmen tend the birds throughout the year, caring for injured swans and rescuing those which have strayed.

Later in the year the Vintners hold a Swan Feast, at which a cygnet is eaten. It is conducted with great ceremony: a fanfare heralds the entrance of the Swan Procession through the Vintners' Hall, then a military band plays 'Greensleeves'. The procession is headed by two Swan Uppers carrying a swan prepared by a taxidermist on a silver dish, followed by the Beadle, Stavesmen, the Swan Warden and the Company banner. The Swan Warden doffs his Elizabethan cap to the Master, with the words: 'Master, I present cygnets for the delectation of your guests'. The Master responds, 'Let them be served, Mr Swan'. The company sing the Song of the Vintners. The Dyers have a similar feast but instead of playing 'Greensleeves' they sing 'The Swan', from John Playford's *The Dancing Master*:

> Look up, my Masters, mark my words
> And hear what we shall sing ye,
> And liverymen all, both great and small,
> Now mark what they do bring ye.
> A swan, an offering fair they bear
> Aven nobilem nunc cantamus.

## Ducks and Cherries

Ducks may not be as glamorous as swans, but they used to be raced in Grove on the first Saturday after 6th July. The ducks were brought to the brook and allowed to swim off, then the men waded into the water and chased after them, each man being allowed to keep the duck he caught. The custom was discontinued because the R.S.P.C.A. considered it to be cruel, but the birds were not harmed. A relic of this is found on the Grove Womens' Institute banner, which shows six ducks in a stream.

The Vale of White Horse was known for the quality of its cherries, and a cherry feast was held on the Saturday following the 6th July at Kingston Lisle. Cherries used to be sold in the street, and it was a day of family reunions.

**Opposite**: The Grove Duck Race in 1957.
Oxfordshire Photographic Archive

# Mock Mayors

**Mock-mayormaking is another example of customs turning life** topsy-turvy and reversing roles: a drunkard or figure of fun represents a civic dignitary, largely seen as a comic character, but at the same time symbolising protest. Mock mayors tended to be elected in areas of towns built outside the original borough boundary, whose inhabitants did not have the right to vote for the town mayor. The ceremony, which has been recorded in Britain since the 15th century, was turned into a festive occasion, often accompanied by drinking, and in the case of Abingdon, morris dancing.

## Abingdon

The mock mayor has, it is said, been elected in Ock Street, a poor area outside the town boundary, at least since 1700. The ceremony is held on

**Above**: Tom Hemmings, the mock mayor of Ock Street, Abingdon in 1953 being chaired along Ock Street. The musician is Major Francis Fryer and the boy walking beside him is Stuart Jackson, who was first elected Mock Mayor himself in 1996.

**Opposite**: Ock Street mock mayor Charles Brett carrying the ceremonial sword and mazer.

Photographs: Abingdon Traditional Morris Men's Scrapbook

the Saturday after 19th June, close to the longest day; an ox-roast followed by a fair used to be held on the 19th to commemorate St Edmund of Abingdon (although his saint's day was actually 16th November).

The polling booth used to be set up outside the Cross Keys in Ock Street. When this closed, the election was transferred to the Crown, which has since also closed. Currently the event is based at the Brewery Tap, but as this does not have its own car park, the election and dancing take place at the Baptist Church, where there is more room. Ballot papers are distributed to residents of Ock Street. The candidates are usually morris dancers or 'retired' dancers, although this is not a formal qualification. *Jackson's Oxford Journal* commented on 25th June 1870:

The qualification for this quasi-dignitary is, we understand, that he boils a pot, or at any rate has a pot to boil, and it would be no disparagement to candidature that he ever sat in the stocks, but he must not be a convicted thief.

ABINGDON. MORRIS. DANCERS.

ELECTION OF MAYOR. SATURDAY, JUNE, 22nd.

POOLING BOOTH " THE CROSS KEYS ". 148, OCK STREET, ABINGDON.

THE BOOTH OPENS AT 12, NOON, UNTIL 4,P.M.

THE CANDIDATES FOR THIS ELECTION ARE,

ARGYLE LESLIE. VOTES RECORDED. 64

BRETT CHARLES. VOTES RECORDED. 205

GRIMSDALE JOHN. VOTES RECORDED. 40

I, the undersigned being the President and, Returning Officer for this Election declare that an Election has been held to-day and,

*Charles Brett*

Has been Elected Mayor of the Abingdon Morris Dancers for the year 1974--1975.

Signed.

Mock mayors have been elected in Ock Street since c.1700. This sheet records the results of the election at the Cross Keys public house in Ock Street in 1975 when Charles Brett was overwhelmingly elected.

Abingdon Traditional Morris Men's Scrapbook

The Hemmings family, who were so influential among the morris men over many decades, often took the role of mayor: Thomas Hemmings, who was born in 1815, claimed to have been mayor about twenty-five times.

Polling ends at four p.m. After the votes have been counted, the result is announced. The mock mayor is presented with his regalia of sash, sword and collecting box (sometimes recently by the actual mayor of Abingdon) and an applewood drinking cup, known as the Ock Street mace or mazer, said to have been carved from the club belonging to one of the Hemmings family at the battle of Ock Street in 1700. Recent additions to the regalia are a gold medallion presented to Abingdon Morris for participating in a five-mile procession round Abingdon's twin town Argentan; a solid silver goblet (from a limited edition of a thousand made to commemorate a thousand years of British monarchy and the coronation of King Edgar in 873 A.D.), presented to the Mayor by the Bathampton Morris men for participation in their festivities; and a Berkshire smock, only worn by the Fool at the mayor-making, donated by the Abingdon Drama Club. The morris also possess an Anglo-concertina presented to William Hemmings in 1922 by the English Folk Dance Society and various medals presented over the years.

Leslie Argyle was elected Mock Mayor on 23rd June 1990, and was then carried on a flower-decked chair up and down the street outside the Cross Keys.

Photograph: Christine Bloxham

The mock mayor used to be chaired, shoulder high, round all the pubs in Ock Street, stopping for refreshment at each, but now few are pubs left, so the procession, led by a man carrying the morris men's famous ox horns, followed by the mayor carried in his chair, then the ex-mayor, the morris Fool and the morris dancers, goes up and down the street, then back to the pub, after which there is a display of morris dancing. For the last few years teams of dancers from different parts of England have been invited to join in the celebrations; for example in 1976 the visitors were Colne Royal and the Lancashire Clog Morris men and Bampton Morris. The whole day is given over to celebration. The 1973 timetable was:

10-11a.m. Ock Street, Cross Keys, Prepare Polling Station

11.10-11.30a.m. Market Place, Queens Hotel, Dance

12-1.30p.m. Boundary House, Oxford Road, Dance and Lunch

1.45-2. 15p.m. Cross Keys, Ock Street

2.30-3.00p.m.Abingdon Hospital, Dance

3.15-3.45p.m. Old People's Home, Ock Street, Dance

3.50-4.00p.m. Morris Men's Voting Time at Cross Keys

4.15-4.45p.m. Election result. Mayor-making ceremony, chairing of Mayor of
    Ock Street. Dancing in of new mayor

4.45-5.50p.m. Morris men to tea

6.00 White Horse, Ock Street

6.30 Air Balloon, Ock Street

7.00 Cross Keys, Ock Street

7.30 Warwick Arms/Crown, Ock Street

8.15 The Market Square

9.00-11.45 Morris men and guests to Railway Inn. (By invitation only)

The guest dancers in 1990 included the Loftus Sword Dancers.

Photograph: Christine Bloxham

That year the guest dancers after the election were morris teams from Bampton, Chipping Campden and Headington Quarry. Retired postman Charlie Brett was re-elected mayor of Ock Street.

## Banbury

New Land Wake, which took place in a poor part of Banbury settled as a new town in the Middle Ages, took place over three days from July 21st. It was described in *Oxfordshire Archaeological Society Reports* for 1904:

> Any inhabitant ... who refused to serve in turn being fined. He was, after the election, chaired round the town, preceded by his mace-bearers carrying large cabbage stalks. It was, as usual then with these festivities, the occasion of a good deal of drunkenness and disorder. Houses in this part were converted into eating-houses, and I was told by an old inhabitant that he had seen about fifty people trying to dance in a small room in a cottage. On July 21st 1890, I happened to be in Fish Street, a street running into Newland, and found flags hanging from some of the houses and children racing for sweets. I asked what was going on, and was told it was Newland Wake. I believe that was the last observance of it ... There was not to my knowledge any mock mayor on that occasion ...

George Herbert wrote in *Shoemaker's Window* (1973) that the latest comer to Newland was chosen as mayor, and that the maces were made from the largest cabbages available with the leaves stripped off the stem. After the mock mayor had been chaired round Newland there were races, with a gaudy waistcoat as prize for the men and a smock or a gown-piece for a woman. The last mock mayor was elected around 1860.

## Old Headington

W. H. Jewitt mentioned a mock mayor in the village situated on the outskirts of Oxford:

We had a mock-Mayor of the village, chaired on men's shoulders, in a bower of evergreens, round its confines on the Wednesday of Whitsun week. This gentleman was generally in a state of doubtful sobriety, having imbibed before setting out 'not wisely, but too well', as had his bearers; and a call being made at each public house (some three in number) and fresh potations indulged in, it may easily be imagined that towards the end of their perambulation most of the performers were more than slightly obfuscated, indeed at times it resulted in a broken limb for the unfortunate recipient of mayoral honours.

*The Antiquary*, 1910

Headington is an untypical place to have a mock mayor, having existed in Anglo-Saxon times, its inhabitants not disenfranchised, or particularly impoverished.

## Oxford

Mock mayormaking was done by a particular group of people in Oxford, the Lower Freemen of the City, who elected a mayor of 'Sloven's Court' which became corrupted to 'Sclavonian'. On election days, it was the job of the court to detect any non-freemen (who were not entitled to vote) in the Town Hall and bring them before the Lord of the Court who sat in one corner wearing mock-regal costume. Any outsider was fined at least sixpence. If the offender refused to pay his fine he was 'cold-burned' – a bucket of cold water was poured down his sleeve.

The *Oxford Times* described the court on 28th August 1886: the 'Court' had thirteen members, corresponding to the officials of the old corporation. John Cooper, born around 1800, who performed the role many times into old age, wore a maroon robe trimmed with white fur at neck and sleeves, and a tawdry crown.

The Lower Freemen attended the Riding the Franchise of the actual Mayor of Oxford, round the city boundaries, providing planks and boats for crossing rivers and ditches. In 1886 the King of the Sclavonians was greeted by the Corporation mace-bearer, Mr Hosier with the words: 'I have great pleasure in offering you the hospitality of the Corporation of the City of Oxford, according to ancient custom and usage, wishing your Majesty a longer life even than you have at present enjoyed, and health and happiness to the last.'

The Mayor of Oxford's officials then provided wine and spirits and gingerbread and all drank to the success of the City of Oxford.

David Steel, in *Riding the Franchise* (1991), commented that in 1984 the Mayor, on Riding the Franchise, 'was received by the King of the Sclavonians at the Free Water Stone near Long Bridges bathing place. This part of the ceremony was not originally an aspect or riding the franchise, but it became a standard feature in the 19th century. The 'King' is a

221

Freeman, usually a waterman, and can best be described as a mock mayor who issues a ritual challenge to authority rather perhaps in the manner of a court jester.'

## Woodstock

Woodstock has an unusual history in that Old Woodstock was probably founded (in the parish of Wootton) to rehouse people ejected by Henry I to enlarge his park. The town of Woodstock was founded by Henry II in 1163 on the opposite bank of the River Glyme. The two were not completely joined until 1887.

It is not known when mock-mayormaking first took place, but it probably predates the mace carried, which bears the inscription: 'This mace was made at the Sole expense of Charles Llewellyn Perkins Esq., Mayor of the ancient village of Old Woodstock – Anno Domini 1786.'

Adolphus Ballard described the custom in the 19th century, practised on Old Woodstock feast day, the Monday after the first Sunday after September 19th, saying that it died out some years before he wrote *Chronicles of the Royal Borough of Woodstock* in 1896:

In the morning there used to be a cricket match and sports, followed at mid-day by a dinner at the Rose and Crown public-house; after dinner the Mayor was elected, and in the evening he was chaired down Old Woodstock and round New Woodstock, stopping at all the public-houses on the way.

Frequently his retinue finished the proceedings by dropping him into the River Glyme at the bottom of Old Woodstock Hill.

Drinking was an integral part of the event and the mayor was notoriously chosen because he was the biggest drinker. Perhaps partly because the two Woodstocks were combined, and partly because drunkenness was increasingly frowned on, the custom declined towards the end of the 19th century but revived in 1910. As the original mace was missing a new one was made from a holly stick entwined with a large cabbage stem, topped with a coronet. The custom lapsed again in the late 1920s and was revived in 1954. The Rose and Crown has remained the venue. The mayor wore a robe made from a red blanket, a chain of office made from curtain rings, and a top hat. Members of his 'Council' mostly wore bowlers and women wore gowns and mortarboards borrowed from an Oxford college. The procession was confined to Old Woodstock, ending as before with a ducking in the Glyme. In 1958 the ceremony was combined with electing a Beauty Queen and holding a flower show.

In 1956 the 18th century mace was found, but not used until 1957 as it required repair. The first woman mock-mayor, Miss K. Castle, was elected in 1956, but was excused a ducking on the grounds of infirmity, and delegated the job to her deputy.

In 1993 the Town Crier introduced the Abingdon Morris men to the assembled crowd at the Rose and Crown at 6.30p.m. After they had danced the candidates for mayor stood in turn on a beer crate and made their electoral addresses, many of which had a comic bent: Edward Saxton apologised

**Opposite**:
**Above**: Candidates at the Old Woodstock mock-mayormaking in 1992 included Carole Simpson, who declared that she had dreamt that the next Olympic Games would be held in Blenheim Park, and promised to promote this.

**Below**: Mel Williams took up the current burning issue: whether or not Woodstock should have a by-pass, and proposed to tax vehicles driving through the town according to the number of wheels they had, then rode off on a unicycle!

Photographs: Christine Bloxham

for having had to postpone the election a week because of bad weather, and said that he had booked a good day with God for the following year. Carole Simpson said she had dreamed that the next Olympics would be held in Blenheim Park. Mel Williams complained about the traffic problem and promised to tax vehicles coming through the town according to the number of wheels they had – and rode off on a unicycle!

After the speeches a secret election was held among the Councillors inside the pub and onlookers were told to watch for the black smoke (which did not actually appear) – a parody on papal elections. The crowd was entertained by morris dancing during the election. Then the new mayor, Edward Saxton, gave a short speech before processing down the hill to the Black Prince and he and others swam across the Glyme to the Woodstock bank and back. The party walked back to the Rose and Crown for a barbecue.

# Harvest Home

**In late summer the harvest was gathered in: the celebration began on** August 1st with Lammas Day, when loaves made with the first of the new season's corn were traditionally blessed. The custom has largely lapsed, but Ellen Ettlinger wrote in the Oxford and District Folklore Society *Annual Record* (1962) that in 1947 the Vicar of Wardington revived Lammas Eve celebrations, decorating the church with sheaves and corn ears from the first two farmers to have cut their corn.

Harvest was the busiest time in the farming year, and upon its success depended the village's prosperity for the coming year, and perhaps because of this importance it was a time for ritual belief and superstition until the pattern changed in the late nineteenth century as machinery took over from men in the harvest field.

In *Lark Rise to Candleford* Flora Thompson gave a vivid picture of harvest in the 1880s, when sail reapers were beginning to appear in the fields, but had not yet threatened men's jobs. She wrote that a Lord of the Harvest was chosen in many villages, who often negotiated a special contract with the farmer for the duration of the harvest. At Cottisford he was known as 'King of the Mowers':

> For several harvests in the 'eighties they were led by the man known as Boamer. He had served in the Army and was still a fine well-set-up young fellow with flashing white teeth and a skin darkened by fiercer than English suns.
>
> With a wreath of poppies and green bindweed trails around his wide, rush-plaited hat, he led the band down the swathes as they mowed and decreed when and for how long they should halt for 'a breather', and what drink should be had from the yellow stone jar they kept under the hedge in a shady corner of the field. They did not rest often, or for long; for every morning they set themselves to accomplish an amount of work in the day that they knew would tax all their powers till long after sunset.

The men had to take advantage of the good weather, as rain during harvest could be catastrophic. Often the whole family would be involved: the children (in the days before regular summer holidays) would play truant from school and come and make straw ropes, which the women used to tie round the sheaves cut by the men. The men worked with sharp sickles or bagging hooks, so the Lord played a vital role keeping them working at a steady pace well away from each other to avoid accidents. At Drayton St Leonard they said that the women could earn enough in the harvest field to keep their children in clothes for the year. Many farmers were superstitious about not beginning to cut the corn on a Friday (an unlucky day to begin any new task).

E. H. Binney wrote about a custom he witnessed at Culham in the 1880s:

Mr J. G. Frazer in *The Golden Bough* quotes (ii, 264) an expression used in the north-east of France: 'When a harvester, through sickness, weariness, or laziness, cannot or will not keep up with the reaper in front of him, they say "The White Dog has passed near him", "He has the White Bitch", or "The White Bitch has bitten him".'

I remember when living at Culham, near Oxford, some fifteen or twenty years ago, hearing almost exactly the same expression used by (among others) a labourer whom I know quite well, and who used it at haytime of anyone who was lazy in the hayfield. My impression however, was that the saying was 'He has <u>lost</u> that little White Dog', and accordingly I took the opportunity of seeing the man in question at Culham this last December asking him what the expression was and what it meant. At first he could not remember much about it, and was inclined to think that the form 'He has lost the little White Dog' was the phrase used, but on my happening to see him again a few days later he told me he had since remembered it all, and the usual expression was 'He's got the Little White Dog'... They used to say it sometimes in haymaking, chiefly at harvest and daytime and 'when the weather's hot' of a lazy man, or 'one as wouldn't work'; but the expression was sometimes used on other occasions. It is still in occasional use I understand. Some say 'The Dog got 'old of 'ee, you know', that means you can't get to work. Again they say sometimes 'the Lawrence got 'im'; it means just the same thing ...

*Folklore* Vol 13, 1902

The last sheaf of corn cut in the field was significant, as it was supposed to represent the Corn Spirit. It was always carried back to the farmyard with great solemnity. At Ducklington, and probably other places, it was done with great theatre too:

On the last night of the harvest, when the last load was to be carted, it was the custom to send down to the field a number of band-boxes containing women's dresses and a good deal of finery for the men and horses.

Four young men then dressed themselves up, two to represent women, and they sat in couples on the four horses that drew the load. Some of the village children sat on the top of the load ... and on reaching the house were treated to cakes etc.

The old farmer himself was bedridden and lay on the ground floor of the house. On these occasions, his bed was drawn up to the window and the wagon stopped in front of it for the old man to see, but as the window was small they had to stop three times for him to see both pairs of horses and the wagon. After this, I believe, the men had a supper.

Clara J. Jewitt, *Folklore*, Vol. 13, 1924

At Sandford the farmer provided a gallon of beer to greet the last load when it arrived back at the farm. A song was often sung as the last load wound its way back, such as:

Harvest home! Harvest home!
Merry, merry, merry harvest home!
Our bottles are empty, our barrels won't run,
And we think it's a very dry harvest home!

Flora Thompson, *Lark Rise to Candleford*

This suggested that they would welcome a drink which the farmer happily provided! Another, from Long Hanborough, suggested they were looking forward to the harvest home:

Hip, hip, hip, harvest home,
A good plum pudding and a bacon bone,
And that's a very good harvest home.

Angelina Parker, *Folklore*, Vol 24, 1913

At Bicester the men shouted 'Harvest home!' as the load progressed back to the farm, and the locals tried to throw buckets of water at them, according to Dunkin's *History of Bicester*.

After the last load was safely in, the church bells were rung to announce that gleaning could begin – the women went into the fields and picked up all the corn stalks left there. It must have been back-breaking work, but it was a valuable perk as with luck they could gather enough to keep them in flour over the winter.

Many people, Mrs Avery of Rotherfield Greys remembered, would gather a 'luck sheaf', a bundle of all the different types of corn they could find, which was hung on the wall to bring good luck and plenty for the year, then replaced with a new one after the next harvest. This is a simplified form of the sheaf made from the last corn to be cut, which was placed in the barn or the farmhouse, sometimes dressed in women's clothes, over the winter, and ploughed back into the fields in the spring to keep the spirit of fertility on the farm. This is also the origin of the corn dolly.

Shortly after this the harvest home dinner was held. It could perhaps be a poignant as well as happy affair, as many of the agricultural labourers were employed on yearly contracts, and would the next day leave the farm, head off for a few days well earned holiday, then attend the nearest hiring fair looking for work, so it would be the last time that that group of people got together.

Flora Thompson vividly described the occasion, and how many people went without breakfast to do justice to the feast:

And what a feast it was! Such a hustling in the farm-house kitchen for days beforehand; such boiling of hams and roasting of sirloins; such a stacking of plum puddings, made by the Christmas recipe; such a rapping of eighteen-gallon casks and baking of plum loaves would astonish those accustomed to the appetites of today. By noon the whole parish had assembled, the workers and their wives and children, to feast and the sprinkling of better-to-do to help with the serving. The only ones absent were the aged bedridden and their attendants, and to them, the next day, portions, carefully graded in daintiness according to their social standing, were carried by the children from the remnants of the feast. A plum pudding was considered a delicate compliment to an equal of the farmer; slices of beef or ham went to the 'better-most poor'; and a ham-bone with plenty of meat left upon it or part of a pudding or a can of soup to the commonalty.

Long tables were set out of doors in the shade of a barn, and soon after twelve o'clock the cottagers sat down to the good cheer, with the farmer carving at the principal table, his wife with her tea urn at another, the daughters of the house and their friends circling the tables with vegetable dishes and beer jugs, and the grandchildren in their stiff, white, embroidered frocks, dashing hither and thither to see that everybody had what they required... It was a picture of plenty and goodwill.

It did not do to look beneath the surface. Laura's father ... used to say that the farmer paid the men starvation wages all the year and thought he made it up to them by giving that one good meal. The farmer did not think so, because he did not think at all.

Flora Thompson, *Lark Rise to Candleford*

Many harvest songs were sung. Angelina Parker (op cit) quoted:

Oliver Cromwell lies in his grave,
Um, ah, dead in his grave.
There grows a green apple tree over his head,
Um, ah, over his head.
The bridle and saddle are laid on the shelf,
Um, ah, laid on the shelf.
If you want you may sing it yourself,
Um, ah, sing it yourself.

Another favourite harvest song was sung at Hanborough:

Here's a health unto our master,
The founder of the feast.
I pray to God with all my heart
His soul in heaven may rest;
And that everything may prosper,
Whatever he takes in hand;
For we are all his servants,
And all at his command.
*Chorus*: Then drink boys, drink,
And see that you do not spill,
For if you do, you shall drink two,
For 'tis our master's will.

Here's health unto our misteris,
The best in one and twenty.
Heigho! is it so, is it so, is it so!
Fill him up a little fuller,
For methinks he seems but empty,
And down let him go, let him go, let him go.
And if he drinks too deep,
He can go to bed and sleep,
And drive away dull sorrow, care and woe.
*Chorus*.

Of course, a little bit of the drink would be 'accidentally' spilt to get more! After dinner there were sports, games and dancing. Harvest suppers like this were held on almost every farm.

Mr Norris, who farmed at Swalcliffe, gave a harvest home for his employees, who were each allowed to invite two friends. Servants such as the butler, coachman, head gardener and others came with their wives. A fiddler supplied music for dancing in the courtyard, and supper was held in the hall. Such dinners ceased in the late 19th century as machines took over from men in the fields.

The first harvest service was devised by George Denison of East Brent, Somerset in the mid-19th century. They rapidly became popular: the church would be specially decorated, with a special sheaf-shaped loaf in pride of place, often, like the one at Westwell, eventually sent to a local hospital. Mollie Harris described the harvest festival at Ducklington in the early 20th century:

The almost bare sanctuary suddenly sprang into life, stooks of wheat greeted us as we entered, outsized marrows filled the windows, onions, leeks and apples were heaped on every ledge, great bunches of Michaelmas daisies and giant dahlias nodded from earthenware jugs, and an unusual crowd filled the pews...

Mollie Harris, *A Kind of Magic*

In many villages a parish harvest supper was organised to replace the one previously held by the farmer, such as this one which Patrick Wise of Burford described to John Simpson of Radio Oxford when talking about harvest suppers at Grafton near Clanfield when he was a child:

They were always a great occasion and eagerly looked forward to by all. It was the one time when the whole of the farming community really got together for a good time. Early on the appointed day some of the farmers and their men would put up a couple of marquees in one of the paddocks. One tent was for the children. During the afternoon the ladies would start bringing the food to put on the trestle tables. There were all kinds of meat and pastries – beautiful home-cooked produce... The children's tent contained oceans of jelly and custard! As evening approached supplies of beer would be stacked up behind a trestle table bar in readiness.

Around teatime everybody would turn up and hang around chatting, waiting for the 'off'. The proceedings were always started by the local vicar saying a few appropriate prayers and then leading us all into a harvest hymn.

Having done his part, the Vicar would join us all at the table and the eating would start. It was the time for a real good blow-out – and next door in the children's tent the jelly was very soon flying through the air! ... Eventually the chattering, eating, drinking and jelly-throwing would start to slacken – and this was the time for everyone to do his or her party piece.

There was always a good singer or two around to belt out 'The Farmer's Boy', and 'The Grandfather Clock', which everybody joined in the choruses. Usually there was a budding Laurence Olivier to do 'a little recitation' on the lines of 'Albert and the Lion' and/or 'There's a little green-eyed idol...'. One of my favourites was a kind of broomstick dance done each year by the late Mr Bobby Hatton... And so the evening wore on, singing and recitations continued as long as there were people to do them, and the more thirsty of the community kept the volunteer barman busy... It was great. It was a way of life that died as I watched it.

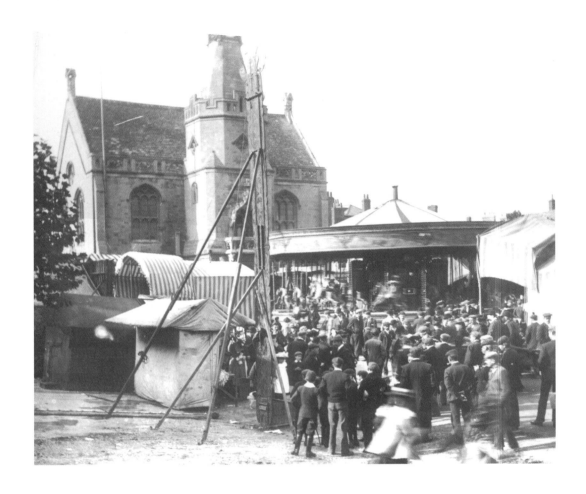

# Fairs and Wakes

As I was going to Banbury,
Upon a summer's day,
My dame had butter, eggs and fruit,
And I had corn and hay,
Joe drove the ox, and Tom the swine,
Dick took the foal and mare,
I sold them all - then home to dine,
From famous Banbury Fair.

*The Cries of Banbury*, Rusher c.1843

**Fairs were an important element of economic life, and formed an** important aspect of the charters granted to towns. Traders often sold items unobtainable in the villages and even elsewhere in the towns and in the

**Opposite**:

A roundabout
outside the Town
Hall at Banbury
Fair.

Banbury Library

Middle Ages strangers, not normally permitted to trade in towns under Guild regulations, were given permission to do so for the duration of the fair. They were a good place to come and look for a new job if you were an agricultural labourer: the hiring aspect grew from the 14th to the 16th centuries, initiated by various Statues of Labourers. Even when these were repealed under Elizabeth I hiring continued, and was still found in the late 19th century.

Gradually the commercial aspect decreased, but the recreational side remained important, as fairs provided one of the few organised entertainments available. People thought nothing of walking ten or twenty miles to visit a local fair, and with the advent of the railways people came from much greater distances. Two hiring fairs a year were held at Abingdon, Bicester, Chipping Norton, Thame, Witney and Woodstock, and annual fairs in Banbury, Burford, Deddington, Watlington and Wheatley.

## Abingdon

As the former county town of Berkshire, Abingdon once boasted seven fairs: the Lent Fair (livestock), the Bull or Lombard Street Fair in May, the Ock Street Fair in June, largely a pleasure fair, St James' Fair in August (largely for lambs' wool), while the September fair featured livestock and cheese.

Hiring fairs were held at Michaelmas, the first on the Monday and Tuesday before October 11th (with a large pleasure element) and a Runaway Fair the next Monday. Those who were not satisfied with the arrangements made for jobs the first week could attend the 'runaway mop' the following week. Prospective servants and labourers stood outside the Red Lion waiting to be hired. A final livestock fair was held in December.

## Bampton

The main fair, on 25th August, was established by William de Valence in the early 13th century, and by 1848 when Dr Giles wrote about it in *History of Bampton* had an important pleasure element. At one time a second fair was held on 24th March, which included an ox roast.

## Banbury

Banbury, as the second largest town in Oxfordshire, had the privilege of holding several fairs, the dates of which have changed over the centuries. In 1698 they were held on:

Thursday after 12th Day
1st Thursday in Lent
Holy Thursday
Feast of Corpus Christi
Lammas Day

Fairs were at one time held at other dates; for example there was a medieval Whitsun week fair. Beesley, in his *History of Banbury*, wrote that the dates after 1836 were:

1st Thursday after Old Twelfth Day and three preceding Days (the Horse Fair)

Third Thursday in February
Third Thursday in March (important for hiring servants)
Third Thursday in April
Holy Thursday (largely a holiday fair by then, but previously for horses, cows and sheep)
Third Thursday in June – for selling stock
Third Thursday in July (the Wool Fair)
Third Thursday in August
Third Thursday in September
First Thursday after Old Michaelmas Day (important hiring fair, also for cheese)
Third Thursday after Old Michaelmas Day (cheese, hops and cattle)
Third Thursday in November
Second Thursday before Christmas (fat cattle fair)

George Herbert, in *Shoemaker's Window*, described the Twelfth Fair which was :

... a pleasure fair entirely, and there were a lot of shows and other amusements. In one of these shows was a 'camera obscura': this was quite a new sight at fairs and obtained a large amount of patronage, but in another part of the same show was a man dead with the small-pox, unknown to the people who visited it, and this was how so many caught the disease ...

Herbert's recollection was slightly wrong – the parish registers show that 73 people died of the smallpox after the Holy Thursday Fair in 1827, but it indicates the inherent dangers of infection.

Thomas Ward Boss remembered the fair in the mid-19th century, when the town was packed with wagons, carts and vans, and people who had walked twenty or thirty miles to visit:

The greater part of the domestic servants only left their places once a year, and this was therefore their only holiday of the year... All stood in the streets in groups, seeking new masters and mistresses, the farmers seeking grooms, wagoners, and shepherds, who stood waiting to be hired... Some had bunches of whipcord, horse-hair or wool in their buttonholes, which represented their respective callings. Dairy maids in those days were largely sought after... Such were the immense crowds waiting between the bottom of Butchers' Row and the bottom of Parson's Street that shopkeepers were compelled to erect hoardings in front of their windows to prevent the pressures of the crowd from breaking them. Hiring was a busy feature for several hours during the Fair, the usual time for the hiring contract being one year, the payment of one shilling over to the servant being the seal of engagement, which was as binding as the King's Shilling is when taken by the new recruit from the Sergeant; the forfeiture of this bond, except by mutual consent, was punishable by imprisonment.

Large refreshment booths were to be found in the Fair, and other parts of the town ...

*Reminiscences of Old Banbury*, 1903

It was considered indecent for the servant girls to consort with the men during the Victorian hirings, so they had to stand in an upstairs room in Parson's Street while the men continued to stand in the street.

When Arthur Jones attended Banbury Fair around 1910 he was entertained by Gage's Boxing Booth, Alf Ball's Wild West Show and a 'Biascope', steam yachts and side shows.

## Bicester

In the 18th century three hiring fairs were held here, one, founded in 1762, on the Friday before 20th June, later changed to October. The fairs were called Hiring, Runaway and Confirmation Fairs. Servants who had been hired pinned a bunch of grey ribbons to breast or shoulder, according to Blomfield. Sid Hedges quoted a little ditty about the hiring:

> Sally be gone to the Hiring Fair,
> Wanting a place below the stair.
> Sally be standing on Market Square –
> Good places going if you be there.
> If place don't suit her, what do she care -
> She can come back at the Runaway Fair!

*Bicester wuz a Little Town, 1968*

The day before the Summer Fair (5th and 6th August), it was announced by a procession including the bellman, collector of tolls, and fiddler. During the fair a sheaf of corn was carried through the fair, followed by a fiddler, which proclaimed the start of the harvest. In King's End inhabitants exercised their right to open 'bough-houses' selling drink, and staples were affixed to the houses to which the green boughs were fastened. It seems a strange time to hold a fair when the agricultural labourers would be busy with harvest.

## Bloxham

Bloxham, as a village rather than a town, was unusual in having a fair, but in the 17th century Dr Plot mentioned a Statute Fair there. *Travellers in Oxfordshire* (1675) gave more details:

> We were very merry at passing thro' a village called Bloxham, on the occasion of a meeting of servants for hire, which the people there call a Mop. This I christen'd by the name of a Jade-Fair, at which some of the poor girls began to be angry, but we appeas'd them with better words.
>
> I have observ'd at some of these fairs, that the poor servants distinguish themselves by holding something in their hands, to intimate what labour they are particularly qualified to undertake, as the carters a whip, the labourers a shovel, the woodmen a bill, the manufacturers a wool comb, and the like.

## Burford

The hiring fair was held on 25th September. Those wanting jobs stood outside the Tolsey. George Swinford commented that at the turn of the century carters carried a whip or wore horsehair, and groom-gardeners carried a piece of sponge. George Pratt Hambridge said that the farmers' wives questioned the servant girls and felt their arms to test their strength. It was apparently not considered seemly for girls to wear bonnets, so they usually went to the fair bare-headed in neat cotton frocks.

Shipton children once parted unwisely with their pennies to see 'the funniest sight you ever did see, the horse's tail where his head should be' – which turned out to be a horse tethered to a manger by its tail.

## Charlbury

Henry II granted Charlbury a fair in 1256, beginning on 14th August, and sent his glove annually as a token that the fair was open. Four fairs were held: a Horse Fair on New Year's Day, a cattle fair in Lent, Cow Fair in May and hiring fair at Michaelmas. Items for sale included Irish linen, Welsh flannels and stockings and Manchester cottons.

## Chipping Norton

Owen's *New Book of Fairs* (1775) listed fairs in Chipping Norton on 7th March, 6th May, last Friday in May, 18th July, 4th September, 8th November and the last Friday in November, which sold horse, cows, sheep, cheese and leather. However in the 19th century, the most important was the 'Mop' on the Wednesday before 11th October, not even mentioned a century before. Here the labourers carried emblems of their trades as usual, and we hear of milkmaids carrying milking stools.

## Deddington

An ox was roasted at the fair held the day after Michaelmas, for which up to fourteen beasts were slaughtered. Customers usually settled their butchers' bills that day. However the most famous fair was the Pudding Pie Fair held on 2nd November. It was announced at 4 a.m. by a watchman shouting 'Four o-clock in the morning, and a fine day for the Pudding-Pie Fair.' Then the town band processed round, stopping at various places, in the morning and the afternoon. The fair was divided into areas: stalls along one side of the Market Place, sheep in the Bull Ring and along Hoof's Lane (now Victoria Terrace) to the Pound, pigs in the middle of the Market Place, horned cattle in the High Street, horses opposite the King's Arms across the Oxford-Banbury Road (sometimes there were as many as 700 horses). Items for sale included leather and winter clothes.

The pudding pies, after which the fair was named, had an outer suet crust filled with boiled plum pudding. After baking the pies were very hard – which inspired a local saying that: 'You could tie a label to one and send it through the post a hundred miles, so hard it was.'

Mary Vane Turner described (*History of Deddington*, 1932) a legend that a King of England was travelling from Woodstock to Banbury and received appropriate local gifts: leather gloves from Woodstock, light cakes from Banbury and from Deddington a pudding pie, a cross between the two: like leather but meant to be eaten. William Course, a local baker, said:

'Deddington people were supposed to save up all the scrapings from the candle-dripping in the lanterns to put in the Pudding Pies.'

The fair was much in decline when George James Dew wrote about it in 1873 (*Oxfordshire Village Life*), but he said that in its hey-day it sold shoes, ready-made clothes, leggings, hats and horses. The pies have not been made since about 1926.

## Eynsham

A medieval edict set up a Pentecostal Fair to be held after a religious procession, which was probably a fore-runner of the Whit fairs. Hot smoked farthings were thrown to the crowd at the fair, and many undergraduates came out from Oxford.

## Faringdon

Horses and cattle were sold at a fair in February, a horse sale was combined with a pleasure fair at Whitsun, and there was a large Statute Fair in the middle of October, followed by a Runaway ten days later.

## Henley

The hiring fair was held on the Thursday after 21st September. In *A Guide to Henley-on-Thames* (1896) E. Climenson commented that the usual tokens worn by the labourers to indicate their jobs had largely been replaced by ribbon streamers. Previously tokens had been exchanged for the ribbons once the men were hired. Entertainments in the 19th century included Wombwell's Menagerie, and stalls sold gilded gingerbread and brandy snaps.

## Nuneham Courtenay

As a small village, Nuneham Courtenay was not entitled to a genuine fair, but an entertainment fair was held in the 19th century:

It was held in the large meadow between the hill and the river. People for miles around would drive through the Park, and there were hundreds of empty vehicles all round the Conduit.

Thousands of visitors went from Oxford and Abingdon by house-boats, barges, and rowing-boats of every description, and for miles around many would walk to this annual outing.

It was a fair of the usual character of the time, booths, shops, cheap-jacks, snuff-boxing, skittles, and other forms of rough amusement. It was ultimately suppressed, I believe, on account of damage sustained by the lawlessness of the rougher elements.

'An Old Freeman', *Early Recollections of Oxford*, 1900

## Oxford

Oxford once boasted several fairs. The Gloucester Green Fair held on May 3rd was also known as St George-in-the-Castle Wake. It was held in

Crowds in St Giles
enjoying the
variety of
entertainments on
offer at St Giles
Fair c. 1904.

Oxfordshire
Photographic
Archive

Broken Hayes, the open space between Oxford Castle and Beaumont Palace until this space began to be encroached around 1660 when the fair was pushed northwards.

Another fair was held in St Clements in late September, which had almost died out by 1927. St Frideswide's Fair lasted for seven days in the Middle Ages, during which the canons of St Frideswide governed the town. At the dissolution of the monasteries the fair was granted to Christ Church, who later sold it to the town, but it died out in the 16th century. There was also a May or Austin fair.

St Giles' Fair, the only remaining fair in Oxford, said to have been held for over 800 years, takes place on the Monday and Tuesday after the first Sunday after St Giles' day, 1st September. It is not a charter fair; it originated as Walton Wakes, a parish feast in Walton manor, situated outside the city boundary and owned by Godstow Abbey. At the dissolution the rights passed to St John's College (which still receives fees from each stallholder). In the 16th century traders sold cloth, crockery, ironmongery and agricultural produce, and there was plenty of food and drink. Over the years it changed to a pleasure fair.

*Jackson's Oxford Journal* of 10th September 1887 reported that one could buy: '... baskets, glass and china ornaments, cheap tools, sweets, gingerbreads, cakes etc., while there were scores of barrows on which were fruit, mostly apparently of a wholesome description, cocoa nuts, hedge nuts, cheap jewellery, photographs, ices, canaries and other cage birds,

St Giles' Fair c. 1910. People came from miles around, dressed in their best.

Photograph: The Oxford Stamp Centre

braces, gilding fluid, potato peelers, name stamps, and other things too numerous to mention.'

Food of all descriptions was for sale, including cakes, chitterlings, fig cake, fried fish, gingerbread, ices, mussels, sausages and tripe. All sorts of novel items were on display, almost like a mini 'Great Exhibition', with demonstrations of riband making, delights such as glass clockwork humming birds and more practical pieces such as Norton's patent incubator. From the 1860s-70s fairground entertainments began to be mechanised and larger roundabouts were possible, together with steam yachts. In the 1880s a 'Sea-on-Land roundabout' appeared ('sailing boats' pitching round on a tramway), then a trapeze railway, a Switchback and in 1895 a Channel Tunnel Railway. Gradually the strolling players, the waxworks and marionettes disappeared, to be replaced by bioscopes. Sideshows included the ever-popular coconut shies, hoopla and shooting galleries, and there were menageries and freak shows.

In the early 20th century crowds of people turned up in the Woodstock Road on Sunday to see the fair paraphernalia waiting to be let into St Giles. Crowds also came at five o'clock on Monday morning to 'see the fair in', and by six thirty the coconut shies were in action and by eleven the rides were working.

There was a dispute with gypsies, who were banned in the late 19th century, leading to a plaintive rhyme 'Mr Mayor, O Mr Mayor':

What have we
Gipsies done or said,
That you should drive us from the Fair
And rob us of our 'customed bread?

237

Dread not the name, good Mr Mayor,
No more the witches' power we claim;
But still we are the Muses care,
And Oxford poets guard our fame.

You welcome lions to the Fair,
Tigers and Monkeys, Punch and Fool;
Then suffer us Another Year,
To hold there our Gymnastic School.

Meanwhile, farewell, good Mr Mayor,
Your frowns dismiss, resume your smiles;
We'll leave off cheating – take to prayer,
And claim thy patronage – St Giles.

*Jean Harrowven, Origins of Rhymes, Songs and Sayings, 1977*

The fair was not held during the first and second world wars, but was revived in 1945. It causes annual disruption to Oxford as major city centre roads have to be closed to accommodate it, but is still a magnet for local people, particularly the young.

## Thame

Fairs were held on 11th October (Old Michael's Day) and the Tuesday of Easter week – the latter was for selling stock, and a pleasure fair, and the former for hiring and for selling horses, particularly black cart colts from Lincolnshire.

## Wallingford

The Michaelmas Fair was held on the last Wednesday in September. The *Berkshire and Oxfordshire Advertiser* wrote in 1904:

In the rush for positions when the Kine Croft was opened ... the narrow streets resounded with the puffing of traction engines, the rattle of horses' hoofs and the crack of innumerable whips... [Waiting to be hired stood] sons of the soil, with sponge or whipcord in their hats ... By midday most of the men were sporting ribbons announcing... their engagement with a new employer.

In 1884 the entertainments included an ugly Zulu and an extraordinarily tall American woman, a photographer's studio, shooting galleries, coconut shies, gingerbread and toy stalls, roundabouts and swingboats, jewellery stalls, cheap johns and the usual array of food.

## Wantage

The town had four fairs, the largest being the Statue fair in mid-October, where cheese and hops featured large, along with domestic items and clothing. A cattle fair was held at Easter, the May Fair specialised in cheese and horses and a Cherry Fair held in mid-July sold locally produced fruit.

Entertainments were often up to date, but it would have taken a lot to beat George Sanger's Peep Show at Wantage Fair in 1833. In *Black Wantage* (1971) Kathleen Philip described how on the night of August 30th barmaid Ann Pullin, age forty, was serving in the Red Lion. One of her customers, George King, a hedger, threw her a coin, which dropped to the floor. When she refused to pick it up King lunged at her with a bean-hook and decapitated her. George Sanger was in the pub that evening and he and his father sat up all night to recreate the murder in a peep show for the fair the next day, which proved very popular.

## Witney Feast

The Feast is believed to be over 750 years old, and was the highlight of the year. It originated not as a fair but as a religious festival commemorating the dedication of the church, and a sermon was usually held in St Mary's on the eve of the Feast, which starts on the Monday after 8th September. It used to be held on Curbridge Down, but moved to Church Green around the 1860s. In 1869 the mass of stalls sold fashionable clothing and second-hand clothes, cakes, fruit, gingerbread, toys, gypsies sold baskets and snuff boxes and cheapjacks shouted their wares. Entertainments included Singer's Royal Wax Works exhibition, Mr Moreland's Theatricals, two cosmoramical exhibitions (which had replaced old-fashioned peep-shows), photographic saloons, and the usual roundabouts etc. There was boxing and dancing. Learned pigs appeared a year later, with a two-headed boy and an armless woman. In 1883 waxworks featured Queen Victoria, biblical scenes such as Daniel in the Lion's Den, and Hamlet. Although it has

Witney Feast has probably been celebrated for over 750 years. Here stalls and swing boats are in evidence.

Photograph: Oxford Stamp Centre

# Minute of Contract of Hiring.

Name of Master *Chas Wakefield* Residence *Langford Downs*

Name of Servant *Philip Winfield* Residence *Filkins Downs*

Hired for *12 months* from *Oct 11th 1918 to Oct 11th 19.*

WAGES *55/- per week*
*and 1 pence drilling money.*

To serve as a *Carter & to do anything else required*
*of him.*

☛ To Work in Haymaking and Harvest as long as required.
If Absent from illness, or other cause, Wages to be deducted.

This agreement is made especially subject to the said
receiving from last Employer a Character satisfactory to the said

Signed { *Chas Wakefield* — Master.
{ *Philip Winfield* — Servant.

Dated *Oct 3rd 1918*

*Ernest money //*

G. D. Halliday, Stationers, Wood Street, Swindon

Contract of hiring, when Philip Winfield of Filkins engaged himself to work as a carter for Charles Wakefield of Langford in 1918.
Christina Hole Collection

decreased in size and importance, it is still an important entertainment in Witney.

## Woodstock

Children used to scramble for pennies on Fair Monday. A pleasure fair still visits the town.

## Wychwood Forest Fair

Witney Feast became notorious for rowdy behaviour and crime in the late 18th century which encouraged the Wesleyans to set up a rival entertainment at Newall Plain near Charlbury on Wake Day. It became established and was known as the Forest Fair. Once over 20,000 attended, enjoying a menagerie, various shows, theatrical performances, a dancing saloon, boxing and stalls, not unlike the Feast. It was patronised by the Duke of Marlborough and his family, but after about fifty years it too became rowdy and the Duke banned it. It was famous for the fabrics sold there.

Charlbury Street Fair is said to be the successor to the Forest Fair. It is an annual event used to raise money for the upkeep of the Corner House and the Memorial Hall. In 1978 the tradition of electing a Fair Maid of Wychwood was revived.

## Village Feasts

Many parishes held annual feasts to commemorate the patronal festivals of the church. They tended to be grouped around Whitsun or from August to November, often beginning on Sunday and continuing for several days. By the 18th century they had lost much of their religious significance, nodded to by a sermon on the Sunday, and had become an occasion for feasting and entertainment.

The Berrick Salome Feast was held on 29th September: at one time it was notorious for the throwing and eating of crab apples. R. E. Moreau wrote (*The Departed Village*, 1968) that at Berrick and nearby Roke similar attractions were found:

There were swing-boats, cheap-jacks, a roundabout, donkey-rides. Usually the roundabout was operated by a man working a crank-handle, but once or twice an ancient steam one turned up.

Banbury Jack used to sell Banbury cakes.

Flora Thompson remembered the Cottisford Feast. On the Sunday:

... strangers, as well as friends, came from far and near to throng the houses and inn ... the big ovens were heated and nearly every family managed to have a joint of beef and Yorkshire pudding for dinner. The men wore their best suits, complete with collar and tie, and the women brought out their treasured finery ... Half-a-crown, at least, had been saved from the harvest money for spending at the inn...

*Lark Rise to Candleford*, 1939

A hundred or so people came from Brackley and nearby villages to participate. The men returned to work on the Monday, but the women and children continued celebrating – many tea parties were held, the chief delicacy being dough cake, which was made for them by the baker, using their own ingredients which he added to his dough. Entertainments included swingboats and stalls. By the end of the 1880s the only relic of the feast was an old woman who turned up with her stall, selling gingerbread babies and various sweets. However Rev. Rayner Smith wrote that it continued until 1914, and that it commemorated the English victory at the battle of Crecy in 1346.

Flora also wrote about the feast at 'Candleford Green' which was probably based on the one at Fringford. As Fringford was a much larger village than Cottisford, the feast was correspondingly more elaborate:

It was essentially a people's holiday. The clergy and the local gentle-people had no hand in it. They avoided the green on that day. Even the youngest of country-house parties had not yet discovered the delights of hurdy-gurdy music and naptha flares, of shouting oneself hoarse in swing-boats and waving paper streamers while riding mechanical ostriches...

For those who liked feasts there were booths and stalls and coconut shies and shooting-galleries and swingboats and a merry-go-round and a brass band for dancing. All the fun of the fair, in fact. From early morning people poured in from the neighbouring villages and from Candleford town...

There were plenty of sweethearts on the green on Feast Monday ... the girls in their best summer frocks, with flowers or feathers in their hats, and the young men in their Sunday suits, with pink or blue ties.

*Lark Rise to Candleford*

At Launton the feast took the form of a roast meal at the Black Bull in August. It was a popular day to have children baptised.

The Souldern Feast was held on the first Sunday after September 18th:

Open house was kept from Saturday till Monday; rich plum puddings were made and joints of beef cooked by all who could afford them, and the poorest cottage had its cake and bottle of home-made wine. Relations and friends from all parts flocked in, old friendships were renewed, and old differences made up.

*Historical and Descriptive Notes of the Parish of Souldern*, Oxford Archaeological Society, 1887

The feast at Uffington took on a far more physical aspect, being a day for wrestling, back-swording and fighting as well as eating and drinking. Stalls of traders and cheapjacks were set up in the field next to the church. There were peep-shows and attractions such as boa-constrictors, pin-eyed ladies and wild Indians, according to Thomas Hughes in *Tom Brown's Schooldays*. Many children who worked away from the village came home for the feast, and housewives prepared home-made wine and cake for visitors.

Wendlebury Feast was held the day after the Harvest Thanksgiving service in the middle of September, until about 1930:

There used to be a grand tea given then in the old club-room of the Red Lion Inn, which was gaily decorated with flags and evergreens for the occasion. Everyone went to this, men, women and children; the children paid three pence each and the adults sixpence. We drank our tea out of half pint mugs that had once belonged to the old Wendlebury Club, and ate huge slabs of dough-cake and vast quantities of currant buns. After the meal was over, sweets, an orange, and an apple were given to everyone present. Then we played games on the cricket-field as long as the daylight lasted, and when dusk fell, we returned to the club-room. The men had arrived by then, and we had singing, in which we all joined, to the strains of an old accordion played by Mr Day of Little Chesterton. Nuts were thrown around the room, and what a scramble there was for them! Sometimes there were enough eatables left over for a sing-song on the following Tuesday and Wednesday nights.

Mrs Samson, *Oxfordshire and District Folklore Society Annual Record*, 1950

Village feasts have not completely died out, and at the Millennium many villages made an effort to organise more communal activities.

# Halloween and Guy Fawkes' Night

**Halloween was not widely celebrated in Oxfordshire, but it was** generally associated with the feast of the dead, and the gap between our world and the spirit world was thought to be at its narrowest.

From around the early 19th century children in many villages, including North Leigh and Great Tew, hollowed out vegetables such as turnips and swedes into the shape of skulls, cutting out holes for eyes, nose and mouth. They put candles inside to make them lanterns, and they were either carried around or put on gateposts, as they were supposed to frighten away ghosts. Pumpkins and mangolds were also used, which Mollie Harris said were often stolen from the fields. North Leigh children jokingly divined the future of their love lives by placing nuts on the hearth – if two nuts burnt together, they believed that their love would flourish.

In the latter part of the 20th century the American idea of trick or treating became established in Britain. It had reached Eynsham by 1978: children asked householders whether they wanted a trick or a treat and if they replied 'trick', produced a pack of cards. However, if the door was closed on them they chucked a clod of earth at it.

At Bampton the brave – or foolhardy – occasionally went to the west door of the church at midnight on October 31st and believed that they would see a procession of all the seriously ill people in the village entering the church, and that those who did not come out again would die within the coming year. A variation of the hempseed divination described earlier was sometimes performed, and a separate divination was done in Oxford:

> On All Hallow's Eve young women who wish to see their future husbands act as follows. The house is brilliantly lighted up before midnight. Two girls then lay a table for four people, two places for themselves, two for the future husbands. A sheet is then hung over the door, and a meal is prepared over the fire in the room. On the stroke of midnight the sheet will be moved aside, and the husbands come in, sit down, take up the knife and fork at the two empty plates, and partake of the meal. They must not be spoken to.

Percy Manning recorded this (MS Top Oxon d.199) from a woman who had tried it out – the result is not recorded.

## Guy Fawkes' Night

Bonfires have been lit on November 5th since the early 17th century. They commemorate the narrow escape of James I and his Parliament from

Bates.        R. Winter.    C. Wright. J. Wright. Percy.    Fawkes.    Catesby.    T. Winter.

**Portraits of the Conspirators in Gunpowder Plot.**

Halloween bonfires were mostly transferred to November 5th after the discovery of the Gunpowder Plot, a supposed Catholic conspiracy to blow up King James I and the Houses of Parliament in 1605. This engraving of the conspirators is from John Brand and Henry Ellis, *Observations on Popular Antiquities*, 1841

being blown up when Guy Fawkes and his fellow Catholic conspirators planted gunpowder underneath the Houses of Parliament. Guy Fawkes was captured in the cellars underneath Parliament, tortured and executed. Parliament decreed that November 5th should be celebrated as a public holiday on which bells should be rung, cannons fired and a service of thanksgiving for the deliveration of the King and Parliament held in every church.

Anthony Wood recorded the events of November 5th in Oxford in 1692:

Gunpowder treason. Mr [Robert] Michel of Trin. Coll. preached. A picture of the pope, with the king of France on his right, and father Peters on the left hand, carried about Oxon from dore to dore upon a stage to be seen by all. Money given at every dore to defray the charge of 4 li. that it cost. At night illuminations in all streets and but few bonfiers. This is the first of Novembers that hath illuminations in windowes. The colleges have bonfiers. Musick at At Marie's after sermon.

ed. Andrew Clark, *The Life and Times of Anthony Wood*, Vol. III

This emphasized the dislike of the Pope and reflected the conflict between France and Britain at that time. It was common practice to burn an effigy of the Pope as well as Guy Fawkes. In the 18th century Pointer wrote in *Oxoniensis Academia* that it was the custom for undergraduates of Pembroke to write verses on November 5th, one copy of which was pinned up in the hall, the other given to the Master; a speech was given before supper.

Over the centuries the night became notorious for riotous behaviour, when the rougher elements held sway. Boys went round begging for – or demanding – wood for bonfires, chanting a rhyme. One Oxfordshire rhyme which gave the history was:

The fifth of November,
Since I can remember,
Gunpowder, treason, and plot;
This was the day the plot was contriv'd
To blow up the King and Parliament alive;
But God's mercy did prevent
To save our King and Parliament.
A stick and a stake for King James' sake?
If you won't give me one,
I'll take two,
The better for me,
And the worse for you.

This was recorded by Pointer in 1749 and by Halliwell, who added:

This is the Oxfordshire song chanted by the boys when collecting sticks for the bonfire, and it is considered quite lawful to appropriate any old wood they can lay their hands on after the recitation of these lines. If it happen that a crusty chuff prevents them, the threatening finale is too often fulfilled. The operation is called 'going a progging', but whether this is a mere corruption of 'prigging', or whether 'progging' means collecting sticks (brog, Scot. Bor), I am unable to decide.

*Popular Rhymes*, 1849

Another Oxfordshire rhyme was:

Let gunpowder plot
Never be forgot.
A stick and a stake.
For King George's sake.
A faggot, a faggot, a faggot.
If you don't give me one, I'll take two,
The better for me and the worse for you.
Hammer and block, beetle and wedges,
If you won't give me a faggot,
I'll cut down your old hedges.

Angelina Parker, *Folklore*, vol 24, 1913

This would originally have referred to King James, and the name changed with subsequent monarchs. Most villages had their own version of the rhyme. The one from Bampton was:

Gunpowder Plot
Shall never be forgot.

This lantern is believed to be the actual 'dark lantern' carried by Guy Fawkes into the cellars below the Houses of Parliament. It has a door which can be pulled across to hide the light from the candle without extinguishing it. It is now displayed in the Tradescant Room of the Ashmolean Museum, Oxford.

Photograph: Ashmolean Museum

A stick or a stake
For King George's sake,
Pray Dame,
Give me a faggot,
If you don't give one,
I'll take two;
The better for me
And the worse for you.

Percy Manning, 'Stray Notes on Oxfordshire Folklore', *Folklore*, vol 14, 1903

The version in Headington, where around 1900 a particularly unpopular local publican was burnt in effigy, was slightly different again:

Remember, remember,
The fifth of November
Bonfire night.
We want a faggot
To make it alight.
Hatchetts and ducketts,
Beetles and wedges,
If you don't give us some,
We'll pull your old hedges,
If you won't give us one,
We'll take two;
The better for us,
and the worse for you.

The Beckley version was slightly less threatening:

Don't you know, 'tis the fifth of November,
Gunpowder Plot?
We've come to beg a stick or a stake
For King George's sake.
If you won't give us one, we'll take two.
Then ricket a racket your door shall go.

Percy Manning, *Folklore*, Vol 14, 1908

The rhyme in the nearby village of Charlton-on-Otmoor went:

The fifth of November since I can remember,
Was Guy Faux, Guy,
Poke him in the eye,
Shove him up the chimney-pot and there let him die.
A stick and a stake for King George's sake,
If you don't give me one, I'll take two,
The better for me and the worse for you.
Ricket-a-racket, your hedges shall go.

*Oxfordshire Archaeological Society Reports*, 1903

In the early 20th century small boys from Charlton, sometimes wearing masks and carrying turnip lanterns, came round singing the rhyme.

Islip parish accounts have a reference in 1700 'for ringing on gunpowder treason, 2s 6d'. The rhyme, recorded here around 1750, with changes in the name of the sovereign, is;

The fifth of November
Since I can remember,
Gunpowder treason and plot;
This is the day that God did prevent,
To blow up his King and Parliament!
A stick and a stake
For Victoria's sake;
If you won't give me one
I'll take two:
The better for me and the worse for you.

John Brand, *Observations on Popular Antiquities*, 1849

Edith Miller (*The History of the Village of Islip*, 1930) wrote that the children begged for money to buy fireworks and held their bonfire party in the school playground.

Ian Yarrow, in *Berkshire Scrapbook*, recorded two rhymes which were probably known in the Vale of White Horse:

Guy Fawkes, Guy – 'twas his intent
To blow up the Houses of Parliament;
By God's mercy he got catched,
Wi' his dark lantern and lighted match.
Guy Fawkes, Guy, – zet up high,
A pound o' chaze to chawke un,
A pint o' beer to wash ut down.
And a jolly vire to ro-ast un.
Up wi' the pitcher an' down wi' the prong,
Gie us a penny an' we'll be gone.

The dark lantern referred to has a panel which can be pulled across to hide the light from the candle without extinguishing it, and is currently on display in the Tradescant Room of the Ashmolean Museum. The other rhyme conjures up the most wonderful image of the tiny figure of Queen Victoria:

Our quane's a valiant zawljer,
Car's her blunderbuss on her right shawlder,
Cocks her pistol, drays [draws] her rapier;
Praay gie us zummit vor her zaayke yer.
*Chorus*: Holler bwoys, holler bwoys, maayke yer bells ring,
Holler bwoys, holler bwoys, God zaayve the Quane.

Bonfires were a common feature in most towns and villages. The one in Charlbury was in the Playing Close. Several bonfires were lit in Blewbury. There are few references to fireworks, which may have been too expensive, but Mollie Harris spoke of having a few sparklers. At Iffley in the early 20th century the boys begged for money as well as wood, and bought fireworks with it. North Hinksey children got together a few pennies to buy fireworks to go with their bonfires.

Guys were another matter – boys dressed guys in any old clothes they could beg, borrow or steal, and took them round when they were begging for wood. Once, according to Edward Cordrey (*Bygone Days at Iffley*, 1956), the Iffley guy was taken to Donnington Farm and suspended between the shafts of an upturned dung cart, then the boys ran off to the carter's house and pretended a man was hanging there. A female neighbour went to look and rushed home screaming, so the guy vanished rather fast and was taken to Iffley Turn where it was laid on the verge to resemble a corpse. It was seen by the people on the horse-bus and as Mr Wilson the schoolmaster tried to move 'the body' it fell in half! One guy in Oxford in the latter 19th century represented an unpopular Alderman.

George James Dew described bonfire night at Lower Heyford over the years. In 1864:

A bonfire in Grantham's field near to the upper turnpike road at 7 o'clock. Mr W. King gave most of the faggots etc. of which there were above two waggon loads. We had a tar tub on a long iron rod, but the flames did not reach it because of the wind. It was a tremendous blaze and could be seen for many miles around ... The fiery sticks after the fire had burned down were thrown about in all directions; I myself as busy as any of them but hands very sore afterwards.

ed Pamela Horn, *Country Life in the 1860s*

In 1867 he wrote that the fire was at 'Grass Seeds', and that after it 'fire balls were swung about and glass bottles charged and exploded.' Two years later he commented on detonators and fog signals being let off. In 1872 there was no bonfire, 'but the ringers gave us a peal instead. I fired some seven and twenty cartridges from my pocket revolver in remembrance of 'Gunpowder Plot'.' In 1976 there were several bonfires and sounds of explosions.

The Shilton bonfires were erected near the school, and later in the cricket field, built up bit by bit in the weeks before, and made up of all sorts of materials such as garden rubbish and cardboard.

In Burford bonfires were erected opposite the Tolsey, and the rougher elements took charge. Muriel Groves was told by her father (*History of Shipton-under-Wychwood*, 1934) that tar barrels were rolled down the hill, pushed with long sticks, and when the local doctor objected to the noise, they deliberately rolled one against his door, shouting all the louder. Tar barrels were also used in the violent struggles between Witney gangs. In the early 19th century these fights, which sometimes began as football matches, were between gangs who lived north and south of the river. In Grove too there were fights up and down the street.

Oxford has suffered over the centuries from fighting between town and gown, and November 5th provided a good excuse. In 1835 shop windows were broken by undergraduates, who stole objects from them to take back to their colleges in triumph, and the next morning the Mercury Fountain at Christ Church was clogged with shop fittings and stolen items. Worse was to come: Mervyn Prower, a student of Brasenose, was stabbed to death in 1857, after the shock of which life calmed down, although Oxford remained notorious:

The streets of Oxford used to be the scenes of great encounters between the townsmen and gownsmen (or college students) on this night, who on any other night in the year, never thought of fighting. Happily in recent years these fights have ceased, but even now the gownsmen are 'gated' on the night of the 5th of November i.e. are confined to their colleges, lest there should be a renewal of these encounters. So severe were the battles in ancient times, that the tower of Carfax Church was lowered because the townsfolk used to ascend thither and shoot their arrows at the undergraduates, and the butchers were obliged to ply their trade beyond the city walls, because they had used their knives and cleavers in their annual fight.

P. H. Ditchfield, *Old English Sports*, 1891

# Christmas Past

**The celebration of Christmas has changed enormously over the** centuries, from the medieval era when the Lord of the Manor gave his villeins, who enjoyed a break of twelve days at this time, a feast (which they mostly provided themselves, as they were obliged to bring him a gift of produce), to a complete ban during the Commonwealth of the 17th century. In the 19th century it became a family-based celebration, which it still is today, although it has become far more commercialised recently.

## Advent

Preparations for Christmas began at the end of November, with the making of the Christmas puddings. The collect for the service held on the Sunday nearest St Andrew's Day (30th November) contains the words 'Stir up, stir up, we beseech thee, O Lord, the wills of thy faithful people, that they plenteously bring forth the fruit of good works...' and housewives have taken this as an indication that the Christmas puddings should be made by then, or immediately afterwards.

The Christmas pudding we know today dates from about 1670, although even then it contained meat. Often puddings were so large that the only way of cooking them was by wrapping them in a muslin bag and boiling them in the washing copper – hence the name 'bag pudding'.

Making the Christmas pudding was a family activity. Often poorer families saved money each week in a Slate Club, which was shared out around the end of November, when the ingredients for the mincemeat could be bought. Isabel Colquhoun described the process at Brightwell-cum-Sotwell:

> Of course the dried fruit did not come packed in cartons, all ready washed. It was bought loose, wrapped in blue paper shaped like a cone, and very much mixed up with grit, so much time had to be spent on cleaning it.
>
> First it was washed in two or three lots of water. Then it was spread out on a tin tray and dried, usually on top of the hob. Candied peel came in big pieces with large lumps of the sugar clinging to it. How we loved to 'pinch' a piece of this while mother's back was turned ... Then the raisins had to be stoned ... what a job. We always had a basin of water and a damp piece of rag on which to wipe our fingers constantly, as, with a knife, we slit open each raisin and got out the stone.
>
> Then there was the suet to be grated ... and the breadcrumbs to be made, the orange and lemon peel to grate and the juice to be extracted. How we loved the smell of all these preparations! Lastly mother would give us a few coppers to go to The Lion for a half-quarter of brandy for the mixing. Everyone present had to stir the pudding and make a wish. If funds allowed, one or two silver threepenny bits, or sixpences were dropped in...

*Pit, Pat, the Pan's Hot*

## St Thomas' Day

December 21st is the feast of St Thomas. It was chosen as a day on which the poor, particularly the elderly, could beg from their richer neighbours. The practice has not been widely recorded in Oxfordshire, but it was a custom among poor widows in Uffington, where it was called 'mumping'.

A special sermon was preached in Taynton that day, and loaves were distributed to the poor. At one time they were thrown down from the church tower and people scrambled for them, according to *Oxfordshire Archaeological Society Reports*, 1905.

The Charity Commissioners recorded in 1825 that at Yarnton a quarter of barley was provided each year by Lord Dynevor, the Lord of the Manor, to make cob loaves. These were traditionally given out to poor children from the parish of Burford in church, when a special sermon was preached, but the children made such a riot that from 1811 the cobs were distributed in a stable.

## Christmas Princes

In the Middle Ages a 'prince' or 'lord' was often elected from the lower orders to preside over merrymaking and ceremonials at the royal court, among the aristocracy, at the Inns of Court and at Oxford and Cambridge colleges. It may have descended from the Roman Kalends custom, celebrated in January, which turned the orders of society topsy turvy and featured men dressing in women's clothes. It was closely related to the Feast of Fools (where the lower orders of clergy 'let their hair down', electing one of them, to whom they gave grandiose titles, to 'rule' the feast, while they dressed in women's clothes and masks, sang and diced) and Boy Bishops.

The custom of electing boy bishops can be traced back to the 10th century: the choirboys chose one of their number as bishop, often on St Nicholas' Day, December 5th, who remained in office until Holy Innocents' Day, December 28th. The ceremonial, processions and services were conducted in a sober and reverent way, and if the boy died in office he was buried with the regalia and ceremony of a real bishop. Boy bishops were chosen at New College, All Souls and Magdalen Colleges before the Reformation.

The Lord of Misrule was a different character – his job was to mastermind revelries from New Year until Twelfth Night. He was usually elected at Halloween and ruled until Candlemas (February 2nd). 'Christmas kings' were elected at Christ Church, Magdalen, New College and St John's, according to Charles Edward Mallet (*A History of the University of Oxford*, vol. 5). The 'Rex Fabarum' at Merton College was mentioned by Anthony Wood:

From the first foundation of the College every year on the Vigil of St Edmund's Day [19th November] the juniors of the Society gathered round the fire in Hall to elect a King of Christmas or Misrule, the 'Rex nostri regni Fabarum'. The outgoing Rex despatched letters under a seal purporting to be sent from some place abroad, and his envoys appeared 'duly robed' and delivered them to the Bachelor Fellow.

These then, standing, sometimes walking, round the fire, there reading the contents of them, would choose the senior fellow that had not yet borne that office, whether he was a Doctor of Divinity, Law, or Physick, and being so elected had power put into his hands of punishing all misdemeanours done in time of Christmas, either by imposing exercises on the juniors, or putting into the stocks at the end of the hall any of the servants, with other punishments that were sometimes very ridiculous. He had always a chair provided for him, and would sit in great state when any speeches were spoken or justice to be executed, and so this his authority would continue till Candlemas.

*Annals of the University of Oxford*

The reference to a chair indicates his status, as most people sat on benches or stools at that time, and chairs were reserved for the most important people present.

Another midwinter custom at Merton was that of 'Regent's Fire' or 'Ignis Regentis', when a regent master would hold a feast for masters and bachelors, accompanied by wine and a magnificent fire and entertainments. The last reference to this was in 1516. A King of the Beans used to be chosen for Twelfth Night, the last one being Jason Heywood, but this ended in 1557.

Trinity College elected a Christmas Prince. The audit book of 1559 has a disbursement for 'pro prandio Principis Natalicii'. A Christmas Prince was elected at Christ Church, and the last one in Oxford was at Magdalen College in 1619.

Percy Manning reconstructed the proceedings at St John's College in 1607 from *An Account of the Christmas Prince as it was exhibited in the University of Oxford in the year 1607* (MD Top Oxon d.199). Proceedings began on October 31st when the fire was lit in the college hall and the Christmas sports began. A quarrel broke out between a second-year student and a freshman and the meeting broke up. The quarrel was resumed the next day and it was suggested that they should choose 'a Christmas Lord or Prince of the Revells, who should have authority both to appoynt and moderate all such games and pastimes as should ensue, and to punish all offenders'.

The motion was carried and a prince was elected. OnNovember 5th a meeting was held to discuss the Prince's rule and raise a subscription to defray the expenses of the revels. The Prince was installed in office on November 30th, St Andrew's Day, and the play *Ara Fortunae* was performed.

On December 21st the Prince's officers were proclaimed and given burlesque titles. The Prince's privy chamber was formally furnished, complete with a carpet (extremely expensive at that time and usually used on tables rather than floors) and a chair of state, with a cloth of state, the symbol of royalty, hanging over it.

On December 25th the Prince was attended to dinner by all the Bachelors and gentleman ushers and he was served a feast of twenty dishes, beginning with the boar's head, carried to table by the tallest of the guard, wearing an empty faucion scabbard held on by a green scarf, accompanied by an attendant with a boar spear, and a huntsman attired in green with 'bloody faucion drawn', two pages dressed in sarcanet taffeta, each carrying a 'messe of mustard'. The leader of the procession sang a boar's head carol, with the last three lines of each verse repeated by the company:

The boar is dead,
Loe, heare is his head,
What manne could have donne more
Then his head off to strike
Meleager like
And bring it as I do before.

He living spoyled
Where good menn toyled
Which made king Ceres sorry,
But now dead and drawne
Is very good brawne,
And we have brought it for you.

Then sette down ye Swineyard
The foe to ye Vineyard,
Lett Bacchus crown his fall
Lett this Boare's head and mustard
Stand for Pigg, Goose and Custard,
And so you are welcome all.

December 27th. The Prince's friends presented a masque or morris.

December 29th. The Tragedy of Philomela was performed (postponed from the previous day).

New Year's Day. Richard Swinnerton, the Prince's squire was sent to the President with the gift of a pair of gloves. charged to say merely: 'The Prince and his counsell in signe of their Loves Present you their President with these paire of gloves.'

The play, *Time's Complaint*, was performed.

The Prince's rule carried on past Twelfth Night (which had no special events).

January 10th. Private performance of *Seven Days of the Week*.

February 2nd. The Scholars decreed that the Prince should stand down. A masque was performed.

February 6th. Egg Saturday. Dancing.

Shrove Tuesday. The Prince resigned. A final play was performed – *Ira sen Termulas Fortunae*.

The Prince's honours were buried and the Prince himself appeared as his own chief mourner, dressed in a scholar's gown.

The Prince that year was Thomas Tooker, who later became a canon of Bristol. It was the first time a Christmas Prince had been elected at St John's College for thirty years, and it was done with great enthusiam. Tooker was endowed with a stream of titles, parodying those claimed by genuine monarchs, based on places in Oxford: 'The most magnificent and renowned Thomas, by the favour of Fortune, Prince of Alba Fortunata, Lord of St John's, High Regent of the Hall, Duke of St Giles's, Marquis of Magdalen, Landgrave of the Grove, Count Palatine of the Cloysters, Chief Bailiff of Beaumont, High Ruler of Rome [a piece of land on the north of Oxford], Master of the Manor of Walton, Governor of Gloucester Green, sole Commander of all Titles, Tournaments, and Triumphs, Superintendant of all solemnities whatsoever.'

## The Boar's Head

In the Middle Ages royalty and aristocracy dined on exotic dishes such as swan and peacock (brought to the table magnificently dressed, complete with feathers, looking like living birds), but the most splendid dish was the boar's head. In Oxford the tradition of serving the boar's head has been continued at the Queen's College since the late 14th century – payment for wild boar appears in the accounts for 1395-6.

There is a picturesque legend attached to the origins of the ceremony. It is said that in the Middle Ages a student of Queen's by the name of Copcot took his Greek textbook (writings by Aristotle) and decided to study in Shotover Forest, a royal hunting forest. He was immersed in his book and did not notice that a wild boar was galloping towards him through the undergrowth. Suddenly he heard the noise and looked up to see the boar approaching fast. It was too late to climb a tree or run away, so with great presence of mind Copcot shoved his text book into the open jaws of the boar, exclaiming, 'Swallow that if you can!' The boar cried out 'Graecum est!' ('This is all Greek to me!'), as it choked to death. It is said that the college in gratitude for Copcot's miraculous deliverance held a boar's head feast. However it is far more likely that a feast was held because the college was kept open at Christmas. The college was founded by Robert d'Eglesfield, a native of Cumbria, who decreed that many of the students should come from Cumberland and Westmoreland, so it would be almost impossible for them to travel home for Christmas.

John Pointer mentioned the custom in 1749:

Another Custom is that of having a Boar's-Head or the figure of one in Wood, brought up into the Hall every Year on Christmas-day, usher'd in very solemnly with an old song, in Memory of a noble exploit (as Tradition goes) by a Scholar (a Tabarder) of this College, in killing a Wild Boar in Shotover-Wood.

*Oxoniensis Academica, or the Antiquities and Curiosities of the University of Oxford*

Whatever its origins, the custom has survived. Pointer's comment on the use of a wooden head is interesting, as during the Second World War, when a boar's head was unobtainable, a papier mâché one was substituted. Henry Taunt described the ceremony around 1900:

And now for the Christmas day festivity. It is only half-past five, but a crowd has collected at the entrance gateway in High Street, and another at the Porter's Lodge in Queen's Lane; ... the doors are opened at six promptly, and in file the

Bringing iu the Boar's Head at Christmas.

visitors from both entrances, all making for the Hall, where they quickly form a dense line on each side of the centre down which the procession will pass. At the further end is the High Table, on a dais, raised slightly above the rest of the Hall, and here are already gathered a number of ladies, friends and guests of the Provost and Fellows... the side tables and stools are soon occupied by a number of persons standing upon them. All classes are represented, dons and citizens elbow each other, with ladies intermingled everywhere and even the young are well in evidence.

The hall is prettily dressed with greenery; holly, and ivy, and laurel, are festooned all round and from picture to picture, whilst in the centre at the end over the Provost's chair, a larger garland is hung with a bunch of mistletoe below. A bright fire blazes in the great open fireplace in the side of the hall, and the incandescent burners furnish enough brilliancy to light up the scene and reveal the delighted faces of the visitors. Soon a procession, headed by the Provost, followed by the Fellows of the college who are in residence, makes its way up the hall and take the places behind the high table, when, all standing, the Provost recites the College Grace...

...In the buttery, another procession is forming, consisting of the Tabarder appointed to sing the Solo of the Carol, the choristers belonging to the college, with the men singers, and the servitors bearing the Boar's Head on its massive silver salver upon their shoulders. The trumpeter with his silver trumpet sounds the ... call twice... The murmur of the crowd in the Hall now dies into silence and every face is turned to the door when the sound of the Chorus, 'Caput apri defero,

A nineteenth-century engraving depicting the boar's head being brought to the table at a medieval Christmas feast.

Illustration from John Brand and Henry Ellis, *Observations on Popular Antiquities*, 1841

256

The Boar's Head ceremony at the Queen's College is one of the highlights of the year for the college chef. It has taken place since the fifteenth century. Here the chef is shown c. 1900 with the boar's head decked and ready to carry to high table, with an orange in its mouth and bearing the college flags.

Oxfordshire Photographic Archive

Reddens laudes Dominus' is heard outside, and, making their way between the throng of spectators, the Tabarder in front, with the bearers of the Boar's Head and choir following, they sing the Carol as they slowly walk up the Hall – each verse of the song being taken up and followed by the Chorus.

At the end of the Carol the dish with the boar's head is lowered and placed on the centre of the table in front of the Provost, while the choir and others crowd around; the Provost then takes the ornaments and three embellishments one by one from the head before him and presents them to the choir boys and visitors, the Solo singer of the year receiving the orange from the boar's mouth. When the ornaments are exhausted the crowd gradually diminishes, and the Provost, Fellows and their favoured guests, are left to enjoy their dinner.

*The Boar's Head at Queen's College*

The ornaments referred to were probably small flags with the college coat of arms and gilded sprigs of holly, mistletoe, rosemary and laurel (which are currently culled from the Fellows' garden).

The carol was already old when it was published by Wynkin de Worde in 1521:

The Boar's Head in hand bear I,
Bedecked with bays and rosemary,
And I pray you, my masters, be merry,
Quot estis in convivio.
*Chorus*: Caput apri defero,

Reddens laudes Domino.
The Boar's Head, as I understand,
Is the rarest dish in all this land,
Which thus bedecked with a gay garland
Let us servire cantico.
*Chorus.*

Our steward hath provided this,
In honour of the King of Bliss,
Which on this date to be served is,
In reginensi atrio.
*Chorus.*

The chef spends weeks preparing the boar's head, which can weigh the best part of a hundredweight on the plate. Taunt said it was first pickled in salt water for several days, cleaned off, immersed in salt water again, then soaked and cleaned, before being tied in a cloth and boiled in a large copper for several hours, then soaked in cold water. It was trimmed and glazed, an orange put in its mouth, a crown on its forehead, with small banners on either side, then once placed on the dish it was decked with bays or laurel and rosemary.

The date of the ceremony was changed in 1961 to the Saturday of the last week of the Christmas term, as few fellows were in residence over Christmas. It is now a private college function, so no outsiders crowd into the hall as in the past.

## College Customs

At All Souls' College it was customary for everyone who worked at the college to be given a mince pie on a plate decorated with the college coat of arms.

The Postmasters (Scholars) of Merton College had their own butcher. Pointer wrote that:

It is a custom for this Butcher of theirs, once a year, about Christmas Time, to invite them all to a Treat at his House; at which time he used to provide a Bull for the Steward (if he pleas'd) to knock down with his own hand, hence this Treat came to be called, The Kill-Bull.

## Christmas Evergreens

**Opposite**:
A postcard showing the boar's head being carried in procession to the high table at the Queen's College.

Photograph: The Oxford Stamp Centre

Holly and ivy, mistletoe bough,
Give me an apple, and I'll go now,
Give me another for my little brother,
And I'll go home and tell father and mother.

This rhyme was sung until about 1825 by Baldon children as they went from house to house, begging for evergreens and apples to decorate their houses and pence for Christmas. Evergreens have been used as midwinter decorations since ancient Egyptian times. Country people gathered them freely from the hedgerows, and townsfolk bought them at the market. They were never put up until Christmas Eve, and were taken down and burnt on 6th January.

John Aubrey wrote about a 17th-century custom:

In several parts of Oxfordshire, particularly at Launton, it is ye custom for the Maid servant to ask the Man for Ivy to dress the House, and if the Man denies or neglects to fetch in the ivy, the Maid Steals away a pair of his Breeches, and nails them up to ye gate in the yard or highway.

*Remains of Gentilisme and Judaisme, 1686*

This may reflect the old belief that smooth ivy symbolised woman and prickly holly man. Ivy was also used in Oxfordshire for divination – if a girl put an ivy leaf in her pocket she believed that the first man she met would become her partner, even if he was already married.

Bay leaves were also incorporated into decorations, as at Lower Heyford church in 1862:

Dec. 25 Christmas Day ... Heyford Church is more neatly decorated this Xmas than it has been before in my recollection. As you enter the church over the porch doorway is 'Emanuel' in large letters made of bay leaves. The front of the gallery has a border of evergreens with 'unto us a child is born' made of variegated ivy, the word 'Child' is on the middle panel and larger than the rest which gives it an appearance of neatness and good style. On the chancel arch is 'Glory to God in the highest' made of holly leaves.

ed. Pamela Horn, *Oxfordshire Country Life in the 1860s: the Early diaries of George James Dew*

Elaborate decorations did not always meet with favour, as they were thought to be too Catholic, and only four years later Dew commented that:

The decoration of the Church this Christmas is extremely simple, and more acceptable to the people than when it was so highly adorned. Last year in particular it was carried to excess ... There are this year wreaths (of holly, ivy etc.) round the heads of the two columns and on the four corbels of the nave arches, with one in the doorway of the chancel screen, and this is all excepting a few leaves in a recess in the north aisle...

Pamela Horn, op. cit.

Mistletoe was forbidden in churches, because of its symbolism as the sacred plant of the pagan Druids. However it was an essential ingredient of the kissing bough (the precursor of the Christmas tree, which did not become popular in England until the Victorian period) which was the chief decoration in many houses, with one kiss permitted for each berry.

The tragic legend of 'The Mistletoe Bough', enshrined in a 19th-century ballad, has been connected with the medieval manor house at Minster Lovell:

The mistletoe hung in the castle hall,
The holly bush shone on the old oak wall,
The baron's retainers were blithe and gay
Keeping the Christmas holiday.
The baron beheld with a father's pride
His beautiful child, Lord Lovell's bride;
While she with her bright eyes seemed to be
The star of that goodly company.
O, the Mistletoe Bough.

'I'm weary of dancing now', she cried,
'Here tarry a moment, I'll hide, I'll hide;
And Lovell, be sure thou'rt first to trace
The clue to my secret hiding place.'
Away she went, and her friends began
Each tower to search, each nook to scan.
And young Lovell cried, 'O, where doest thou hide,
I'm lonesome without thee, my own dear bride.'
O, the Mistletoe Bough.

They sought her that night, and they sought her next day,
They sought her in vain till a week passed away
In the highest, the lowest, the loneliest spot,
Young Lovell sought wildly, but found her not.
And years flew by, and their grief at last
Was told as a sorrowful tale long past.
And when Lovell appeared the children cried:
'See, the old man weeps for his fairy bride.'
O, the Mistletoe Bough.

At length an old chest that had long been hid,
Was found in the castle – they raised the lid;
And a skeletal form lay mouldering there
In the bridal wreath of a lady fair.
O, sad was her fate, in sporting jest,
She hid from her lord in the old oak chest.
It closed with a spring, and her bridal bloom
Lay withering there in a living tomb.
O, the Mistletoe Bough.

Several old chests have been sold at auction with the claim that they were 'the authentic' mistletoe bough chest. One is displayed in Greys Court, Henley-on-Thames. The story has been connected with several places, including Bramshill in Hampshire, Dalby Hall near Melton and Exton Hall, but in fact it comes from a 16th century Italian story, so has no basis in historical reality in Oxfordshire.

The White Hart in Old Headington was still hanging mistletoe on Christmas Eve in 1950, and decorated the inn sign with a garland. The

Magdalen Arms in Iffley Road used to hang a crossed hooped garland or kissing bough decorated with evergreens on its sign over Christmas.

Christmas is regarded as the festival of light, coming as it does in the darkest part of the year, so candles formed an important element of decorations. In Oxford people used to light a triad of candles in their windows on Christmas Eve as a symbol that any passer by was welcome to come in and partake of refreshments – this has echoes of the current custom of having Scandinavian bridges of electric candles in the window, but few would be so foolhardy today as to invite strangers into the house.

St John's College had a stone candle socket ornamented with the image of the Lamb of God on which the Christmas candle was placed on high table for the twelve nights of the Christmas festival.

## Christmas Music

Some carols date back to the Middle Ages, and new ones were published over the centuries, particulary in the 19th century. This encouraged a revival of carol singing: as well as singing in church, parties went round from house to house, not just the children who come round now singing a couple of verses, but groups of adults:

Dec 24... At Steeple Aston several parties came singing Christmas hymns and Carols at Miss Dandridge's kitchen door. One party consisting of a man with a concertina and several young women sang very nicely indeed. I gave them a fourpenny piece which I had in my pocket...

ed Pamela Horn, *Country Life in the 1860s*

Groups went round many villages, including Great Tew. In Adderbury around the 1830s and 1840s waits, made up from working-class men, went from house to house singing at Christmas. They sang post-Reformation carols rather than medieval ones and music was provided by the village orchestra which in the 1840s included violins, bass viol, flutes, a hautboy, serpent and clarinet, played by labourers and artisans. One of their carols, quoted by Michael Pickering in *Village Song and Culture*, was written by local man Tom Hayward, and entitled 'Adderbury Church':

All glory to God, and peace upon earth
Be published abroad at Jesus' birth;
The forfeited favour of heaven we find
Restor'd in a Saviour, the friend of mankind.

Our newly born King by faith we have seen,
And gratefully sing his goodness to men,
That all men may wonder at what we impart,
And joyfully ponder his love in our heart.

Then let us behold Messiah the Lord
By prophets foretold, by angels adored.

Let every believer his mercy adore
And praise him forever when Time is no more.

It is not known whether the waits hoped for monetary contributions, but poorer singers without musical accompaniment also went from house to house singing 'Good mortal men remember ...' which asks for alms in the words:

Good master and good mistress
As you sit by the fire
One ha'penny or one penny
As much as we desire.
All in joy! All in joy!
I hope you will remain
All in joy!

A bit o' your good wittles ma'am
And a drop o' your good beer
Will send you a merry Christmas
And a happy new year.
All in joy! All in joy!
I hope you will remain
All in joy!

Michael Pickering, op. cit.

The waits at Swalcliffe sang 'While Shepherds Watched their Flocks by Night' and 'Good King Wenceslas'. After the mid-19th century carol singing by adults mostly took place in church and the waits disappeared. The brass band at Shilton played for several social functions around Christmas, and on Christmas Eve went to the mansion at Bradwell Grove to play, then came back to Shilton and played 'Christians Awake' by the village pond. However children carried on going from house to house in small groups singing carols, as in Ducklington. At Iffley the choirboys went round singing carols over several nights.

Wassailing too goes back several hundred years. An early example was recorded from Henley-on-Thames on Twelfth Eve in 1555, when Henry Machin recorded in his diary (ed. J. Nichols, Camden Society, 1848) that party guests were entertained by 'twelve wessels with maidens singing, with their wessels; and after came the chief wives singing with their wessels; and the gentlewoman had ordained a great table of banquet, desserts of spices and fruit, as marmalade, gingerbread, jelly, comfit, sugar plate and divers others.' It is not recorded whether this was a private entertainment, or whether the women were going from house to house.

Wassailers went round the Vale of White Horse singing:

Wassail, wassail all over the town,
Out toast it is white, and our ale it is brown;
Our bowl it is made of a sycamore-tree,
And a wassailing bowl I will drink unto thee.

263

They carried round a large wassail bowl, which they hoped would be filled at each house with Lamb's Wool, a drink made from hot ale, sugar, spices, eggs and roasted apples, sometimes mixed with cream, with sippets of bread. A wassail bowl is preserved at Jesus College, Oxford.

Bellringing took place at midnight on Christmas Eve, often incorporated into midnight mass. A more recent service popular in many churches in the late 20th century (although it was first held in Moravia about 1747) is the Christingle, which is often used to raise money for the Children's Society. The children present are each given a candle symbolising the light of the world set in an orange (representing the world), with sweets and nuts impaled on cocktail sticks attached to the orange which stand for the harvests of the four seasons.

## Christmas Treats

Many farmers would reward their labourers by killing a bullock and giving each one some beef. This was the practice at Wytham, but on a larger scale:

An estate bullock was killed every year for distribution to everyone in the village on the basis of one pound of meat per person, men, women and children. The cuts were graded to some extent according to the social status of the receiver. The farmer, for example, could expect to receive a piece of sirloin and a piece of steak, and the cottagers would meet to compare notes as to what they had in their turn.

There was also the annual Christmas party for the children. This started with a meeting in the large servants' hall for tea at which invariably one or two people made themselves ill by eating or drinking too much. This was followed by a visit to the large Christmas tree in the main hall of the Abbey where Lord and Lady Abingdon and the children were present to distribute the presents.

G. R. L. Potter, *Life in a Berkshire Village*, 1970

Christingle services, which originated in Protestant Moravia in the mid 18th century, are now often held around Christmas to raise money for such organisations as the Church of England Children's Society. Children carry an orange (originally earned by giving donations to the poor), which represents the world, the candle is for the light of the world, the raisins on cocktail sticks represent the harvests of the four seasons. Here Richard and Peter Blanks are seen at a service held in St Andrew's Church, Headington in the mid 1990s.

Many children's parties were held in the villages. Alice M. Harvey recalled them at North Hinksey:

> Miss Toynbee ... often gave parties in the school and at Christmas there was a big Christmas tree loaded with presents. We had games and sang carols and afterwards all had sweets and oranges to take home. I remember one year especially – there was a big fairy at the top of the tree and all the girls wanted it. When it was time for the presents to be given we were all excited wondering what sort of present we would have. All the children had a present (thanks to the kindness of Miss Toynbee), however, this particular year three girls had been forgotten and I was one of them. So it was decided to put our names in a hat and the first girl's name to be pulled out should have the fairy doll, and that the other two would also have smaller dolls from the tree. We stood and waited and to my delight it was my name that came out first. I was very thrilled as I had not had a real doll before (only rag dolls that I had made myself at home).

*Memoirs of a Country Childhood, 1975*

## Christmas Eve

Many preparations for Christmas began surprisingly late to our mind: Mollie Harris wrote that it was not until her stepfather came home from work at six o'clock on Christmas Eve that her mother rushed off from Ducklington to Witney to buy the children's Christmas presents – the shops used to stay open until ten that night. The family made Christmas decorations at home from coloured paper and flour paste.

It was on Christmas Eve that the decorations were put up – mostly evergreens, and few poor families could afford a Christmas tree. However Jack Gibbard, the son of the village blacksmith at Great Tew, remembered making paper chains as a child around 1910, and his family had a tree lit by candles and decorated with glass baubles and sugar mice with a fairy doll on the top.

A Kingham woman remembered that around 1750 her grandfather used to stay up on Christmas Eve to see whether the animals would begin to eat, drink and talk. As the clock struck midnight the horses did eat and drink, but he heard no talking.

## Christmas Day

Poor children did not expect presents from anyone except their parents, and perhaps immediate family, but even though the contents of their Christmas stockings were meagre, they were much anticipated and enjoyed. Jack Gibbard's stocking was typical, with an apple in the toe, nuts and dates wrapped in coloured paper and a few small toys and an orange in the top. At Leafield Mrs Burrows remembered that in the early 20th century she was given a new handkerchief with a penny tied in the corner, plus an apple, an orange, nuts, sugar animals and small toys. One year she received a wooden peg doll, for which she made the clothes. Isabel Colquhoun recalled the excitement:

What a thrill ... to feel the stocking bulging with who knows what. I was supposed not to touch it until mother came in later and gave me a light, but excitement and curiosity often proved too strong and in the dark I emptied the contents and felt them to see what they were. Nothing very special, of course, but priceless treasures to me. Most stockings were filled with the same kinds of presents: an orange, an apple, a few nuts, dates and figs, some sweets, perhaps a new handkerchief or a piece of new hair ribbon, a hair-slide or an inexpensive brooch or bracelet, with often a halfpenny, penny or sixpence (what wealth!) in the toe. Simple things, but what delight they brought! And the children really believed in Father Christmas.

*Pit, Pat the Pan's Hot,* 1975

Some families attended church on Christmas morning, like Alice Harvey, dressed in her best clothes and shoes, carefully put out ready the day before.

Lower Heyford children often walked round to see Mrs Evans at The Beeches, who gave each child who visited a Christmas card and a penny. She gave each of her tenants a Christmas pudding.

The Christmas dinner was usually something special – beef, or, as in Mollie Harris' home, rabbit.

Flora Thompson recalled the quiet Christmases at Juniper Hill:

The men had a holiday from work and the children from school and the churchgoers attended special Christmas services. Mothers who had growing children would buy them an orange each and a handful of nuts but, except at the end house [her home] and the inn, there was no hanging up of stockings, and those who had no kind elder sister or aunt in service to send them parcels got no Christmas presents.

Still, they did manage to make a little festival of it. Every year the farmer killed an ox for the purpose and gave each of his men a joint of beef, which duly appeared on the Christmas dinner table together with plum pudding – not Christmas pudding, but suet duff with a good sprinkling of raisins. Ivy and other evergreens (it was not a holly country) were hung from the ceiling and over the pictures; a bottle of home-made wine was uncorked, and a good fire was made up, and ... they all settled down by their own firesides for a kind of super-Sunday.

*Lark Rise to Candleford*

A more festive time was had by widow Eliza Haynes who was born on Otmoor, and worked as a servant. After she was widowed she moved to Oxford to work as an under-scout at Oriel College. When she celebrated Christmas around 1900:

Christmas Day itself started with the ceremonial emptying of stockings, usually dates wrapped in coloured paper, an orange, apple and some nuts. The turkey came up to all expectations, a golden, sizzling creature now, on a big willow-patterned dish, after which the blinds were drawn and Eliza brought in a holly-topped, sugar-sprinkled pudding, which had been set alight with brandy ... Usually, there was a bottle of wine, or lemonade, according to taste, and the whole family stood for what was known to them as the family 'Toast'.

'Here's to them that we love,
And to them that love us.
Here's to all them that love them,
That love them, that love us.'

In the evening there were games, the favourite of which was 'Snap-Dragon'. Raisins spread on a large flat dish were fired with brandy, so that one was obliged to grab quickly from the flames as many raisins as possible. These were afterwards counted and the possessor of most raisins, awarded a small prize.'

Phyllis Surman, *Eliza of Otmoor,* 1976

At Eynsham people made their own entertainment and popular games in the early 20th century were Hunt the Slipper, Charades and Sardines. In Headington people went into their gardens at mid-day to look and see whether the sun shone through their apple trees – if it did they looked forward to a good crop the following autumn.

At Cumnor after evening service all the parishioners who were liable to pay tithes claimed the right of an invitation to the vicarage for bread, cheese and ale. According to Chambers' *Book of Days* the Vicar had to provide four bushels of malt brewed into ale and small-beer, bread made from two bushels of wheat and a hundredweight of cheese. Any food left over after the evening's entertainment was given to the poor the next day.

A similar custom took place at Kidlington:

Given and allowed out of the Vicaridge three quarters of beef, half a quarter or four bushels of Wheate, and half a quarter of Mault out of the Parsonage for the providing of a breakfast on Christmas Day in the morning, to be dressed and disposed of and spent at the Vicaridge House yeerely amongst the Parishioners of Kidlington.

Mrs Bryan Stapleton, *Three Oxfordshire Parishes,* 1893

# The Twelve Days of Christmas

**The twelve days began on Boxing Day, and continued until Twelfth Night, January 6th.** In the Middle Ages most villeins took a holiday over the twelve days, but this became eroded, particularly during the 19th century with the movement away from the land and the increase in industrialisation, with manufacturers anxious to keep their machines in use.

## Boxing Day: December 26th

This is the amalgamation of the feast days of two St Stephens: the early Christian martyr and a 9th century Swedish missionary who was the patron saint of horses. Horses were supposed to be especially well treated that day and were often bled to make them healthy. Perhaps because of this Boxing Day fox hunts were popular as shown in this article in the *Oxford Times* of 23rd January 1877:

> The fine frosty weather of Christmas Day was continued on Boxing Day, and as this is the most generally observed of the four Bank Holidays ... large numbers of pleasure seekers were able to avail themselves of a day's outing.
>
> From an early hour St Aldate's Street was crowded with pedestrians en route for 'The Fox' where it had been announced that the hounds would meet; and at the appointed hour several hundreds of lovers of this sport had congregated.
>
> This was the principal attraction during the day but the votaries of teetotalling were gratified by the visit of the Grand Lodge of England... The admirers of the histrionic ... were also able to indulge their predilection by a visit to the theatre where ... a French drama entitled 'The Two Orphans' was successfully placed on the boards.
>
> Christmas Day at the workhouse, with 'a feast which left nothing to be desired' was observed in the normal way... Then there was the annual dinner of destitute children...

However Boxing Day has acquired its name from the custom of emptying the poor boxes in the church that day and distributing the contents, and apprentices visiting their masters' customers to ask for tips. In Bicester the poor took matters into their own hands:

> ... immediately after breakfast on Boxing Day, many of the poor assemble together, in a body, visit the houses of the gentry and tradesmen to ask for a Christmas box. As they expect a penny for every adult and a half-penny for each child, the total number of applicants sometimes amounts to a hundred, for each family assembles in full strength.

J. Dunkin, History of Bicester, 1816

In Bampton the Parish officials, according to Dr. Giles in his *History of Bampton* (1847), 'with smiling faces, claim their Christmas boxes.' Giles also wrote about the St Stephen's breakfast held before enclosure in 1812:

> ... it appears that those who rented the tithes used to boil a large quantity of beef early on the morning of St Stephen's day, and send it, smoking hot, to the three vicarages, where it formed the centre of a large circle of farmers and others who were assembled to partake of the breakfast. What other solemnities accompanied the feast, I have not been able to ascertain, but there is no doubt that the rest of the day was devoted to jollification, and that no one, who had been in any way connected with the breakfast, ever conceived a thought of returning to his labour until the next morning.

December 27th was the feast of St John the Evangelist, the 28th Holy Innocents' Day, commemorating the massacre of small children by Herod. The feast of Thomas Becket was celebrated on 29th December, but there were no special customs for these days, or for 30th December.

## New Year's Eve

Preparations for the New Year were carefully organised, because it was thought that if New Year's Day was a good one, it would be followed by good luck for the rest of the year.

At Merton College Scrutiny Night was held on New Year's Eve:

> 'Tis a Custom on the last Night in the year, (call'd Scrutiny Night) for the College Servants, all in a Body, to make their Appearance in the Hall before the Warden and Fellows (after Supper) and there to deliver up the keys, so that if they have committed any great Crime in the Year, their keys are taken away and consequently their Places, otherwise they are of course deliver'd to 'em again.

At the opening of the Scrutiny, the Senior Bursar made this short speech:

> In hoc Scrutinio haec sunt proponenda, Mores Servientum, Numerus Portionistarum, Electio Hortulanorum.
>
> <div align="right">John Pointer, <i>Oxoniensis Academia</i>, 1749</div>

In ordinary homes people made preparations for the New Year. Some followed the Scottish custom of first footing: the idea being that the first person to enter the house after midnight on New Year's morning should be dark haired and carrying a piece of coal, a piece of bread or cabbage leaf, and either money or salt, to magically ensure that the family visited would enjoy warmth, food and wealth for the next year. Sometimes he also carried a sprig of evergreen to symbolise continuing life. An old man in Bodicote in 1954 said that as the bells rang in the New Year at midnight he went out and brought in some greenery, even if it was only a leaf, which is a similar idea. Leafield farmer John Simpson Calvertt recorded in 1888 that he brought an ivy leaf into the house on New Year's morning to bring good luck.

Bringing in fresh water from the well was also thought to bring good luck for the coming year.

Mrs Gasson from Kencott believed that people should bring in coal as soon as they came down on New Year's morning to ensure plenty for the year. She said that many people placed it on the doorstep in readiness the night before. A Chipping Norton woman in the late 19th century always organised for her dark-haired milkman to come first footing.

Good luck was encouraged in other ways: at Headington Quarry, Wootton, and possibly elsewhere, people danced round a candle at midnight on New Year's Eve, and if the candle was still alight at the end of the dance, they would enjoy good luck.

The boys of Burford greeted the New Year with a rhyme:

I wish you a merry Christmas, a happy New Year,
A pocket full of money, and a cellar full of beer;
A good fat pig to last you all the year,
Please to give me a New Year's Gift.

## Needle and Thread Ceremony, The Queen's College

The College was founded in 1341 by Robert de Eglesfield, who decreed that a custom in remembrance of him should be held each New Year's Day. It was described by Celia Fiennes in the 17th century:

There is a very odd custom in Queen Coll. for every new years-day there is a certain sum laid out in Needles and Thread which was left by the Founder, and every Gentleman of that Colledge has one given him with these words: Take this and be thrifty.

ed Christopher Morris, *The Illustrated Journeys of Celia Fiennes*, 1982

This is done as a rebus on the name of the Founder: 'aiguille et fil' or 'needle and thread'. A special dinner is held on New Year's Night, to which guests are invited, and each person present is given a needle and thread as described above. The *Oxford Times* of 1st January 1921 had a story about it:

The story goes that Henry IV, whose son Prince Hal was an undergraduate of somewhat riotous habits, complained to the authorities of the expense and wastefulness of the College. It is assumed that on this the Prince was sent for and admonished by the Provost, for on his next appearance before his royal father he presented himself with needles hanging from the eyelet holes of his doublet, a testimony, as the scapegrace must be supposed to have meant to the newly-learnt thrift and regularity of his habits. How his father took the joke is not recorded.

The Bursar, (the Rev. G. R. Cronshaw) observed the ceremony on Saturday night, and on approaching each priest inquired his degree, whether of Law, Medicine or Divinity. Needles threaded with silk thread - red, blue and black were then presented, a Doctor of Laws receiving a blue one and a Doctor of Divinity a black. He then uttered the time-honoured wish - 'take this and be thrifty'. Having completed the round, he handed to each guest the remaining threads that had not been claimed, and wished them a happy New Year. Each guest fixed the needle in the lapel of his gown, and winding the threads round it left the ends hanging.

The story about Prince Hal is spurious, as the ceremony was decreed by Robert de Eglesfield himself.

## Twelfth Night

The holiday continued until Twelfth Night, although with no special celebrations. January 6th was the Feast of the Epiphany, when the Magi were believed to have visited the Christ child, bringing word about him to the gentiles.

Riotous parties were held, a main feature of which was the cake, into which were baked a bean and a pea, the finders of which became the King and Queen for the evening. They were the main cakes baked over the festive period, rich fruit cakes decorated with icing, the precursor of the Christmas cake. Bakers in Oxford and other towns were justly proud of their Twelfth Night confections, one of the highlights of their year. They advertised in the local papers and filled their shop windows with cakes of various sizes, which they claimed would suit all tastes and all purses.

Parties seem to have declined in the late 19th century, but another Twelfth Night custom is still in force: taking down the Christmas decorations. At Spelsbury and many other places it was the custom for the evergreens to be brought in on Christmas Eve and removed on Twelfth Night. At Kencott the evergreens were always burnt to keep the Devil from the house.

The next day, it was back to work for the coming year.

# Mummers' Plays

**The mummers are still a familiar, if anachronistic, sight, in their** paper or theatrical costumes, performing around the Christmas period in Abingdon, Bampton, Headington Quarry and a few other places. The nature of the mummers' play, with its theme of death and resurrection and its swashbuckling hero such as Saint or King George fighting an enemy such as the Turkish Knight, together with its use of man-woman figures, suggest it goes back at least to the Middle Ages, if not being pagan in origin. Surprisingly there are no references to the play before the 18th century, as medieval references to mummers were not to this type of play. It seems likely that the plays flourished mostly during the 18th and 19th centuries, carrying on in a lesser way, and in some cases revived, in the 20th century.

Most villages had a version of the play, performed by labourers and artisans, many of whom were illiterate, so the text was passed down by word of mouth, often from father to son. This meant that it changed as people misheard words (for example the 'Turkish Knight' occasionally became the 'Turkey Snite', as in Headington Quarry), and there must have been ad-libbing as there is today, which gives the plays contemporary relevance. The Chadlington play, recorded in 1893, had gaps in the dialogue between Jack Finney and the Doctor, designed to be improvised. At Christmas 1990, on the brink of the Gulf War, the Abingdon mummers included extensive patter relating to Saddam Hussein, which had disappeared the following year. It is by changing in subtle ways like this that the custom retains relevance. Contemporary mummers have much patter around reviving the dead man, and employ all sorts of devices such as drenches, electric shock treatment from car batteries and even 'the pill' (i.e. a contraceptive!), and this part of the play can last several minutes.

The plays are short and informal, and like morris dances, tended to be performed in the street, or in private houses (and more recently in pubs) or in courtyards, not in a theatre. The performers sometimes created a space for a 'stage' by walking round in a circle as the play began.

The plays performed in Oxfordshire are of the hero-combat type (sword plays and wooing plays are found in other parts of the country), in which the hero meets his enemy, they fight, one is killed, the quack doctor revives the dead man, and various comic characters come on, with Father Christmas usually master of ceremonies. The actual characters varied greatly. In the Islip version, the oldest recorded in Oxfordshire, said to date from 1780, the master of ceremonies is Anno Domini, the combatants the Royal Duke of Blunderland (possibly suggesting some of the Georgian royal dukes?) and Earl or King Percy, accompanied by a Herald, Doctor Spinney, Salt Peter, Fat Jack, a Pedlar Chap and Father Christmas. In nearby

Kirtlington the enemy was the Duke of Thumberland. In Burford St George had to fight not only the Turkish Knight but the Dragon and other characters included the Giant and the King of Egypt. The Giant Blunderbore and Dragon appeared in another version labelled as 'Oxfordshire' (probably from Thame) with King Alfred, King Alfred's Queen, King William and Old King Cole. An Africky King appeared at Steventon, a French Officer at Brightwell, while in Bloxham the play was based on Robin Hood and Little John. St George often became King George – a compliment to the actual King Georges of England. The French Officer may have been a reference to the Napoleonic wars.

Sometimes the performers dressed in 'paper' costumes, with paper attached to smocks or shirts. In Long Hanborough the mummers used to go from house to house before Christmas asking for old newspapers and coloured papers. Disguise was important: Angelina Parker wrote in 'Oxfordshire Village Folklore' (*Folklore* 1913, vol. 24): 'When we saw them perform, it was a great part of the fun to guess who they were, for they were literally covered from head to foot with narrow strips of paper'.

At Brightwell-cum-Sotwell the mummers had costumes largely made from wallpaper, and blacked their faces. Percy Manning recorded (MS Top Oxon d.199) that the Kirtlington mummers wore rags and paper. Molly, the man-woman character, dressed as an old woman, wore a large cap and carried a broom, the Duke of Thumberland wore a paper coronet and carried a wooden sword, while King George had a paper crown and a wooden sword, Dr Good a dress coat, Mr Finney was clad as a broken-down gentleman, Beezlebub had a rabbit skin tied round his head and anything else he could lay his hands on which would give him an ugly appearance while another man dressed as the doctor's horse. The Aston Upthorpe and Aston Tirrold mummers wore paper-fringed coats, according to the *Berkshire Book*. A Cholsey resident told Steve Roud that each character made his own costume: 'using crepe paper and other old materials accordingly – for instance the person acting King George would make his own crown from cardboard and silver paper, and where a beard was necessary a part of an old woollen shawl would be shaped for attachment to the face – likewise the character using a sword or dagger would make his own from wood or stiff cardboard and cover with silver paper or paint.' (*Berkshire Mumming Plays: A Geographical Index and Guide to Sources*, 1991). The East Hagbourne mummers decorated long coats with paper, and wore hats decorated with crimped paper streamers. Paper costumes were worn over ordinary clothes at Stanford-in-the-Vale, where men did not blacken faces. Ribbons were added to the paper on Uffington costumes. At Islip mummers either wore masks or blacked their faces and tied hay bands round their arms and bodies, according to Brand's *Popular Antiquities*.

Sometimes the men acquired theatrical type costumes. At Drayton around 1930 James E. Vincent (*Highways and Byways of Berkshire*, 1931) saw the local mummers:

Into the hall walked a ploughman's boy, white bearded, in a tall hat and an overcoat of immemorial age, who reeled off a long speech in broad and rapid

Berkshire, of which the intelligible part was a fervent hope that 'Father Christmas won't never be forgot.' Next entered 'King George', and after him a 'knight from furring parts', both gaudily attired, partly in portions of cast off uniforms of the British army ... Followed a terrific combat with wooden swords, after the first bout of which King George fell, 'wounded in the knee', and grinning. But a doctor, summoned from without, after a recital of the merits of his medicines, some of them 'strong enough to kill any tu,' (sic) cured King George and bade him 'rise and foight thy foe agin'. So King George rose and laid about him with a will, until the foreign knight fell. Him, a stranger, fantastically attired, tended, and the combat ceased. Next came 'Merrian', a carter's boy with a shirt over his muddy corduroys, and bright blue eyes brimming over with fun, who recited at breakneck pace a number of lines, consisting, so far as they could be followed, of wild paradoxes. 'I zaw a cow black as snow' was one of the few phrases that could be distinguished, and then, upon modest largesse, followed singing.

The Clifton mummers performed in Deddington until about 1928, collecting money for local charities. Songs such as 'My Grandfather's Clock' were added to their repertoire, plus concertina playing and dancing. One character with a blackened face, playing Beezlebub, wore decorated flannel trousers and a beribboned top hat. In the 19th century the mummers had dressed in rags, and one character was 'Mother Wallopsee' who had a blackened face. Silk top hats were worn by the Great Tew mummers, who also had blackened faces. The Middle Barton mummers had accessories such as a metal helmet, and a top hat for the doctor. The Chipping Norton mummers 'all wore masks and dressed up very grotesquely' (Mrs Norgrove, *Birmingham Weekly Post*, 4th October 1884). The Ordish collection has a note that Beelzebub at Culham wore a tall hat, black coat (stuffed to give him a hunchback appearance) and carried a knobbed stick over his shoulder.

It is possible that some of the plays were derived from versions published as chapbooks, and adapted to local usage. Occasionally, as at Bampton, a play was 'created' for them: one written by Dr Giles, a 19th-century local historian, was performed in 1847. Giles wrote as an introduction to his text: 'The following verses are principally the author's own composition being written in imitation of what he remembers to have heard in Somersetshire many years ago, when Mumming and many other customs were still in use.'

He wrote a hero-combat play featuring St George and the Turkish Knight, with a doctor, Father Christmas, Robin Hood and Little John. Much of this became incorporated into the remains of the original Bampton play, giving it two fights, between King George and the Turkish Knight and King George and the Bold Slaughterer (it may originally have been between the King of Prussia and the Bold Slaughterer, as the former appears in a superfluous role). This was published by P. H. Ditchfield in *Old English Customs Extant at the Present Time* (1896). A third version was recorded from Bampton, Aston and Chimney by Alfred Williams about 1910 which is different again, featuring Father Christmas, the Valiant Soldier (Slasher), the Royal Russian King (who also calls himself the 'Turkish Knight'), the doctor and Jack Vinney.

The mummers performed at Bampton until the outbreak of the Second World War, and the play was revived in 1946. The men reviving it learnt their words from the pre-war performers. What they learnt was an almost complete version of Dr Giles' play, followed by a version similar to Ditchfield's version. It is obvious that the text in the late 19th century was fluid in character, with words being spoken by varying characters. The play has now been taken over by the Bampton morris men, who proudly perform it each year.

In some places such as Bloxham, when the mummers' plays fell out of favour around the time of the First World War, they were replaced by 'niggering'. There were strands of similarity between the two; Yvonne Huntriss has studied them (*Cake and Cockhorse*, autumn 1978) She wrote:

Mr William Woodford ... remembers seeing the mummers when he was a small boy [late 19th century] but cannot remember much about them except that they had handkerchiefs and ribbons and came round on Boxing Day. Mr. Preedy remembers that they came down the street on Boxing Day; some wore masks, those that had no masks had faces blacked with cork and candle. They were either four or five in number. He remembers that the first mummer would come across with a besom and sweep the doorsteps, and up and down the middle of the road. Then the members would do a dance similar to the morris dancers. The one with the besom would suddenly shout out: 'Here comes old Father Beelzebub, and in his hand he carries his club.' Other remembered words were: 'For where is he that will bid me stand? I'll knock him down right in the sand. I'll cut him up as small as flies, and then you can have him to make mince pies.' He would then run at the crowd with his club which was a knobbly stick and frighten the children to death. One mummer was dressed as a woman and was called Sally.

Interestingly all the memories Mrs Huntriss heard about the mummers were from men – it was considered 'men's business'. The niggering was easier to maintain as only three men were needed. They too went round on Boxing Day, wearing red mufflers, pearl-buttoned flashy waistcoats, black trousers, long tail coats decorated with ribbons (often borrowed from the gentry and their servants) and tall silk hats and blackened their faces using burnt cork dipped in milk. The 'nigger' characters were Bumper Jones with a tambourine, Uncle Neddy who played the bones and Sally on the melodeon (Sally was also a character in the mummers' play). They started out at about seven o'clock in the morning, parading the streets and stopping at some of the houses to sing and dance. The day after Boxing Day they went to some of the 'toffs' houses', where they got mixed receptions, and in the evenings they went to the pubs. Each man could expect to make about thirty shillings each day, or three pounds if they toured local villages. The niggers began by singing the songs which the mummers had incorporated into their play. Often the words became distorted and some of their songs sound as though they were designed for niggering, such as this one quoted by Mrs Humphriss:

If the man in the moon was a coon, coon, coon, what would I do?
No courting in the moonlight night,

No courting in the pale moonlight,
If the man in the moon was a coon.

Niggering carried on in Bloxham into the 1940s and was recorded in the 20th century in Lower Heyford (which was perhaps close enough to have been visited by the Bloxham niggers), Finstock and Ramsden.

Mummers' plays were widespread, and have recently been catalogued in two handlists: *Mumming Plays in Oxfordshire: An Interim Checklist* by Stephen Roud, published by the Traditional Drama Research Group in 1984 and *Berkshire Mumming Plays: A Geographical Index and Guide to Sources* by Stephen Roud and Malcolm Bee, published by Folklore Society Publications in 1991. These can be consulted for more details, but the following gazetteer gives a flavour of the information on mummers, which is often fragmentary.

## Abingdon

The play was said to have been performed originally by men from the Vineyard, but by 1939, when it was last recorded, the mummers came from Sunningwell. It was revived around the 1980s by the Abingdon morris men, who use a version of the play which they call the Sunningwell play. The play is performed to raise money for charity, and the men perform at the annual Advent weekend at Manor Farm Cogges near Witney at the beginning of December, and around the Abingdon area, usually before Christmas.

## Ardington

Mumming was performed here until the 1890s.

## Aston Tirrold and Aston Upthorpe

The fight was between King George and Slasher. Doctor Jack Finny, who claimed to be able to cure a magpie with toothache, brought the slain man back to life.

## Barton – Steeple, Middle and Westcott

The play was introduced by the Foreman, the combatants were the Royal Prussian King and King George, the latter was killed, then cured by the Doctor, aided by Bighead. The performers wore clothes covered with rags and ribbon streamers, wore grotesque masks and paper head-dresses. The text was printed in *Oxfordshire Archaeological Society Reports*, 1904.

## Blewbury

The play included a sword dance (most unusual for Oxfordshire), in which the swords were crossed and the men danced round them.

## Bodicote

The mummers performed until the late 1870s. Their play featured King

The Abingdon mummers are drawn from the AbingdonTraditional Morris team. They perform regularly at the Cogges Manor Farm Advent weekend in early December and around Abingdon before Christmas, raising money for charity. Here they are seen at Cogges in 1991. The characters are, from left to right: King George, the Quack Doctor, the Turkish Knight, the Molly and Father Christmas.

Photograph: Christine Bloxham

George and the Turk, the Doctor, Beezlebub or Great Head, a man with a besom who swept the floor and a couple of other characters. O. V. Aplin remembered that the Doctor came on saying:

> Here's the Doctor come from Spain
> As can bring the dyead to life again
> I cure the hip, the pip, the palsy ...

He cured the slain Turk with a pill and drew a tooth, which was 'pulled out' by all the performers taking each other by the waist and pulling until they all fell over backwards, at which the 'tooth' (that of a sheep or pig) was held up triumphantly. The Doctor exclaimed:

> He's not dead,
> He's in a trance
> Rise up, 'Father Abraham'
> And we'll have a dance.

*Cake and Cockhorse*, Spring 1967

## Brightwell-cum-Sotwell

The characters were King George, a gay French Officer (the word 'gay' would not have had its modern connotation of homosexuality, but meant 'cheerful'), Molly, Jack Finney as the Doctor and a comic fiddler. Molly opened the play with the words:

A room, a room I do desire for all my brave and gallant souls.
Stir up the fire and make a light and see and act this noble Knight.
Acted by age, acted by youth, acted on this stage tonight.
If you don't believe in what I say, walk in King George and clear the way.

Nigel Hammond, White Horse Country, 1972

Isabel Colquhoun (*Pit a Pat the Pan's Hot*) wrote that the mummers' sweep was played by the local chimney sweep, Mattie Warwick. Before the First World War the mummers wore curly black wigs and King George used to be cured with a cobweb – an old country remedy to stop bleeding.

## Buckland

Mummers performed until before the Second World War. Characters included Molly Tinker, who wore a skirt, blouse and bonnet, and two people dressed up as a horse.

## Charlton-on-Otmoor

The play was performed until c.1903. Molly led the way into the house, sweeping so vigorously that older people sometimes felt intimidated. Characters were Molly, the Turkish Knight, King George, Doctor, Mince Pie, Saucy Jack and Father Christmas. The text was printed in *Oxfordshire Archaeological Society Reports*, 1903.

## Chilson

The play included a dragon, King George, a Dentist and a Doctor.

## Chipping Norton

St George fought the Turkish Knight, the Doctor pulled a large tooth (a clothes peg) from the Turkish Knight, and a character called Jumping Jack carried his family (balloons) on his back.

## Cholsey

The characters included King George, Tipton Slasher, Doctor, Father Beezlebub and Tom the Tinker.

## Cumnor

Fred Coster recalled:

It is performed by seven persons, all attired in multi-coloured paper strips with hats to match, except the Donkey who wears a donkey mask with long ears. To obtain the correct dress wallpaper pattern books are got, the whole pages removed and cut into strips, leaving a two inch margin at the top, these pages are then sewn onto a coat until it is completely covered. The hat is made of newspapers, 'Admiral's' shape and then covered with the pattern paper. 'Props' needed are two wooden swords, a 'doctor's' bag, pair of large spectacles, pair of pliers, short poker, a horse's tooth, a pill box, an inflated pig's bladder tied onto a short stick.

Stephen Roud and Malcolm Bee, *Berkshire Mumming Plays ...*, 1991.

## Drayton (near Abingdon)

The man-woman figure was called Merrian, King George fought a knight 'from furring parts'. A text in the Helm collection has notes that the performers wore paper strip costume, apart from the Old Woman, who wore women's clothes. These were later replaced by a red cloak and pointed hat for Father Christmas, plus a long beard and a bag of rubbish, King George wore blue trousers with a red stripe, red jacket, black hat with red band, sword and belt, Beau Slash a khaki uniform, sword and belt. The doctor wore a top hat, tail coat and grey beard and carried a stick. Jack Vinney had a white smock, slouch hat, bag of props and blackened face and the Old Woman, who spoke with a falsetto voice, a blouse, skirt, hat with a veil and umbrella. (Stephen Roud and Malcolm Bee, op. cit.)

## East Hagbourne

The mummers wore paper costumes and hats and travelled round the neighbouring villages.

## East Hendred

A text was recorded from here in the Carpenter collection.

## Finstock and Ramsden

Mike Heaney recorded William Pratley, who recited a fragment of the play in a fast mutter:

My name's Mr Spinney
What canst thee do then Jack?
Cure a man from having the toothache.
How doest thou do that then Jack.
Cut his head off, stick his body in the wall.
Ooh you cruel fellow; no cruelty at all.
As I was going down the lane
I saw a pigsty
Built with apple dumplings
Thatched with pancakes
Knocked at the door
In felled the windows

Out come the maid
What dost thee want then Jack?
A glass of bread 'n' cheese
Oh yes, if you please.

## Glympton

This play was published in *Folklore*, vol. 72, 1961. The characters were:

Molly. A stalwart man dressed in a woman's gown, shawl and bonnet, with a besom in his hand, and a ludicrous imitation of a woman's voice.

King George. A big man dressed as a knight, with home-made helmet, sword, etc.

French Officer. A thin man with cocked hat, sword, epaulettes and uniform.

Doctor. Dressed in a very long tail-coat, pigtail, knee breeches etc.

Jack Vinney. Dressed as a jester, with a kind of tall fool's cap.

Happy Jack, In tattered garments.

Old Beezlebub. As Father Christmas.

## Goring and Streatley

In 1907 the *Abingdon Herald* reported that Mrs Stenney-Rawson wrote a short play for the mummers with 'an amusing dialogue and topical songs'.

## Hatford

Characters were the Foreman, Slasher, St George, the Doctor (who also claimed to cure a magpie with toothache), Jack Vinney and Mary.

## Headington Quarry

Two versions of the play were known in Headington at the end of the 19th century, one featuring King George, Turkey Snite (a corruption of Turkish Knight), Doctor Brown, Almond Nick and Jolly Jack. The second version, which William Kimber was taught by his father, included Father Christmas, the Prussian King, the Duke of Cumberland, Doctor, Jack Finney and a fiddler. Mumming died out in 1914 when the men went away to war.

The Headington Quarry W.I. published a version recorded from a former mummer in *History of Headington Quarry and Shotover* in 1933, with characters including Father Christmas, the Turkey Snite, Jack Finney, Doctor, Beelzebub and a Fiddler. This was performed by several different groups over the years and the tradition is now continued by members of the Headington Quarry morris dance team, who perform on Boxing Day, dressed in theatrical costumes. The performance now starts with a group of local women performing on hand bells, followed by the play, an Because many of the original words have disappeared, the men ad lib. Bringing in matters of current interest, and the play varies according to how many pubs have been visited around the Quarry!

Father Christmas enters, 'Welcome or welcome not...' Then King George, 'a man of courage bold' enters, and is challenged by the Turkey

Snite who claims he has 'come all the way from Tyrkey-land to fight', as they quarrel over who shall have the King of Egypt's daughter (who does not actually appear). During the fight King George is wounded in the heart so the Doctor is called, who claims he can cure

'All sorts of diseases such as the hipsy, the pipsy, and the gout,
  Pains within and pains without.
  If the devil's in him, I'll fetch him out.
  A touch on the heart and a touch on the knee,
  Rise up, King George and follow me.'

**Above**:

The Headington Mummers now perform on Boxing Day. This photograph shows the play being performed in 1901 at the meeting place of Court Napoleon 6829 of the Order of Foresters at the Chequers, Headington Quarry. The photograph was taken by E. H. Binney who wrote of it 'King George is dead. Turkish knight on the left.'

Photograph: Headington Quarry Morris Dancers' Scrapbook

Beelzebub comes on carrying his club, followed by Jack Finney and the Fiddler.

After the play members of the Headington Quarry morris team perform a sword dance – this is a northern tradition, taught to the Quarry men by Dr Robin Parsons, who became affiliated to the Quarry morris in 1953 while he trained at the Radcliffe, and by Bob Clarkson, a Geordie stationed

**Right**:

King George is revived and greeted by the Fool of the morris men.

Photograph: Christine Bloxham

**Left**: John Graham is the musician and Robin Ainly is Father Christmas, 1967. Photograph: Headington Quarry Morris Dancers' Scrapbook

**Below**: 'In comes I...' Robin Ainly as Father Chistmas, 1967. Photograph: Headington Quarry Morris Dancers' Scrapbook

at Cowley Barracks, who taught elements from a different sword dancing tradition. The sword dancing is only performed on Boxing Day, never as part of the traditional morris dancing.

## Holton

The characters were Foreman, King William, the Duke of Cumberland, Jack Finny, the Doctor, an old man and his wife.

The Doctor claimed:

Oi can cure all kinds of diseases. Everything my medicine pleases ipsy pipsy palsy and the gout pains within and pains without. Not only that but last Moonday noight oi asked King Garges wife to weigh me out noine pounds of butter and she was hup in a old olly bush weighing out eight pounds of steel to pay er rent with. She drops er gert butter dragger on my 'ead and knocks me right from bottom to top takes to my eels and I runs down a long short narrer lane and there I met a live lion stuffed with straw 'e run me to a mouse 'ole and there I met poor old Mrs Indle Crinkle bless er old 'eart oi knowed and you knowed and we all knowed her only nobody knowed nothing at all about 'er and I goes down a little bit further and out comes a black blue bark 'e dogged at me, 'oi gives 'im such a ead over rattler I never sees no more on im. And I goes down a little bit further and oi coomes to the dook's 'ouse, 'oi knocks at the do'er and out coomes the maid such a roush. She asks me if oi'l 'ave a bit o beer and a glass 'o bread and cheese, oi says yes thank her no if yer

please and oi goes down a little bit further and oi sees two dead men a foighting and two blind men lookin on to see fair play and two dumb men shouting 'orray.

Christina Hole Collection

## Iffley

Beezlebub was master of ceremonies, King George killed the Turkish Knight in battle, and Dr Brown restored him to life. Father Christmas and a character with a money box also featured.

## Islip

See Appendix III for the text of the 1780 play. The characters in this were Anno Domini, The Royal Duke of Blunderland, Earl or King Percy, Herald, Pedlar Knave, Quack Doctor Spinney, Salt Peter, Old Fat Jack and Old Father Christmas.

Percy Manning recorded another, presumably later, version which included the Duke of Northumberland, King George, the Doctor, Beezlebub and Jack.

## Lockinge

Characters included Hearty King George. Old Beelzebub as Father Christmas, Happy Jack Winney (or Jack Finny, who combined with the doctor) and Molly (or Mary Tinker or Tom the Tinker). The last performance was at Lockinge House for Lady Wantage in 1881.

## Longcot

There is a version of a play from here in the Ordish Collection.

## Long Hanborough

The men appeared covered from head to foot in narrow strips of paper, knocking at people's back doors, and once given permission swept into the room, while a space was created for them by a man walking in a circle with a stick. This character seems to have fought with a French Officer:

'I am the French Officer, officer I,
Many long fields I have battled to try,
So guard thy head and mind thy blows, head, face, also,
So a battle, a battle, betwixt thee and I,
To see which shall be on the ground dead first. Shall I?'

The first speaker was wounded and cured by noble Dr Airo, who then introduced Jack Finny, dressed as a clown, who demanded to be known as 'Mr Finny':

'Don't you know I'm a man of very great fame.
Last year when I cam here,
You never asked me to taste your beer.
Now I have come with bladder and besom,
To sweep the cobwebs from your room.'

Angelina Parker, 'Oxfordshire Village Folklore', *Folklore*, 1913, vol. 24

## Long Wittenham

Characters included King William and a doctor called Jack Binny or Pinny.

## North Newington

The play was performed until about 1914, featuring Father Christmas, Jack Finney, Belbug, Billy the Sweep and Bighead.

## Old Marston

Characters were St George, the Turkey Snipe, Doctor Brown, Almond Nick and Jolley Jack.

## Pusey

The mummers wore paper costumes and had blackened faces. Characters included King George and Beelzebub.

## Radley

The mummers' costumes were made from shreds of calico and coloured paper. The hero was St George.

## Souldern

All the mummers wore scarecrow-like costumes. The part of Molly was taken by the largest young man available. After the fight the doctor arrived on a hobby horse and after reviving the dead man, pulled a tooth the size of a decanter stopper from Molly. He was accompanied by Jack-pudding:

Ear comes I, as never come yet,
With my gret yead, and my little wit;
My head is gret, my wit is small,
I'll do my dooty to plaze you all.

Oxfordshire Archaeological Society, *Historical and Descriptive Notices of the Parish of Souldern*

## Stanford-in-the-Vale

The men wore strips of paper attached to their own clothes, and Molly Tinker wore a sunbonnet and blackened 'her' face.

## Steventon

King George called himself the 'Africky king' and fought Beau Slasher, the French Officer who was at one time known as Jack the Slasher. The man-woman figure was Molly Tinker. The performances used to be after church on Boxing Day. Costumes were made over Christmas and consisted of paper strips pasted on to thicker paper, worn over ordinary clothes.

## Stoke Talmage

Once the players were admitted to a house, they were led in by Father Christmas with the words:

In comes old Father Christmas
Welcome him, or welcome not
I hope old Father Christmas
Will never be forgot.
Christmas comes but once a year
And when he comes it brings good cheer
Roast beef, plum pudding and mince pies
Who likes them any better than you and I?

King George then threatens the Valiant Soldier, Tip and Slasher:

In comes King George, this Turkish Knight
I come back to England for to fight
I've travelled to Ireland through France and Spain
And over the hills and back again.
Where is that man,
Who dare bid me stand?
I'll cut him down with my created hand.
I'll cut him, I'll slash him, as small as flies,
And send him to the cook shop to make mince pies.
Mince pies hot, mince pies cold, I'll lay him his grace
Before he's three days old.

West Oxfordshire Oral History Group, Broadsheet No. 1

Tip and Slasher is followed on stage by Mr Big Head and Mr Beezlebub.

## Sunningwell

Characters included King George, Bold Slash, and the Announcer, who wore coats with wallpaper fringes, Old Woman Ann in women's clothes and the Doctor. The play continued to be performed later than in many places, perhaps because of Sunningwell's proximity to Boars Hill, which had many wealthy inhabitants who would contribute money. It was common in the 1930s and was revived after the Second World War, dying out around 1951. The Sunningwell play has been taken over by the current Abingdon mummers.

## Sutton Courtenay

Characters when the play was revived in 1933 by boys included the Royal Persian King, who wore a blue and gold robe, Bull Slasher in rough army clothes, the Doctor in a blue suit and top hat, Beelzebub as an old tramp and the Broken Kneed Pony with a flat wooden head on a pole on pram wheels. (Stephen Roud and Malcolm Bees, op. cit.)

## Uffington

Mummers dressed in paper costumes with ribbons, with characters including King George, Father Christmas, the Doctor, Beelzebub Mother Vinney, the Doctor's Boy and Starcher. Traditional mumming died out before 1930 but it was revived for the Festival of Britain in 1951, in 1965 for a television programme by John Betjeman and again in the 1970s.

## Wantage

The revived play performed by the Icknield Way Morris Men has a play featuring King Alfred (the real King Alfred is said to have been born in Wantage), who is killed by a French Officer and brought back to life by the Doctor. The *Oxford Mail* of 28th December 1977 wrote that the play that year featured a punk rocker and a buxom wench.

## Waterstock

R. J. E. Tiddy recorded the play in 1914. The hero, King George, fought Captain Slasher, and George was killed, then cured by the Doctor, and featured a foreman and Jack Finney.

## West Hendred

The mummers included King George and the Doctor and a white horse formed part of the company.

# Appendix 1:
# The Mallard Song

**A more modern version of the Mallard Song is quoted by Montagu Burrows** in *Worthies of All Souls*:

> The Griffin, Bustard, Turkey and Capon
> Let other hungry mortals gape on,
> And on their bones with stomach fall hard,
> But lett All Souls men have their Mallard.
> *Chorus*:
> O by the blood of King Edward,
> O by the blood of King Edward,
> It was a swapping, swapping Mallard.
>
> The Romans once admired a Gander
> More than they did their best Commander,
> Because hee saved, if some don't fooll us,
> The place named from the scull of Tolus.
>
> The poets fained Jove turnd a Swan,
> But lett them prove it if they can;
> To make appeare it's not att all hard.
> He was a swapping, swapping Mallard.
>
> The lett us drink and dance a Galliard
> In the remembrance of the Mallard,
> And as the Mallard doth in poole
> Lett's dabble, dive and duck in bowle.

In the early 18th century the third line of the third verse was altered to:

As for our proof it's not at all hard.

# Appendix II:
# Abingdon Bun Throwing

**This is an occasional rather than a seasonal custom, which seems to have** begun either in 1760, on the accession of King George III, the first Hanoverian King to have been born on British soil, or a year later on 22nd September to mark his coronation. Loaves were distributed free in the market place, and throwing them from the roof of the County Hall seems to have developed from that. Mieneke Cox wrote:

> In Abingdon the coronation of George III has been tentatively regarded as the beginning of the quaint tradition of bun-throwing. It was customary to distribute cakes and ale in the Bury at celebrations, but one day a spark had the bright idea to throw buns from the flat roof of the Market House to the population gathered below.
>
> *Abingdon: An 18th Century Market Town*

The tradition was recorded in the *Oxford Herald* in 1819 when the Corporation celebrated the Golden Jubilee of George III, and the paper commented that Mr John Waite said that he 'caught' the cake in 1761, although the local paper of that date said they were 'distributed'.

In 1820 at the coronation of George IV a thousand buns were thrown by the Mayor and Councillors. In 1831 five hundred cakes were thrown from the tops of

Abingdon bun throwing probably originated in the 18th century to celebrate a coronation. It is now often performed to commemorate a royal occasion, such as the celebration of the hundredth birthday of Her Royal Highness Queen Elizabeth the Queen Mother on 4th August 2000. Unfortunately on this occasion the County Hall was under repair and shrouded in scaffolding. As crowds gathered in the Market Place they were entertained by a band.

Photograph: Christine Bloxham

The crowd in the market place eagerly tried to catch the buns, sometimes resorting to holding up coats between them to increase their chances!

Photograph: Christine Bloxham

houses, and in 1837 the Corporation accounts referred to throwing buns 'according to ancient usage'. Two thousand five hundred buns were thrown to celebrate Victory Day in 1946 and the fourth centenary of the borough in 1956. Queen Elizabeth II visited Abingdon in 1956 and witnessed a special bun throwing.

The Mayor, aldermen and councillors process from the Guildhall to the roof of the County Hall (now the site of Abingdon Museum). The mace-bearer then calls for three cheers for the Sovereign, and after the Mayor has thrown the first bun the others join in.

Bun-throwing has been done recently to mark royal weddings, Queen Elizabeth II's Silver Jubilee in 1977, the 80th birthday of H.R.H. Queen Elizabeth the Queen Mother in 1980, and most recently the Millennium and on 4th August 2000 to celebrate the hundredth birthday of H.R.H. Queen Elizabeth the Queen Mother.

On that occasion people congregated in the Market Square, listening to a band, then at seven o'clock in the evening the Mayor and Corporation, led by the mace-bearer and accompanied by the Oxford West and Abingdon member of parliament, Evan Harris, paraded from the council offices under the Abbey archway to the County Hall. They stood for a moment to greet the crowd, but no speeches were given, and they proceeded up the stairs to the top of the building. Unfortunately it was covered with scaffolding (although a banner declaring the reason for the bun-throwing was attached to the facade) so it was impossible to see them throwing the rain of buns from the parapet – just the occasional glimpse of a hand. The rain of buns continued for about a quarter of an hour. Most people relied on their hands to reach up and catch them, but a couple of people held up a jacket between them, and there was at least one open umbrella held upside down. Many people were able to collect several buns apiece, and some locals pride themselves on their collections of buns built up over the years.

# Appendix III:
# The Islip Mummers' Play

**This is in the Percy Manning Collection (d.199pp299-306) in the Bodleian** Library, and is said to date from around 1780, from a manuscript which belonged to Thomas Johnston of Islip, clerk of the Parish, making it the earliest version written down in Oxfordshire.

*Characters*
Anno Domino (female)
Pedlar Knave
Old Doctor Spinny (Doctor Quack)
Salt Peter
Old Fat Jack
Old Father Christmas
Royal Duke of Blunderland
Earl or King Percy
Herald

*Play text*
ANNO DOMINO *enters, carrying a besom or broom*
'What ho! What ho! make room for mummers and old Anno Domino.
I have brought my champions brave,
Fighting men and Pedlar Knave,
Old Doctor Spinny, sometimes called Quack,
His man Salt Peter, and Old Fat Jack,
Old Father Christmas, so old and white
He has promised to look in tonight.
Act 1st. Come in my eldest son and show how battles are lost and won.'

DUKE OF BLUNDERLAND:
'Here comes I the Royal Duke of Blunderland
With my Broad Sword all in my hand.
Where is the man that does bid me stand?
I'll slay him and cut him as small as flies,
And send him to the cookshop to make mincepies,
Mincepies hot or mincepies cold
I'll send him to the Devil before he['s] three days old.'

*Enter* EARL *or* KING PERCY:
'I am the man that dares bid you stand,
Altho' you swaggers and swears, that with your courageous hand,
You will slay me and cut me up as small as flies,
And send me to the cookshop, to make mince pies.

Defend yourself for I show no mercy.
I fight to the death as sure as I am Percy.'
(*Instructions: decide which is to be dead man and make a good fight*).

HERALD:
'Call the Doctor, call old Quack.
Take my donkey and bring him back.'
(*Knock on door*)
'Come in Doctor Quack.'

DOCTOR:
'I am not a Quack, as you may see
I am Dr. Spinny with a big M.D.'
(*Doctor enters mounted, nag restive, kicks doctor off. Blame Salt Peter for giving the nag too many beans.*)

DUKE or PERCY:
'Doctor, doctor, I have killed a man.'

SALT PETER:
'Kill'd a man, kill'd a Monkey.'

HERALD:
'Doctor, doctor, do your part
The king is wounded to the Heart,
As you can plainly see.'
(*Dr. Spinny examines the dead man and calls Peter to bring him his bag of tools. Doctor sews up a wound and speaks*):

DOCTOR:
'I am a Doctor, a Doctor Good,
Who's hand were never stained with Blood,
I can cure the itch, the Pox, the Palsy and the Gout, Pains within and pains without,
If the Devil [is] in I can fetch him out.
I have Plaster and Potions, Poisons and Pills,
Some to cure and some to kill.
I have travelled thro' England, Ireland, France and Spain,
Been to Europe and back again.
Hocus Pocus Alecampain
Take one of my Pills, Dead Man, rise and fight again.'
(*Dead man is alive again. Singing heard outside.*)

SONG:
'I am a button maker by my Trade,
Till I was ruined by a Maid,
Dam such maids so said I
Fall, rall riddle roll ido.'
(*Enters Fat Jack, drunk.*)

FAT JACK:
'Here come I old Fat Jack,
At fighting I can do my whack.
By day or Night, or candlelight,

Old Jack will Fight, with all his Might
Wrong or right, sober or tight.'
(*Jack staggers and falls and knocks Anno Domino down. Anno Domino groaning is examined by Doctor Spinny.*)

SALT PETER:
'She's got the toothache.'

DOCTOR SPINNY:
'The Tooth Ache why she is quite big and will bring forth a New-Heir-Year, on the
    31st of December at 12 p.m.
Peter fetch (my)★ Pinchers and we will have a tooth out, and make sure, it will make
    the Bill longer.'
(*He pulls tooth out and gives a pill. Anno Domino right again. Knock at door.*)

PEDLAR:
'Here comes I a Pedlar Chap,
On my shoulder I car's my pack,
I have ribbons for the ladies fair,
Ornaments to deck their Hair,
Patches for their Pretty Faces,
High heeled Boots and fine Laces,
Toys to please both great and small,
And I've brought my fiddle to please you all.'

(*All dance the Morris. Enters Father Christmas. Performers all dance round him and sing*):
'A Virgin unspotted the Prophets foretold
Should bring forth a Saviour Child which are no (sic) behold,
To be our redemption from Death, Hell and Sin,
Which Adam's transgressions involved us in.
So let us be merry, cast sorrow away
Christ Jesus our Saviour was born on this day.'


★ erased in original

# Appendix IV: Oxfordshire Christmas Miracle Play

**Published in *Notes and Queries*, 5th series, Vol II, 26th December 1874,** contributed by Dr. Frederick George Lee who collected it in Thame in 1853 from a performer. The play was performed for Lord Wenman at Thame Park in the late 18th century and for various local nobility and gentry in the early 19th century.

DRAMATIS PERSONAE
King Alfred
King Alfred's Queen
King William
Old King Cole (with a wooden leg)
Giant Blunderbore
Little Jack
Old Father Christmas
St George of England
The Old Dragon
The Merry Andrew
Old Doctor Ball
Morres-men

(*All the mummers come in singing, and walk round the place in a circle, and then stand on one side.*)

*Enter King Alfred and his Queen, arm in arm:*
'I am King Alfred, and this here is my ride,
I've a crown on my pate and a sword by my side.'
   (*Stands apart*)
*Enter King Cole.*
'I am King Cole, and I carry my stump,
Hurrah for King Charles! Down with old Noll's Rump!'
   (*Stands apart*)
*Enter King William.*
'I am King William of blessed me-mo-ry,
Who came and pulled down the high gallows-tree,
And brought us all peace and pros-pe-ri-ty.'
   (*Stands apart*)
*Enter Giant Blunderbore.*
'I am Giant Blunderbore, fee, fi fum,
Ready to fight ye all - so I says, "Come,"'
*Enter Little Jack (Blunderbore continues).*
'And this here is my man Little Jack,
A thump on his rump and a whack on his back.'

293

*(Strikes him twice.)*
'I'll fight King Alfred, I'll fight King Cole,
I'm ready to fight any mortal soul;
So here I, Blunderbore, takes my stand,
With this little devil, Jack, at my right hand,
Ready to fight for mortal life, Fee, fi, fum.'
    *(The Giant and Little Jack stand apart)*
*Enter St. George*
'I am St George of Marry Eng-land,
Bring in the morres-men, bring in our band.'
    *(Morres-men come forward and dance to a tune from fife and drum. The dance being*
    *ended, St George continues.)*
'These are our tricks. Ho! men, ho!
These are our sticks, - whack men so.
    *(Strikes the Dragon, who roars, and comes forward. The Dragon speaks.)*
'Stand on head, stand on feet,
Meat, meat, meat for to eat.'
    *(Tries to bite King Alfred)*
'I am the dragon, here are my jaws,
I am the dragon, here are my claws.
Meat, meat, meat for to eat,
Stand on my head, stand on my feet.'
    *(Turns a somersault and stands aside)*
*All sing, several times repeated.*
'Ho! ho! ho!
Whack men so.'
    *(The drum and fife sound. They all fight, and after general disorder, fall down.)*
*Enter Old Doctor Ball*
'I am the doctor, and I cure all ills,
Only gullup my portions [?potions] and swallow my pills;
I can cure the itch, the stitch, the pox, the palsy and the gout,
All pains within and all pains without.
Up from this floor, Giant Blunderbore!'
    *(Gives him a pill and he rises at once)*
'Get up King; Get up Bride;
Get up Fool, and stand aside.'
    *(Gives them each a pill and they rise)*
'Get up King Cole, and tell the gentlefolks all,
There never was a doctor like Mr. Doctor Ball;
Get up, St. George, old England's knight,'
    *(Gives him a pill)*
'You have wounded the Dragon, and finished the fight,'
    *(All stand aside but the Dragon, who lies in convulsions)*
'Now kill the old Dragon, and poison old Nick,
At Yule-tyde both o'ye, cut your stick.'
    *(The doctor forces a large pill down the Dragon's throat, who thereupon roars, and dies*
    *in convulsions)*
*Then enter Father Christmas*
'I am Father Christmas! hold, men, hold!
Be there loaf in your locker, and sheep in your fold,
A fire on the hearth, and good luck for your lot,
Money in your pocket, and a pudding in the pot.'
*He sings,*

'Hold, men, hold!
Put up your sticks,
End all your tricks;
Hold, men, hold!'
    (*Chorus - all sing while one goes round with a hat for gifts*)
'Hold, men, hold!
We are very cold,
Inside and outside,
We are very cold.
If you don't give us silver,
Then give us gold
From the money in your pockets -'
    (*Some of the performers show signs of fighting again*)
'Hold, men, hold!'
    (*Song and chorus*)
'God A'mighty bless your hearth and fold,
Shut out the wolf, and keep out the cold;
You gev' [have given] us silver, keep you the gold,
For 'tis money in your pocket. - Hold, men, hold!'
    (*Repeat in chorus*)
'God A'mighty bless, etc.'
    (*Exeunt omnes*)

# Appendix V: The Mummers' Play from Westcott Barton

**Written down for the Rev. J. Marshall in 1870 and printed in the *Oxfordshire*** *Archaeological Society Reports* for 1904.

CHARACTERS
Foreman
Royal Prussian King
King George
Doctor
Bighead

THE TEXT
(*Foreman steps out from among the company with an old besom and begins:*)
'Sweep, sweep a room for me
And all my jolly company;
Sweep, sweep, old pots to find,
Brass nails and rusty pins, they
Run upon my mind.
Sweep, sweep, ye gallants all,
And give me time to rise.
I am come to show you a bit of activity
This merry Christmas time.
Walk in the Royal.'
(*The Royal walks in.*)
'I am the Royal the Prussian King,
Born to find the Christian King,
If any Spanish, French or Turk think they can do
Me any harm or hurt, let him come and try.
I would cut him up as small and numerous as flies,
And send him to Jamaica to make mince pies.
So I pray let all your voices sing
For the sake of the Prussian King.'
*Foreman*: 'Walk in King George.'
(*King George walks in blowing.*)
'I am the man that dare bid thee stand,
Though thou saidest thou would cut me down with thy hand,
Though you said you would cut me up as small and numerous as flies,
And send me to Jamaica to make mince pies.
I have fought my battles in a field of clover,
I have fought my battles till the blood ran over,
I have fought my battles through France and Spain,
And here I am to fight again.

So a battle, a battle betwixt you and I,
To see which on the ground first shall lie.'
(*The Royal and King George have a conflict in which King George receives his death-wound and falls down.*)
*Foreman:*
'King George is wounded through his heart and likewise through his knee.
Fifty pounds I'd freely give if only that noble old Doctor was here,
Doctor, doctor, stop nor stay,
But mount old Dobbin and come this way.'
*Doctor:* 'I come from Portugal, France and Spain
To fetch dead people to life again.'
*Foreman:* 'Pray noble doctor, what can you cure?'
*Doctor:* 'All manner of diseases,
Just what my pills pleases,
Hard corns, soft corns, the itch, stitch, palsy, and the gout, pains within and pains without.
Bring me an old woman seven years dead,
And seven years laid in her grave,
I would give her pills to work her stomach through and through, incline her body and stomach too. If she haven't got one tooth in her head, if she can rise and crack one of my pills, I will be bound to fetch her to life again. My man Jack - '
*Bighead:* 'Yes, sir.'
*Doctor:* 'Bring those pills.'
*Bighead:* 'Fetch em.'
*Doctor:* 'I say bring them,
Think I am going to keep a dog and bark.'
(*Doctor runs after him.*)
*Bighead:* 'I be gwewing as fast as I can, sir.'
(*Doctor comes in with the pills.*)
*Doctor:* 'These are the pills that cure all ills,
And work the old stomach through and through.
Work the old stomach down to the knee.
Fifty pounds I would receive if any man can do more than I can.'
(*Doctor gives the dead man a pill*).
*Doctor:* 'My man Jack.'
*Bighead:* 'Yes, sir.'
*Doctor:* 'Softly hold up the head of the man, for I find the breath is nearly come into his old body again.'
(*The performers run round the dead man to find his head.*)
'Is this it? Is that it? Is this it? Is that it?'
*Doctor:* 'Softly lay down his head for the breath is come into his old body again. If I break his old neck I'll set it again. Rise up, King George, and fight again.'
(*The Doctor helps him up.*)
*Foreman:* 'Walk in Beelzebub.'
*Bighead:* 'In comes I, so han't been hit,
With my big head and little wit,
My head is so big, and my wit is so small,
But I'll endeavour to please you all.
In come I old Beelzebub,
And on my shoulders I carry a club,
And in my hand a dripping pan,
And don't you think I'm a merry old man.
Good dog, good dog, lay down your bones,

And wrinkle up your ribs,
My bonnie boys cock up one leg,
And we will have a merry jig.'
(*They all dance and the performance is ended.*)

It looks as though the characters of Bighead and Beelzebub were originally separate.
There may be other characters missing, as there is no man-woman figure included.

# Appendix VI: Calendar of Customs to Visit in Oxfordshire

**Easter**: Egg Rolling at Shotover Hill, Oxford. Organised by Oxford City Council.

**May 1st**: May Morning at Magdalen College.
Around May 1st: May Day celebration at Charlton-on-Otmoor. Contact the Primary School for details.
Various other villages also have May celebrations.

**Ascension**: Beating the Bounds – Oxford. This is organised by the different parishes in Oxford. (Ascension Day is the Thursday ten days before Whit Sunday.)

**Whit Monday**: Bampton: morris dancing and garlands. (Whit Sunday is the seventh Sunday after Easter.)

**Morris Dancing** can be seen in many parts of Oxfordshire throughout the summer. Contact local teams for details, especially Abingdon, Bampton and Headington Quarry.

**Trinity Sunday**: Kirtlington Lamb Ale. Weekend of morris and folk dancing held in Kirtlington. (Trinity Sunday is the Sunday after Whit Sunday.)

**Saturday after 19th June**: Abingdon Mock-Mayormaking. Election, mock-mayor-making ceremony and morris and folk dancing held in Ock Street, Abingdon. Contact Abingdon Tourist Information Centre for details.

**Around 24th June, St John the Baptist's Day**: Burford Dragon. Held in the evening, either on 24th June or the Saturday nearest to it. Contact Burford School for details.

**July**: Swan Upping, River Thames. Organised by the Worshipful Companies of Dyers and Vintners, City of London.

**August**: Woodstock Mock-Mayormaking. Evening of election and folk dancing.. Contact Woodstock Tourist Information Centre for details.

**September**: Monday and Tuesday after Sunday after St Giles' Day, 1st September: St Giles' Fair, Oxford.

**September and October**: Fairs are held in many towns, including Abingdon, Banbury, Thame, Witney and Woodstock.

**December**: Christingle Services. Held in many Church of England churches. Contact individual churches for dates.

**December**: Mummers' Plays

Abingdon Mummers perform at the Advent weekend at Manor Farm Cogges, Witney, on the first weekend in December, and around Abingdon during December.

Bampton mummers perform in Bampton around Christmas.

Headington Quarry mummers perform in all the public houses in Headington Quarry on Boxing Day, starting at the Crown and Thistle in Old Road at 11.30a.m.

**Abingdon Bun Throwing** is an occasional custom and will probably next be performed to celebrate the Golden Jubilee of Her Royal Highness Queen Elizabeth II in 2002. Contact the Abingdon Tourist Information Centre.

# Bibliography

Alexander, Sally, *St Giles' Fair*, History Workshop Pamphlet, 1970
'An Old Freeman', *Early Recollections of Oxford*, 1900
Anon, *Travellers in Oxfordshire*, 1675
Anon, *Shilton – A Village Scrapbook*, O.R.C.C., 1972-3
Anon, *The History of the Famous Maypole at Ewelm in Oxfordshire...*, 1702
Aubrey, John, MS Lansdowne
Ballard, Adolphus, *Chronicles of the Royal Borough of Woodstock*, Oxford, 1896
Banbury Historical Society, *Cake and Cockhorse*
Beesley, Alfred, *History of Banbury*, 1841
Beesley, Sarah, *My Life*, 1892
Bennet, John, *Poems on Several Occasions*, 1774
Berkshire Federation of W.I.s, *The Berkshire Book*, 1939
Binney, E.H., in *Folklore*, Vol 13, 1902
*Birmingham Weekly Post*
Blair, John, *Bampton Folklore*, Merton Priory Press, 2001
Bliss, Philip, *Reliquae Hearnianae*, Oxford, 1857
Blomfield, J.C., *History of Fritwell*, 1893
Boss, Thomas Ward, *Reminiscences of Old Banbury*, Potts, 1903
Bradford, J.E. and F., *The History of Thame and its Hamlets*, 1860
Brand John and Ellis, Henry, *Observations on Popular Antiquities*, 1841
Briggs, K.M., *Folklore of the Cotswolds*, Batsford, 1974
Brody, Alan, *The English Mummers and their Plays*, Routledge and Kegan Paul, n.d.
Buckland, Theresa and Wood, Juliette, *Aspects of British Calendar Customs*, Sheffield Academic Press, 1993
Burns, J.S., *A History of Henley*, London, 1861
Burrows, Montagu, *Worthies of All Souls*, 1874
Burrows, Montagu, *Collectanea*, Oxford, 1890
Carleton Williams, Ethel, *Companion into Oxfordshire*, Methuen, 1941
Carr, William, *University College*, London, 1902
Cawte, E.C., Helm, A, and Peacock, N., *English Ritual Drama*, Folklore Society, 1967
Chandler, Keith, *Ribbons, Bells and Squeaking Fiddles*, Hisarlik Press, 1993
Chandler, Keith, *Morris Dancing in the English South Midlands, 1660–1900*, Hisarlik Press, 1993
Chaundy, T.W., 'William Kimber. A Portrait by T.W. Chaundy', in *Journal of the English Folk Dance and Song Society*, vol. 8, no.4, 1959
Clark, Andrew, *The Life and Times of Anthony Wood*, Oxford, 1894
Clark, Andrew, *The Colleges of Oxford*, 1892
Colquhoun, Isabel, *Pit, Pat the Pan's Hot*, Oxford, 1975
Coppock, G.A. and Hill, B.M., *Headington Quarry and Shotover*, Oxford University Press, 1933
Corbett, Elsie, *History of Spelsbury*, Cheney, 1962
Cordrey, Edward, *Bygone Days at Iffley*, 1956

Cox, Mieneke, *Abingdon: An 18th Century Country Town*, Abingdon, 1999

Crusha, Rev. E.H.W., *May Day at Charlton-on-Otmoor*, 1977

Davison, G.M., *The Story of Swalcliffe*, 1943

Ditchfield, P.H., *Old English Customs Extant at the Present Time*, 1896

Ditchfield, P.H., *Old English Sports*, Methuen, 1891

Dunkin, J. *History of Bicester*, 1816

Early, Charles & Co., *A Visit to Witney and Witney Mills*, 1898

Edwards, H., *Old English Customs*, 1842

Ettlinger, Ellen, 'Monuments of Folklore', in *Oxford and District Folklore Society Annual Record*, 1962

*Folk-lore*, 'Oxfordshire Mummers', *Folklore*, Vol V, 1894
  'The Glympton Mummers' Play', *Folklore* Vol. 72, 1961

*Gentleman's Magazine, The*

Frazer, J.G., *The Golden Bough*, Macmillan, 1967

Giles, J.A., *History of Bampton*, 1848

Goshawk, Evelyn, *Idbury History*, 1961

Gough, Mr & Mrs., *Historical and Descriptive Notices of the Parish of Souldern*, 1887

Gott, Charles and Joan, *The Book of Witney*, Barracuda, 1986

Graham, Malcolm, *Henry Taunt of Oxford*, The Oxford Illustrated Press, 1982

Grant, Bob, Heaney, Mike and Judge, Roy, 'Copy of gp of Morice Dancers Mr Manning', in *English Dance and Song*, vol. 43, no.2, 1981

Grant, Bob and Heaney, Mike, 'In Steps I', in *English Folk Dance and Song*, Vol. 423, No. 4, 1981

Groves, Muriel, ed., *The History of Shipton under Wychwood*, London, 1934

Green, David, ed., *An Oxfordshire Christmas*, Alan Sutton, 1992

Halliwell, J.O., *Popular Rhymes and Nursery Tales*, 1849

Hammond, Nigel, *The White Horse Country*, William Smith, 1972

Harris, Mollie, *A Kind of Magic*, Chatto & Windus, 1969

Harrison, Brian and Trinder, B.S., 'Drink and Sobriety in an Early Victorian Town', in *English Historical Review*, 1969

Harrop, Peter, 'Mumming in Bampton', in *Folk Life*, Vol. 18, 1980

Harrowven, Jean, *Origins of Rhymes Songs and Sayings*, Ward, 1977

Harvey, Alice M., *Memoirs of a Country Childhood in North Hinksey Village*, 1975

Hassall, W.O., *Wheatley Records*, Oxfordshire Record Society, 1956

Hayden, Eleanor, *Travels Round Our Village*, 1901

Hedges, Sid, *Bicester wuz a Little Town*, Bicester Advertiser, 1968

Helm, Alex, *The English Mummers' Play*, D.S. Brewer, 1981

Henderson, Bernard, *Merton College*, London ,1899

Henman, Velda, *Islip, Oxfordshire*, 1987

Herbert, G., *Shoemaker's Window*

Hobson M.G., and Price, K.L.H., *Otmoor and its Seven Towns*, 1961

Hole, Christina, *English Customs and Usage*, Batsford, 1941

Hole, Christina, *British Folk Customs*, Hutchinson, 1976

Hole, Christina, 'The North Newington Mummers' Play', in *Oxford and District Folklore Society Annual Record*, No. 8, 1956

Hone, W., *Year Book*, 1838

Horn, Pamela, ed., *Oxfordshire Village Life*, Beacon, 1983

Horn, Pamela, ed., *Country Life in the 1860s: The Diaries of George James Dew*, Beacon, 1986

Howard, Alexander, *Endless Cavalcade*, Barker, 1964

Howkins, Alun, *Whitsun in 19th Century Oxfordshire*, History Workshop Pamphlet, 1973

Howse, Violet M., *Hatford - A Parish Record*, 1976

Huntriss, Y.S., 'Mummering and Niggering in Bloxham', in *Cake and Cockhorse*, Autumn 1978
Jackson Coleman, S., *Tales and Traditions of Berkshire*, Folklore Fellowship, 1949
Jewitt, Clara J., 'Collectanea', in *Folklore*, Vol. 13, 1902
J.H.S., *The Pancake Bell and Other Jingles*
*Jackson's Oxford Journal*
Judge, Roy, 'May Morning and Magdalen College', in *Folklore*, vol.97, 1986, i.
Judge, Roy, *The Jack in the Green*, Brewer, 1979
Kibble, John, *Historical and Other Notes on Charlbury*, Oxford, 1927
Kibble, John, *Historical & Other Notes on Wychwood Forest*, Oxford, 1928
Lockhart, J.G., *Cosmo Gordon Lang*, 1949
Lowe, Barbara, 'Early Records of the Morris in England', in *Journal of the English Folk Dance and Song Society*, Vol. VIII, no. 2, 1957
Macarthur, Wilson, *The River Windrush*, Cassell, 1946
Mais, S.P.B., *Our Village Today*, 1956
Malcolmson, R.W., *Popular Recreations in English Society*, Cambridge University Press, 1973
Mallett, Charles Edward, *A History of the University of Oxford*, vol. 5, 1924
Manning, Percy, 'Bringing in the Fly', in *Folklore*, Vol 25, 1914
Manning, Percy, MS Top Oxon, Bodleian Library
Manning, Percy, 'Stray Notes on Oxfordshire Folklore', in *Folklore*, Vol 13, 1902
Manning, Percy, 'Some Oxfordshire Seasonal Festivals', in *Folklore*, Vol. 8, 1897
Mason, Violet, 'Scraps of English Folklore', in *Folklore*, Vol. 40. 1929
Meades, Eileen, *The History of Chipping Norton*, Alden Press, 1949
Miller, Edith, *The History of the Village of Islip*, Oxford, 1930
Miller, Ella, ed., *Forest Hill Village Book*, Oxford, 1933
Monk, William J., *By Thames and Windrush*, Oxford, 1926
Moreau, R.E., *The Departed Village*, Oxford University Press, 1968
Morris, Christopher, ed., *The Illustrated Journeys of Celia Fiennes*, Macdonald, 1982
Morris, James, *Oxford*, Faber, 1965
Nichols, J., ed., *The Diary of Henry Machyn*, Camden Society, 1848
Northeast, Peter, *This Venerable Village*, Blewbury Local History Group, 1975
Norwood, R.P., *History of Kiddington*, 1930
*Notes and Queries*
Opie, Iona and Peter, *The Oxford Dictionary of Nursery Rhymes*, Oxford University Press, 1951
Opie, Iona and Peter, *The Lore and Language of Schoolchildren*, Oxford University Press, 1959
*Oxford and District Folklore Society, Annual Record*
*Oxford Chronicle*
*Oxford Mail*
*Oxford Times*
*Oxfordshire Archaeological Society Reports*, 1904, 1905
Palmer, Geoffrey and Lloyd, Noel, *A Year of Festivals*, Warne, 1972
Palmer, William, ed., *Kilvert's Diary*, 1977
Parker, Angelina, 'Oxfordshire Village Folklore', in *Folklore*, vol. 24, 1913
Parker, J.H., *Glossary of Architecture*, 1840
Parkes, George David and Mary, *May Day at Iffley*, 1934
Pickering, Michael, *Village Song and Culture*, Croom Helm, 1982
Pimlott, J.A.R., *The Englishman's Christmas*, Harvester, 1978
Plot, Robert, *The Natural History of Oxfordshire*, 1676
Plummer, Alfred and Early, Richard, *The Blanket Makers*, 1969

Pointer, John, *Oxoniensis Academia, or the Antiquities and Curiosities of the University of Oxford*, 1749

Ponsonby, Col. Sir Charles, *Wootton: The Anatomy of an Oxfordshire Village, 1945-1968*, 1968

Potter, G.J.R., *Life in a Berkshire Village*, 1976

Potts, William, Manuscript Collection, Banbury Library

Powell, G.H., *Stonesfield Through Two Centuries*

Pumphrey, C.M., *The Charlbury of Our Childhood*, Sessions Book Trust, 1990

Quiller Couch, Lilian, *Reminiscence of Oxford by Oxford Men*, Oxford Historical Society, 1892

Rayner Smith, Rev. C., *Cottisford and its Church*, 1972

Rix, Mary Bright, *Boars Hill, Oxford*, 1941

Roud, Stephen, *Mumming Plays in Oxfordshire: An Interim Checklist*, Traditional Drama Research Group, 1984

Roud, Stephen and Bee, Malcolm, *Berkshire Mumming Plays*, Folklore Society Publications No. 7, 1991

Samuel, Raphael, ed., *Village Life and Labour*, Routledge and Kegan Paul, 1973

Sharp, C.J., and Macilwaine, H., *The Morris Book*, E.P., 1974

Shortt, Hugh, *The Giant and Hob Nob*, Salisbury Museum, 1972

Simpson, Jacqueline, *British Dragons*, Batsford, 1980

Stapleton, Mrs., *History of Kidlington, Yarnton and Begbroke*, Oxford, 1983

Steel, David, *Riding the Franchise*, Oxford City Council, 1991

Stewart, Sheila, *Country Courtship*, Roundwood Press, 1975

Strutt, J., *Sports and Pastimes of the People of England*, 1801

Stubbes, Philip, *Anatomy of Abuses*, 1563

Sturge Gretton, M., *Burford Past and Present*, Blackwell, 1920

Sturge Gretton, M., *A Corner of the Cotswolds*, Methuen, 1914

Surman, Phyllis, *Eliza of Otmoor*, Oxford, 1975

Taunt, H.W., *The Boar's Head at Queen's College, Oxford*, n.d.

Taunt, H.W., 'Reviving Merrrie England: May Day Ceremonies', in *The Sphere*, 1908

Taylor, Leslie and Griselda, *Within Living Memory*, 1978

Thompson, Flora, *Lark Rise to Candleford*, Oxford University Press, 1939

Tiddy, R.J.E., *The Mummers' Play*, Clarendon Press, 1923

Tomalin, G.H., *The Book of Henley*, Barracuda, 1975

Tuckwell, Rev. L.S., *Some Reminiscences of 30 Happy Years of Clerical Work in the Parish of Standlake*, 1918

Turner, Mary Vane, *The Story of Deddington*, 1932

*Victoria County History of Oxfordshire*

Vincent, James E., *Highways and Byways of Berkshire*, Macmillan, 1931

West, Martin, *The All Souls Mallard*, All Souls College, 2000

West Oxfordshire Oral History Group, *Broadsheet Number One*, n.d.

Wheatley, Henry B., ed., *The Diary of Samuel Pepys*, Bell, 1952

Williams, Alfred, *Villages of the White Horse*, Duckworth, 1913

*Witney Express*

*Witney Gazette*

Wodhams, J.R., ed., *The Midland Garner*, 1884

Wood, Anthony, *History and Antiquities of the University of Oxford*, 1674

Wright, A.R. and Lones, T.E., *British Calendar Customs*, Vol. I, Glaisher, 1936

Yarrow, Ian, *Berkshire Scrapbook*, 1952

# Index

## THE SALT OF THE EARTH

Diary of a poor family in Woodstock, 1900

**Dorothy Calcutt**

One year in the life of a large family living on the edge of the Blenheim Palace estate in Woodstock, Oxfordshire in 1900. The author's mother, Dora, told her daughter many tales of her childhood at the turn of the century, and this book is based on those stories.

Includes contemporary photographs of the people and places in the story.

£8 paperback  120pp  1 902279 06 9

## BORN IN A STABLE

The true story of John Ashton, illegitimate son of a Northumberland nobleman and an Oxfordshire village barmaid

**Dorothy Calcutt**

Leo has inherited the family mansion in Northumberland, but is frustrated in his desire to have a son to continue the name and inherit his estate. To 'prove' his manhood, he is unfaithful to his wife. The barmaid at an inn in the Oxfordshire village of Long Hanborough (Emma, the author's great-grandmother) bears him a son, John.

This book tells the story of Leo's ambitions, of John's birth in extreme poverty in a farmyard stable, and of his upbringing and occasional meetings with his father.  The events take place half a century before those in *The Salt of the Earth*.

£7.50 paperback  1 902279 13 1  80pp

## DISCOVERING WYCHWOOD

An illustrated history and guide

**Charles Keighley** (Editor)

The history and guide for visitors and residents alike, and the only book of its kind.

*Includes about 100 photographs and line drawings, and two colour plates*

£8.99 paperback  168pp  1 902279 09 3

## CHARMING CHARLBURY, ITS NINE HAMLETS AND CHIPPING NORTON

**John Kibble**

John Kibble published *Charlbury and its Nine Hamlets* in 1927 and *Charming Charlbury* in 1930. Re-issued for the first time in a single volume, these two books give a tantalising and unique insight into two hundred years of life in this quiet corner of the Cotswolds, conveyed in the memories, stories and records of the people Kibble knew and met.

£10 paperback  224pp  1 902279 05 0

## A HISTORY OF CHARLBURY

**Lois Hey**

*With a study of the town's geology by Professor Geoffrey Walton*

The history of the Cotswold town of Charlbury, from pre-history to the present day. Illustrated with many historical photographs from local collections. Includes chapters on dissenters, schools, pubs and the gloving industry.

£8.99 paperback  144 pp  1 902279 03 4

# ALSO PUBLISHED BY THE WYCHWOOD PRESS

## THE FOREST THAT SAILED AWAY
**Poems by Elizabeth Birchall**

*Illustrations by Amanda Henriques* ·

A beautifully illustrated homage to ancient woodlands and to the sailors whose ships were built from them. It draws on the mythic meaning of individual trees and original accounts of historic voyages, and closes with poems celebrating renewed sensitivity to ecological balance and diversity.

£7.99 paperback   64pp   1 902279 10 7

## 'WALK HUMBLE, MY SON'
Growing up in Ascott-under-Wychwood, 1918–1939

**Eric R. Moss**

*Including* My Personal Memories, *by Doris Warner*

A graphic and moving account of life between the wars in a poor family that can trace its ancestors back to the seventeenth century. Doris Warner won first prize in a county competition for her *Memories*, which include both world wars and their impact on Ascott life.

Illustrated with many historic photographs.

£8 paperback   144pp   1 902279 07 7

## WYCHWOOD: THE EVOLUTION OF A WOODED LANDSCAPE
**Beryl Schumer**

Foreword by Harold Fox, Head of the Department of English Local History, Leicester University

The history of the woodland, showing exactly how extensive the tree cover was in the Norman period, and which settlements were already in existence. It traces later developments which have created the landscape of today.

£7.50 paperback   128pp   1 902279 02 6

## WYCHWOOD FOREST AND ITS BORDER PLACES
**John Kibble**

Foreword by Roy Townsend

Like his father and grandfather before him, John Kibble was a stonemason. Born in 1865, his memories are of people who lived and worked in, and remembered the life of, the forest villages in the 1700s and 1800s.

£7.50 paperback   128pp   1 902279 00 X

## WINCHCOMBE
A history of the Cotswold borough

**D. N. Donaldson**

The story of life in Winchcombe from earliest times. The book is illustrated with many old photographs, drawings and plans.

£14.95 paperback   272 pp   1 902279 12 3

## IRON AGE AND ROMAN WYCHWOOD
The Land of Satavacus and Bellicia

**Tim Copeland**

The continuity between the people living in Wychwood before the arrival of the Romans and those who worked the land for centuries after that event. The Iron Age and Roman periods in Wychwood still have an impact on the area today.

£12 paperback   144pp   1 902279 14 X